Formalist Criticism and
Reader-Response Theory

transitions
General Editor: Julian Wolfreys

Published Titles
NEW HISTORICISM AND CULTURAL MATERIALISM John Brannigan
POSTMODERN NARRATIVE THEORY Mark Currie
FORMALIST CRITICISM AND READER-RESPONSE THEORY
   Todd F. Davis and Kenneth Womack
MARXIST LITERARY AND CULTURAL THEORIES Moyra Haslett
LITERARY FEMINISMS Ruth Robbins
DECONSTRUCTION•DERRIDA Julian Wolfreys
CHAUCER TO SHAKESPEARE, 1337–1580 SunHee Kim Gertz
MILTON TO POPE, 1650–1720 Kay Gilliland Stevenson
BURKE TO BYRON, BARBAULD TO BAILLIE, 1790–1830 Jane Stabler
JACQUES LACAN Jean-Michel Rabaté
BATAILLE Fred Botting and Scott Wilson

Forthcoming Titles
NATIONAL IDENTITY John Brannigan
IDEOLOGY James Decker
QUEER THEORY Donald E. Hall
POSTMODERNISM•POSTMODERNITY Martin McQuillan
RACE Brian G. Niro
MODERNITY David Punter
PSYCHOANALYSIS AND LITERATURE Andrew Roberts
SUBJECTIVITY Ruth Robbins
TRANSGRESSION Julian Wolfreys
IMAGE TO APOCALYPSE, 1910–1945 Jane Goldman
POPE TO WOLLSTONECRAFT, 1713–1786 Moyra Haslett
PATER TO FORSTER, 1873–1924 Ruth Robbins
ORWELL TO THE PRESENT, 1945–1999 John Brannigan
DICKENS TO HARDY, 1837–1884 Julian Wolfreys
TERRY EAGLETON David Alderson
JULIA KRISTEVA AND LITERARY THEORY Megan Becker-Leckrone
HÉLÈNE CIXOUS: WRITING AND SEXUAL DIFFERENCE Abigail Bray
ROLAND BARTHES Martin McQuillan
ALTHUSSER Warren Montag
HOMI BHABHA Eleanor Byrne

Transitions
Series Standing Order
ISBN 0–333–73684–6
(*outside North America only*)

You can receive future titles in this series as they are published by
placing a standing order. Please contact your bookseller or, in case of
difficulty, write to us at the address below with your name and address,
the title of the series and the ISBN quoted above.

Customer Services Department, Palgrave Distribution Ltd
Houndmills, Basingstoke, Hampshire RG21 6XS, England

transitions

Formalist Criticism and Reader-Response Theory

Todd F. Davis and Kenneth Womack

palgrave

First published 2002 by
PALGRAVE
Houndmills, Basingstoke, Hampshire RG21 6XS and
175 Fifth Avenue, New York, N.Y. 10010
Companies and representatives throughout the world

PALGRAVE is the new global academic imprint of
St. Martin's Press LLC Scholarly and Reference Division and
Palgrave Publishers Ltd (formerly Macmillan Press Ltd).

ISBN 0–333–76531–1 hardback
ISBN 0–333–76532–X paperback

This book is printed on paper suitable for recycling and
made from fully managed and sustained forest sources.

A catalogue record for this book is available
from the British Library.

Library of Congress Cataloging-in-Publication Data
Davis, Todd F., 1965–
    Formalist criticism and reader-response theory/Todd F. Davis
    and Kenneth Womack.
    p. cm. – (Transitions)
    Includes bibliographical references and index.
    ISBN 0-333–76531–1 – ISBN 0–333–76532–X (pbk.)
    1. Formalism (Litrary analysis) 2. Reader-response criticism.
    I. Womack, Kenneth. II. Title. III. Transitions (Palgrave (Firm))

PN98.F6 D38 2000
801'.95–dc21   2001058649

10 9 8 7 6 5 4 3 2 1
11 10 09 08 07 06 05 04 03 02

Printed in China

Contents

General Editor's Preface   viii

Acknowledgements   x

Introduction: Moving beyond the Politics of Interpretation   1

Part I   Formalist Criticism and Reader-Response Theory: A Critical Introduction   **11**

1. Twentieth-Century Formalism: Convergence and Divergence   13
   - Separate yet human: Humanism and formalist conventions   17
   - Moving from theory to practice: The legacy of I. A. Richards and Cleanth Brooks   22
   - Another way of knowing: Formalism as literary discourse   26
   - The limits of formalism: Universalism, eclecticism, and morality in the work of F. R. Leavis and Kenneth Burke   28
   - The evolution of formalism: The case of Northrop Frye   33
   - Formalist concerns in the present   36

2. Russian Formalism, Mikhail Bakhtin, Heteroglossia, and Carnival   39
   - Signs, signifiers, and the Prague Linguistic Circle   44
   - Bakhtin and the narratological revolution   47

3. Reader-Response Theory, the Theoretical Project, and Identity Politics   51
   - Transactional reading in the theories of Louise M. Rosenblatt and Wayne C. Booth   53
   - Reader-response theory, narratology, and the structuralist imperative   57

- A subjectivist feast: Reader-response theory and
  psychological criticism   63
- Searching for the gendered self: Reader-response
  theory and feminist criticism   73

4. Stanley Fish, Self-Consuming Artifacts, and the
   Professionalization of Literary Studies   80
   - 'Meaning as an event': The evolution of Stanley Fish's
     reader-response theory   82
   - 'Reading' critical theory, professionalization, and the
     lingering problem of intentionality   86

**Part II   Readings in Formalist Criticism and
Reader-Response Theory**   **91**

A: Formalist Critical Readings

5. Travelling through the Valley of Ashes: Symbolic Unity in
   F. Scott Fitzgerald's *The Great Gatsby*   93
   - Nick Carraway's narrative of hope and wonder   96
   - *The Great Gatsby*, the romantic tradition, and narrative
     transcendence   103

6. Charlotte Brontë and Frye's *Secular Scripture*: The Structure
   of Romance in *Jane Eyre*   107
   - Romance and its contexts: The archetypal play of form
     and feeling   107
   - Romantic expectations: Heroes, heroines, and their quests   112
   - Descent and ascent: The structural movements of Jane
     and Rochester   117

B: Reader-Response Critical Readings

7. 'Telle us som myrie tale, by youre fey!': Exploring the
   Reading Transaction and Narrative Structure in Chaucer's
   Clerk's Tale and *Troilus and Criseyde*   123
   - Chaucer, narrative discourse, and the *Clerk's Tale*   124
   - Chaucer and the transactional possibilities of literary
     parody   129

8. Addressing Horizons of Readerly Expectation in Joseph
    Conrad's *Heart of Darkness* and Ford Madox Ford's
    The Good Soldier, or, How to Put the 'Reader' in 'Reader
    Response'   136
  - Engendering reader-response through Conrad's and
    Ford's literary impressionism   138
  - Marlow's journey to the ethical void   140
  - Dowell's narrative circumlocution and the ethics of
    storytelling   145

Conclusion: Beyond Formalist Criticism and
    Reader-Response Theory   154

Notes   157
Annotated Bibliography   169
Works Cited   177
Index   188

General Editor's Preface

Transitions: *transition-em*, n. of action. 1. A passing or passage from one condition, action or (rarely) place, to another. 2. Passage in thought, speech, or writing, from one subject to another. 3. **a.** The passing from one note to another **b.** The passing from one key to another, modulation. 4. The passage from an earlier to a later stage of development or formation . . . change from an earlier style to a later; a style of intermediate or mixed character . . . the historical passage of language from one well-defined stage to another.

The aim of *Transitions* is to explore passages and movements in critical thought, and in the development of literary and cultural interpretation. This series also seeks to examine the possibilities for reading, analysis, and other critical engagements which the very idea of transition makes possible. The writers in this series unfold the movements and modulations of critical thinking over the last generation, from the first emergences of what is now recognised as literary theory. They examine as well how the transitional nature of theoretical and critical thinking is still very much in operation, guaranteed by the hybridity and heterogeneity of the field of literary studies. The authors in the series share the common understanding that, now more than ever, critical thought is both in a state of transition and can best be defined by developing for the student reader an understanding of this protean quality.

This series desires, then, to enable the reader to transform her/his own reading and writing transactions by comprehending past developments. Each book in the series offers a guide to the poetics and politics of interpretative paradigms, schools, and bodies of thought, while transforming these, if not into tools or methodologies, then into conduits for directing and channelling thought. As well as transforming the critical past by interpreting it from the perspective of the present day, each study enacts transitional readings of a number of well-known literary texts, all of which are themselves conceivable as having been transitional texts at the moments of their first appearance. The readings offered in these books seek, through close critical reading and theoretical engagement, to demonstrate certain possibilities in critical thinking to the student reader.

It is hoped that the student will find this series liberating because rigid methodologies are not being put into place. As all the dictionary definitions of the idea of transition above suggest, what is important is the action, the passage: of thought, of analysis, of critical response. Rather than seeking to help you locate yourself in relation to any particular school or discipline, this series aims to put you into action, as readers and writers, travellers between positions, where the movement between poles comes to be seen as of more importance than the locations themselves.

Julian Wolfreys

Acknowledgements

Special thanks are due to Julian Wolfreys, the *Transitions* series editor, for his steadfast encouragement, abundance of generosity, and general goodwill. We are also grateful to Margaret Bartley, Felicity Noble, and Anna Sandeman for their efforts on behalf of this volume, as well as to James Decker, Dinty Moore, and Gary Weisel for their friendship and advice. As always, we owe particular debts of gratitude to our wives, Shelly Davis and Neneng Womack, for their kindness, tolerance, and support as we saw this volume through to its completion.

Introduction: Moving beyond the Politics of Interpretation

> What, beyond reinforcing status, is the function of criticism?
>
> (Paul Lauter, *Canons and Contexts*)

> Issues of value and evaluation tend to recur whenever literature, art, and other forms of cultural activity become a focus of discussion, whether in informal or institutional contexts.
>
> (Barbara Herrnstein Smith, *Contingencies of Value*)

> Literary studies have not yet found a way to institutionalize the lesson of recent criticism that no text is an island, that every work of literature is a rejoinder in a conversation or dialogue that it presupposes but may or may not mention explicitly.
>
> (Gerald Graff, *Professing Literature*)

In *Professing Literature: An Institutional History* (1987), Gerald Graff contends that 'no text is an island' (10). We might add that no form of theory or act of criticism is an island either. What critic or theorist can claim to lounge comfortably upon the unblemished sands of some uncharted isle sipping fresh guava juice, somehow untainted and untouched by the interpretive activity of past centuries? Indeed, all theory and criticism must claim its place in an ever-growing family tree. Over the course of the twentieth century – and sadly it appears to have continued into the twenty-first – critics and theorists alike have repeatedly ignored or done battle with their precursors, sometimes to the scholarly equivalent of death. How much richer and, perhaps, more valid might our reading strategies and the various readings they produce be if, instead of ridiculing our theoretical predecessors, we actually listen and examine how their legacy plays a role, albeit a subtle one, in our various acts of interpretation. It may be difficult for some progeny to sit at the feet of their ancestors, listening as the elderly speak lovingly and nostalgically about the good old days when criticism actually made sense. But the desire for another generation to recall longingly how at one time criticism heeded the formal detail of a given literary work, offering a close reading and an appraisal of it, or how in yesteryear criticism actually believed there was a connection between the text and the world beyond the text, suggesting that the teaching of literary works might actually impact how we live beyond their bookish margins, should not be interpreted as a sign of critical dementia. Regardless of our level of comfort, we surely would gain a greater appreciation for the work that preceded us and the manner in which that work informs our own acts of interpretation if we would take a moment to listen to such voices, engaging with them in a dialogue that seeks to better understand the other, rather than attacking the other with an aggressive monologue designed to drown out competing voices.

Perhaps the most famous – and maybe the most ridiculous – theoretical example of this kind of academic jousting between parent and child may be found in the oedipally driven theory of Harold Bloom. While no one can contest that the *Anxiety of Influence: A Theory of Poetry* (1973) represents a landmark work of criticism in the twentieth-century book of letters, its own influence and ensuing damage to the profession of criticism should be noted. The violence at the root of Bloom's theoretical perspective – that somehow the child must kill the parent to advance artistically – seems to have found a comfortable home in an academy where graduate students are encouraged to publish while they are in school in hopes that they might compete in an ever-challenging job market, where young professors may be expected to publish at least two books within their first few years on the job if they hope to be granted tenure. Yes, an artist or critic must in some way find his or her own voice, moving beyond the merely derivative.[1] But does such a move necessitate an act of aggression? Perhaps one reason for the success of Bloom's theory is that it fits well within a capitalistic economic framework. In order to determine ownership of a work of art, shouldn't the artist have to demonstrate how his or her work is radically different than other art that has come before? If an artist were to emphasize instead how the new painting or sculpture or novel was derived from or influenced by other artists or teachers, regardless of the competency of the technique and the overall success of the composition, in the current cultural climate that artist would be assured of failure. Similarly, the professionalization of English studies over the course of the past century appears to have been heavily influenced by capitalism. Such a system demands that critics and artists alike understand originality – the creation of new knowledge – as more about explaining how others are wrong and less about describing what is right in previous criticism or art and then building upon it.[2] Sadly, in far too many instances, originality is defined as a breaking with the past, a movement forward that attempts to demonstrate that those who came before had it all wrong. The trouble with such a system – outside of its arrogance and ignorance – is that the cycle of intellectual violence must be perpetuated if the system is to continue to exist. Such a system of knowledge demands that intellectual violence be passed from generation to generation. A note to those who will very soon step into the arena: We who attempt to usurp the critical throne must inevitably become critical fathers or mothers ourselves, and thus face the prospect of death at the hands of our own academic children. If such a picture proves unseemly and absurd, what, then, are the alternatives?

Perhaps we should begin by revisiting Bloom's use of the Oedipus story as a metaphor for artistic and critical formation. The most important aspect of Sophocles's tale – and its main function within the religious festival when it was first staged – has far less to do with the belatedly appended Freudian notion about sons and fathers and their fated clash over mothers and far more to do with Oedipus's tragic mistake. The hubris out of which Oedipus acts leads to his downfall, and it is hubris that the viewers of this play may avoid if they attend to Sophocles's counsel. We have no control over our fate, Sophocles suggests. The gods will do with us as they please. But we do have the ability to control our own responses to that fate, to act with humility. We would do well as critics to heed Tiresias's warning and move forward with some degree of modesty and respect for the lessons of the past. By doing so, we may avoid hurting others or ourselves with criticism's current language of conquest and violence. We are not arguing, however, for the end of argument. The academy would lose its integrity if we did not demand that the work of our intellectual ancestors be examined and tested, that the validity of their theories and readings be scrutinized. If new knowledge is to be made, the makers cannot simply accept the lessons of the past without reflection and care; to do so would be tantamount to stagnation, an intellectual death of another sort. Yet something has been lost over the course of the past century. In a system – perhaps industry is the more appropriate word – that demands more and more intellectual product from its members, it is inevitable that instead of regarding seriously the rich inheritance of the past – stopping to analyze how we continue to use principles and methods from this inheritance – we disparage it, relegating it to some academic nether region for the outdated and unfashionable. While we admit that all acts of criticism are political, that no interpretative performance exists outside the hermeneutic circle of power, we would suggest that a healthier approach to the act of literary criticism might involve the notion of theoretical collaboration.[3]

As Graff has already established, no book stands alone. In fact, the very book you hold in your hands is connected to myriad other texts, including the texts that comprise the *Transitions* series to which it belongs. Indeed, the series' nomenclature itself points toward the idea of the kind of collaboration that is of most interest to us. To be in transition is to move from one place to another; in that movement, however, one always brings part of the place one leaves to the new place where one has just arrived. In this way, criticism might be compared to the houses we have lived in and the neighborhoods where we have played. While we may never see those neighborhoods or live in those houses again – likely not even knowing who lived or played there before us – they nonetheless continue to shape who we are in the present moment.[4] Correspondingly, those who have lived in the homes we inhabit leave part of who they are behind when they start on their journey toward a new destination. Our life is joined to their life – even if we never meet them – because of the artifacts they leave behind: the color of paint on the walls, the built-in bookshelf in the corner. In other words, who we are and how we think and act is always a collaboration with the past, a creation that represents a transition from one thing to another. How many critics have begun their careers living in one theoretical neighborhood only to move to another in mid-life? A fine example at present is the celebrated critic Susan Gubar. With the publication of such works as *The Madwoman in the Attic* (1979) and *No Man's Land* (1988-94) with Sandra M. Gilbert, Gubar established herself as a feminist critic of great influence and scholarly depth. Since that time she has gone on to write about the issues of race in *Racechanges* (1997) and is currently exploring ethnicity and suffering in terms of the Holocaust and Jewish identity. Not surprisingly, with each transition Gubar has not abandoned her past. Instead, at every turn her past interests and discoveries inform her present thought. Thus, gender and race issues impact her present work on the Holocaust, allowing for the production of a rich and variegated criticism that helps us to see how her range of concerns are interrelated, not separate or distinct issues. In other words, transition allows us to see more holistically – a healthy idea for a world that grows smaller by the day due to technological advances. At this point in history, we cannot afford to build ideological and theoretical walls within our criticism; it should not be our goal to isolate ourselves from other critics and their interpretative strategies. Rather, if we have any hope for healthy growth in our discipline, we should seek to communicate openly with one another despite our differences, exchanging ideas and building upon the insights that each may bring.

Language is also in flux at all times, as is the criticism created from that language. We may attempt to capture language by producing dictionaries and grammars and other static instruments that offer the illusion of control and consistency, but those who use language to tell new stories of our experience inevitably find fresh and inventive ways to employ words, circumventing all of the tools that seek to harness them. As with language, criticism and theory must be in flux, in transition, in order to maintain its health. As Ralph Waldo Emerson contends, 'He in whom the love of truth predominates will keep himself aloof from all the moorings, and afloat. He will abstain from dogmatism, and recognize all the opposite negations between which, as walls, his being is swung' (21). Without transition – the state that Emerson refers to as 'repose' – we are left with nothing more than the mechanical, the rote; no new thought will lead us into a more profound wonder of our condition and the art that represents it. Without the ability to move, to remain unattached, we can do little to protect ourselves from the critical pundits who rise up, espousing some singular, controlling school of thought. At the root of transition is the idea that we might have the ability to transcend our limitations, our finite condition as humans, by moving from one idea to another, and the most productive and viable manner to make such a move is through collaboration, a joining with the Other who may help us to see what we have never even imagined. From decade to decade, the critical vogue that determines what most readers focus upon in the act of reading undergoes a series of transformations, often in dramatic and provocative ways. Such transformations are not the only shifts, however. Even within a given decade, transitions and negotiations occur as critics engage in scholarly dialogue. Sadly, over the last several decades, less and less dialogue appears to be occurring. A critical climate in which critics of a like mind gather at the same meetings or read exclusively one another's texts, never encountering critics of different and diverse persuasions who might actually disagree with their thoughts, is an unhealthy one. No collaboration or transition can take place in such an atmosphere, and, as a result, the academy suffers in terms of the kinds of knowledge that it might create.

Think of the potentially fruitful conversations that might occur between a New Historicist and a Formalist as they examine a work by John Irving, for instance. Each critic brings a particular strength to a reading of Irving's *The World According to Garp* (1978) but, as is often the case, each has difficulty seeing what the other sees. Whether the critic ignores certain aspects of the work intentionally or simply cannot see them as a result of years of training and practice is irrelevant. Without some kind of collaboration, potential knowledge is lost. In lectures, the evolutionary biologist and celebrated paleontologist Stephen Jay Gould often points toward the ways other disciplines offer the key to unlock the doors to problems that have left certain narrowly focused, disciplinary thinkers dumbfounded. The inescapable result of wearing the 'glasses' of only one discipline or critical theory is that one can see only what such glasses reveal. The New Historicist, if he or she is unwilling to cross theoretical boundaries in order to learn from the Formalist, will perceive only the ways the 1970s cultural and political scene impacts Irving, leading him to include such themes in his novel as feminism, gender formation and transformation, the changing family structures of the period, and the political climate of post-Vietnam America. The Formalist, needless to say, will fare no better. Instead of understanding the role history and culture plays in the creation of Irving's fictional world, he or she likely will focus exclusively upon Irving's use of a Dickensian narrative style, his textual argument with postmodern fiction and the metafictional forms it uses, and the symmetry and balance of his novel, which concludes with a final chapter, 'Life After Garp,' that offers fictional resolution. Needless to say, if the two critics can engage one another in a critical conversation, their understanding of the work will be far more comprehensive, and as they continue to write criticism in the future, they will be forced to consider the principles of the other's discipline. While this consideration may not be explicit within the frame of their own essay, it implicitly shapes what is produced in an important and vital manner.

Invariably, how one reads texts determines what kinds of texts one reads, and with the professionalization of literary studies in the academy, those who hold seats of power – namely, the professors – have in large part determined what texts enter the canon and which texts from the canon are most regularly taught to students so that the cycle might once again begin. In *The Political Responsibility of the Critic* (1987), Jim Merod explains that 'intellectual authority and the authority of scholars and critics are the first of all guild creations, products of the credentials conferred by schools that exercise their norms of judgment in order to reproduce themselves' (65). Whether one agrees with Merod's politics and his interpretation of scholarly activity and teaching in the academy is of little consequence, but it is difficult to argue with his observations about the guild system that serves as the foundation for the university. Such a system does not necessarily perform a sinister function, however. We often teach what we love, and, in turn, those we have taught often go on to teach in a similar fashion using similar texts. But this seems little more than an observation of human nature; this is the manner in which stories have been passed from generation to generation for aeons – long before literary criticism or English studies entered the academy, even before an academy existed, for that matter. How, then, might we construe differently the idea of 'responsibility' that Merod alludes to in his title? The answer already exists in the model of collaboration mentioned earlier. Graff contends that history need not repeat itself, but 'it may do so if the institutional arrangements that encourage repetitive patterns are not recognized and altered' (249). As with Graff, we do not believe that history necessarily must repeat itself. Unlike Merod or Patrick Colm Hogan, however, we do not argue for the destruction of the scholarly 'guild system' – only a reworking of it. We cannot imagine a time when – nor an 'objective' space where – teachers would teach against their learned values and literary inclinations. More to the point, this desire to teach what one has passion for would appear to be a potential strength, not a weakness, in our exploration of texts both in the classroom and in our writing. Thus, in our desire to see teachers and critics work within the midst of their passion, on the very subjects and texts that mean most to them, as well as our desire to see a more diverse academy where a wider range of texts are taught and more dialogue takes place between different theoretical schools of thought, we turn to the role of collaboration once more.

By creating space in the contemporary university for dialogue – a space that the *Transitions* series has the potential to help open – we expose ourselves to the possibilities of a critical collaboration that moves from text to text and from theoretical concern to theoretical concern. James H. Kavanagh describes the relations of ideology as the 'systems of representation that are its products and supports – through which individuals of different class, race, and sex are worked into a particular lived relation' (319). Such a succinct and clear description, by comparison, helps us think about the interrelationships that exist between different theoretical schools and also suggests the role formalism and reader-response theory plays in the cycle of critical consideration. How much more profound our critical activity would be if we considered the impact of other forms of theory upon our own theoretical perspective. Since the rise and eventual fall of formalism and reader-response theory, critics have continued to consider aesthetic and readerly implications as they choose the kinds of texts they examine and the manner in which they examine them. The lived relation of critic to critic depends upon the structures established over the course of the history of literary studies and helps us understand the kinds of decisions each critic makes – decisions that often demonstrate no direct relation to the critic's own theoretical school, but nonetheless are significant in terms of the kinds of texts that will be examined. For example, while few critics align themselves with formalism or New Criticism at present – Murray Krieger being the last 'pure' formalist perhaps – aesthetic evaluation plays a role in literary criticism for virtually all critics. While we may find some critics who do not consider the aesthetic quality of the work they study – either consciously or unconsciously – such critics are in the minority. What human being has not been socialized to think about the aesthetic quality of given objects or landscapes? Who among us does not have a particular kind of painting or music or story that causes us to contemplate its beauty? From culture to culture across the planet, we encounter human communities that have established methods of evaluation to define what they consider to be beautiful. After such communities define what they find to be aesthetically pleasing, those in their group respond to and praise objects that fit within the boundaries of the rubric. Thus, it would be absurd to say that aesthetic evaluation has disappeared from literary criticism or the human cultures that make such forms of criticism possible. To the contrary, whether the critic be a feminist, an ethical critic, a psychoanalytic critic, or a critic of some other feather, the narrative or poem that the critic engages most likely will hold some aesthetic appeal. This is part of the legacy of formalist criticism. What has been discarded from the formalism espoused and practiced in the first half of the twentieth century by the likes of T. S. Eliot, Robert Penn Warren, I. A. Richards, and John Crowe Ransom is the rigid and dogmatic assertions that the aesthetic principles established by these select few should be subscribed to by the many. The elitism that formalist thought suffered from grew out of a blindness to the individual reader. Searching for some universal system of aesthetics did not allow formalists to examine the myriad elements that impact how a reader may perceive what he or she is reading.

It is here that transition and collaboration serve as the catalyst for critical change on a larger scale. Unlike the work of early formalist critics, the reader-response critic contends that not all humans are acculturated in the same manner, nor do they live within the same socioeconomic structures or the same geographical locations or historical periods. Building upon this contention, the reader-response critic argues that the formalist has chosen an arbitrary set of aesthetic values that do not apply to all art forms or all cultures. Simple observation reveals that different cultures often embrace radically divergent or contrary aesthetic forms. Yet the reader-response critic cannot ignore the role aesthetics play for both the reader and the artist without simply closing her eyes or plugging his ears. Although a 64-year-old, white, male farmer of Dutch Calvinist descent living in Iowa may have very different aesthetic values than a 14-year-old African-American girl who attends an African Methodist Episcopal Church and lives in the Cabrini Green public housing projects of Chicago – both still do have aesthetic values that play a vital role in the ways they respond to and interpret the artistic texts in their lives. If formalist concerns may be joined with reader-response interests, then a hybrid critical model evolves that does not abandon or ignore formal consideration of the work, nor does it disregard the role that the reader plays in the act of interpretation.

In *Formalist Criticism and Reader-Response Theory*, we attempt to offer a succinct overview and history of formalism and reader-response criticism. But our aim in doing so has very little to do with a desire to return to the good old days when these forms of criticism reigned. In fact, the very idea that a form of criticism should 'reign' disturbs us. Such a model implies that criticism is a game or contest to be won. That there are winners and losers in the act of interpretation seems strange indeed. We doubt that this is the desired outcome of a storyteller when beginning to write, and we are certain that the reader who reads for the sheer pleasure of it – when not participating in a classroom or symposium – does not think about proving that he or she understands the narrative correctly and others incorrectly. At the conclusion of the book, we hope each reader examines his or her own critical methodology in light of formalism and reader-response theory's intellectual riches. Outside of those who campaign for a particular school of theory – critical pundits who expend enormous efforts for rather small returns – most of us more likely have an eclectic hermeneutic, comprised of a variety of theories working together at once. Understanding where such critical tenets come from represents an important first step in moving beyond the politics of interpretation and into the promising future of collaborative criticism.

Part I

Formalist Criticism and Reader-Response Theory: A Critical Introduction

1 Twentieth-Century Formalism: Convergence and Divergence

> Criticism must become more scientific, or precise and systematic, and this means that it must be developed by the collective and sustained effort of learned persons – which means that its proper seat is in the universities.
>
> (John Crowe Ransom, *The World's Body*)

> The business of the critic is simply to show how the machine is meant to work, and therefore to show all its working parts in turn.
>
> (William Empson, *Seven Types of Ambiguity*)

> Theory, which is expectation, always determines criticism, and never more than when it is unconscious. The reputed condition of no theory in the critic's mind is illusory.
>
> (John Crowe Ransom, *The World's Body*)

Perhaps the most dominant and influential of all forms of criticism during the twentieth century, formalist thought likely remains the most misrepresented. While the far-reaching political and ideological force of Anglo-American formalism's New Criticism cannot be denied, it is all too often caricatured as a monolithic reading strategy, one somehow devoid of any theoretical acumen. In *Professing Literature: An Institutional History* (1987), Gerald Graff contends that although contemporary 'defenders of theory tend to equate the New Criticism itself with unreflective empiricism . . . in its time the movement stood for theoretical reflection against the primitive accumulation of data' (247). Ransom's decree that literary criticism need become 'more scientific, or precise and systematic' points away from a naïve perspective that reading and interpretation are somehow natural activities. Sadly, Ransom's assertion includes a more elitist demand that such activity should occur behind the walls of universities and colleges. But we should not assume that Ransom's desire to shift the power of reading and interpretation to the academy was shared by all New Critics. A group whose margins and membership remains unclear in many ways,[1] the New Critics represent only one strain of formalism, and, even within this particular group, much diversity and tension existed. Because of New Criticism's reign in the academy from roughly 1940 to 1960 – and, perhaps more significantly, the programmatic institutionalization of its standards as the normal or natural practice of reading for several generations of students and teachers in secondary schools in America – the New Criticism became the target or scapegoat of competing forms of criticism – even while many of its specific strategies or skills remain the basis for other more overtly ideological forms of reading.

New Criticism claims such diverse and noted practitioners as William Empson, T. S. Eliot, I. A. Richards, Allen Tate, W. K. Wimsatt, Monroe C. Beardsley, John Crowe Ransom, Cleanth Brooks, René Wellek, Kenneth Burke, F. R. Leavis, and Yvor Winters, among a host of others. The sheer number and diversity of names in this list implicitly points toward the marked differences that existed within the named boundaries of this group. Yes, all of these critics undertook a shift away from the various forms of biographical, moral, and sociological criticism practiced by a previous generation in order to focus upon the formal aspects of the art object, but such a shift inevitably led each critic down different roads, offering markedly different perspectives of the same artistic scenery.

The story of the New Criticism begins in the 1920s, when seeds for an explicit turn to formalism were planted and began to take root in America and England. In America, such groups as the Fugitives and the Agrarians articulated a shift away from historical or biographical criticism toward an emphasis upon close reading. In such journals as *The Fugitive*, the *Southern Review*, the *Kenyon Review*, and the *Sewanee Review*, critics waged a battle for the work of art itself, stridently proclaiming that we must honor art for art's sake, not for the sake of the artist's life or for some political cause. Under the editorship of such noted critics and poets as Ransom, Tate, and Robert Penn Warren, these journals not only established a forum for such critical discussions but also published many of the poems that would later come to embody the very critical standards championed by the New Criticism. In England, a similar movement was underway. Under the tutelage of Eliot, some of the same concerns were mirrored in the pages of *The Criterion*, as well as in the work of Empson and Richards.

Although most literary historians agree that Eliot moved beyond the New Criticism during the 1930s and 1940s – shifting his role from literary critic to that of social critic – his influence upon British and American formalism continues to manifest itself most dramatically in the idea of the text as *sacred*. In his authoritative treatise *The Sacred Wood* (1920), Eliot advances the idea that the decadent devolution of the contemporary world represents a marked turning from the ordered, unified world whose very creation implies a sacrosanct, higher order – a complexity and wholeness that can only be found in a turn away from skepticism and science. The alienation of modernity, Eliot suggests, results from our turn to secularism and industrializa-tion, a condition that may only be overcome in a return to myth and religion. Not surprisingly, then, Eliot champions texts and forms of criticism that value what he calls a 'unified sensibility' – a complexity of thought and wholeness birthed from some religious or mythical order. For this reason, Eliot champions a poet like Dante and dismisses a poet like Blake: the former works toward unity and claims a traditional mythological framework, philosophy, and theology, while the latter does not subscribe to any set of accepted or tradi-tional ideas. For Eliot, the sacred unity found in the poetry of the highest order is born out of a homogenous (in his case, a Christian) cultural inheritance. While Eliot's work marks a significant turn toward a formalist study of literature, the breadth of his career cannot be characterized in the same terms as those who more passionately championed the New Criticism. Rather, Eliot saw his own work in less exclusive terms, explaining in *To Criticize the Critic* (1965) that 'it is impossible to fence off *literary* criticism from criticism on other grounds, and that moral, religious, and social judgments cannot be wholly excluded' (25).

While not all formalists aligned themselves with Eliot's religious views, their actual practice of literary criticism mirrored the idea of the text as *sacred*. Much of the world beyond the text – and even more to the point, beyond the security of the walls of academe that guarded the most influential formalists – crumbled beneath the weight of wars and economic depression, beneath the onslaught of radical shifts in social and intellectual thought. Not surprisingly, in a climate of cataclysmic upheaval, the role and meaning of a given text altered radically, taking on the increasingly important but harrowingly illusive role of stabilizer. The stability or security of a given text – most often a poem for the formalists – was found within itself. According to formalist thought and practice, the chaotic world beyond the borders of the text need not intrude; within the boundaries of the text all might be saved.

As Wallace Stevens's poetry proposes, what the poet seeks to create is a supreme fiction, a world made of words complete in and of itself, able to order and secure its own domain – to offer a stay against the confusion that rages beyond the text, somehow complete and sepa-rate. Given this shift in the poetry of such major writers as Stevens and Eliot and Auden, literary critics no longer needed to consider an author's life or the cultural or political milieu in which the text was born – as the previous generation had done. While the sustaining structures of nineteenth-century life disappeared in the face of war, depression, and the ever-shifting ground of new theoretical thought that pointed toward ideas of relativity, critics thrust the text into an increasingly important and exalted role. In 'The New Criticism: Pro and Contra,' Wellek furthers Stevens's idealization of the text, contend-ing that science and a move away from organicism to industrialization created a damnable mess that only the restorative powers of the poetic text might restore. Like the Agrarians, Wellek's scathing critique of scientific progress asserts that science 'is the villain of history which had destroyed the community of man, broken up the old organic way of life, paved the way to industrialism, and made man the alienated, rootless, godless creature he has become in this century. Science encourages Utopian thinking, the false idea of the perfectibility of man, the whole illusion of endless progress' (618-19). Such a philosophical and ideological position undergirds and unites many formalist critics during the first half of the twentieth century in ways that individual practices and interpretive techniques necessarily did not.

As late as the 1970s, Murray Krieger diligently and persuasively defended formalism and New Criticism, serving as the final apologist for the New Critical faith. Beset on all sides by a variety of theoretical schools that caricatured formalism as nothing more than a stridently banal reading paradigm and that made New Criticism the scapegoat for a variety of critical and social ills, Krieger portrayed the ever-more pervasive turn to theory – especially the work of Derrida, which Krieger confronted in *Theory of Criticism: A Tradition and Its System* (1976) – as a crisis of faith. Placing himself in line with Matthew Arnold's modernist humanism, Krieger explained in *Poetic Presence and Illusion: Essays in Critical History and Theory* (1979) that if we share Arnold's loss of faith, we can go either of two ways: we can view poetry as a human triumph made out of darkness, as the creation of verbal meaning in a blank universe to serve as a visionary substitute for a defunct religion; or we can – in our negation – extend our faithlessness, the blankness of our universe, to our poetry. . . . Stubbornly humanistic as I am, I must choose that first alternative: I want to remain responsive to the promise of the filled and centered word, a signifier replete with an inseparable signified which it has created within itself. But I am aware also that my demythologizing habit, as modern man, must make me wary of the grounds on which I dare claim verbal presence and fullness. (173)

Krieger's daunting and perilous balancing act represents the transparent culmination of the faithful desire for *meaning* found in the practice of formalists in general and in that of the New Critics in particular. Despite the continued onslaught of damning historical events and theoretical shifts, Krieger admits to the anxiety he – and such formalists as Eliot and Warren before him – feels as he places his faith in the idea of verbal presence and fullness over that of absence and infinite cultural and linguistic negotiation. In their shift from the old historicism – with its reliance upon biographical and sociological evidence – New Critics worked with hope toward the idea that some universal might exist, that in the creation of the text some order might be established which transcended cultural and temporal considerations. In the present era, when the idea that a given text might be separate – an object removed from temporal and social consideration – has been so radically overturned as to make such an assertion appear embarrassingly naïve, Krieger's continued defense of such a position serves as a nagging reminder that contemporary criticism may have lost a crucial element in its deconstruction of formalist thought: the ability to consider how literature ennobles and sustains the human experience.[2]

Separate yet human: Humanism and formalist conventions

In *Practicing Theory and Reading Literature* (1989), Raman Selden accuses the New Critics, as so many other theorists have done before him, of a bold deception: the hidden agenda, he claims, of New Criticism, quite simply, is a 'humanistic and moral crusade' (26).

Clearly Selden's accusation ignores not only Krieger, but Eliot and a host of other critics who made no apologies for the humanism that served as the foundation for their desire to see literature as 'the poet's rage for order, the struggle to unify disparate experience' (26). In light of Selden's judgment, it is important for us to understand how Eliot's ideas of impersonality and W. K. Wimsatt and Monroe C. Beardsley's intentional and affective fallacies relate to humanism. At first glance, Eliot's radical crusade against the private experience of the author seems in opposition to humanism's concern for the interests, needs, and welfare of others. Isn't the author's experience part of the human condition? If the author writes out of this experience, won't the power of that experience be transformed by the formal considerations of the poem or novel in such a way that the readers will also be transformed? Shouldn't artists be encouraged to create directly out of their own emotional experiences, to delve deeply into their own place in time and culture so that a greater degree of truth and feeling might be achieved?

Like the asceticism of Benedictine nuns who were encouraged to never love any single person with too great a passion or commitment so that in turn they might be able to love all persons, Eliot's poetics of impersonality insinuates that in order for the artist to speak universally the poet must leave the baggage of personal experience behind. In 'Tradition and the Individual Talent,' Eliot contemplates the role and work of the poet in relation to the universal, the timeless, in hopes of establishing a program of sorts for identifying those poets and poems worthy of praise. Early in the essay, Eliot explains that good poetry 'involves, in the first place, the historical sense, which we may call nearly indispensable to anyone who would continue to be a poet beyond his twenty-fifth year; and the historical sense involves a perception, not only of the pastness of the past, but of its presence' (784). For Eliot, one significant step toward the creation of art that is universal in its range is a recognition that the past must always be part of the present. The poet must understand how his or her creation relates to tradition, to the many works that have come before and that will continue to exist alongside the new creation as it takes its place in the inherited community of high art. Such a notion fits comfortably with present ideas of intertextuality and the way textual forces come together in the creation of new texts. What distinguishes Eliot's ideas of tradition and the role it plays in the creation of art from the idea of intertextuality, however, is his elitism in defining what texts are truly worthy of inclusion. Like F. R. Leavis who would later write of the 'great tradition,' Eliot concerns himself with the construction of boundaries between high and low art, between the popular or the contemporaneous and what he believes is for the ages. Eliot's tradition is exclusive and hierarchical and does not account for the many other cultural forces that might make a popular novel or rock lyric or situation comedy as important in the creation of a given text as Dante's *Inferno*. Aren't all of the forces the artist experiences important in the culminating art object? Eliot responds with a resounding 'no' and asserts that if we approach a poet with his idea of tradition in mind, 'we shall often find that not only the best, but the most individual parts of his work may be those in which the dead poets, his ancestors, assert their immortality most vigorously' (784). As the voices of other poets enter the work of the present, Eliot argues, the poet's own personality must depart. 'The emotion of art is impersonal. And the poet cannot reach his impersonality without surrendering himself wholly to the work to be done,' Eliot explains. 'And he is not likely to know what is to be done unless he lives in what is not merely the present, but the present moment of the past, unless he is conscious; not of what is dead, but of what is already living' (787).

But how might the poet escape from his or her personality, escape from the emotional power of the inner life so commonly associated with romantic art? With apparent disdain for romanticism, in 'Hamlet and His Problems' Eliot conceives of a technique that serves as the foundation for his poetics of impersonality – the *objective correlative*. As he explains, 'the only way of expressing emotion in the form of art is by finding an *objective correlative*; in other words, a set of objects, a situation, a chain of events which shall be the formula of that *particular* emotion; such that when the external facts, which must terminate in sensory experience, are given, the emotion is immediately evoked' (789). According to Maud Ellmann, for Eliot the 'only antidote to the "slither" of Romantic individualism was a fierce renunciation of the self' (4), and this renunciation of self led in the direction of classicism, objectivity, and impersonality.

Eliot's dominance in both poetry and criticism during the first half of the century helped determine in large part the course and preoccupation of a discipline that was in its infancy as a profession.[3] His strident insistence that art's creation, as well as its interpretation, be kept free of the taint of the *personal* clearly influenced the work of Wimsatt and Beardsley, leading to their formulation of two of the most powerful concepts in New Critical theory and practice. Disavowing any genetic or receptionist form of criticism, Wimsatt and Beardsley's work might best be seen as a culmination or codification of the arguments that already were being made by other critics about the misuse of biography or cultural and historical artifacts. Originally published in the *Sewanee Review* and later reprinted in *The Verbal Icon* (1954), 'The Intentional Fallacy' (1946) and 'The Affective Fallacy' (1949) outline in clear, almost pedantic language, the foolishness in considering biographical or extra-textual information of any kind. Wimsatt and Beardsley dogmatically assert the preeminence of the literary art object – its position outside the constraints of authorial intention, cultural influence, or historical forces. As they explain:

> Judging a poem is like judging a pudding or a machine. One demands that it works. It is only because an artifact works that we infer an intention of an artificer. 'A poem should not mean but be.' A poem can *be* only through its *meaning* – since its medium is words – yet it *is*, simply *is* – in the sense that we have no excuse for inquiring what part is intended or meant. Poetry is a feat of style by which a complex of meaning is handled all at once. Poetry succeeds because all or most of what is said or implied is relevant; what is irrelevant has been excluded, like lumps from pudding and 'bugs' from machinery. In this respect poetry differs from practical messages, which are successful if and only if we correctly infer the intention. (4–5)

What good might the knowledge of the author's intention serve in the act of literary criticism? Wimsatt and Beardsley's resounding and preemptive response – 'No good whatsoever' – finds its main defense in the fact that artists do not always accomplish what they intend; moreover, much finds its way into the poem or novel or painting that the artist might not have intended. A criticism constrained by authorial intention, formalist thought contends, gives far too much credence to what we think the artist intended and may have accomplished and far too little to the work itself. Formalism disregards altogether authorial intention and cultural influence, proclaiming that the art object alone is all that is needed to work critically towards a single, correct meaning. Unlike much contemporary criticism wherein the critic – depending upon the theoretical lens used to 'read' the work – offers only one potential interpretation in a range of interpretations, New Criticism worked with the assumption that one *true* reading of a work did exist, somehow inextricably bound in the formal construction and organic unity of a given art object and not in our conception of an author's intention.

New Critics viewed the poem as a well-wrought urn, impersonal and ahistorical, and the very existence of the poem implied that in some platonic fashion there also existed – waiting to be discovered by the diligent critic who studied the construction of the poem for efficiency and balance – some ideal reading of that object. To this end, Wimsatt and Beardsley furthered their practical rules for critical activity by explaining in 'The Affective Fallacy' that the critic also should not look to the poems impact upon the reader – in other words, the reader's response should be given no deliberation. Theories of catharsis, didacticism, or delight, Wimsatt and Beardsley insist, should not be considered when evaluating or judging art. 'The affective fallacy,' they explain, 'is a confusion between the poem and its *results* (what it *is* and what it *does*)' (21). What this leads to is a kind of criticism that attempts to measure the psychological effects of a given work, and such activity, they argue, invariably 'ends in impressionism and relativism' (21). Given this statement, we can see that impressionism and relativism are the very things that Wimsatt and Beardsley wish to fight against. It is their desire to fix the meaning or emotional content of a poem, to make their evaluation of it as *beautiful* withstand the ever-changing forces of culture and history. Wimsatt and Beardsley do not ignore entirely the idea that a poem possesses an emotional content, however, but they do maintain that it is only through an objective evaluation of the poem – one that makes use of formalist techniques – that the measure of its true emotional content might be achieved:

> Poetry is characteristically a discourse about both emotions and objects, or about the emotive quality of objects. The emotions correlative to the objects of poetry become a part of the matter dealt with – not communicated to the reader like an infection or disease, not inflicted mechanically like a bullet or knife wound, not administered like a poison. . . . Poetry is a way of fixing emotions or making them more permanently perceptible when objects have undergone a functional change from culture to culture, or when as simple facts of history they have lost emotive value with loss of immediacy. (38)

Similar to Eliot's poetics of impersonality, Wimsatt and Beardsley fashion a poetics that rejects temporality, the very strictures of human finitude. Instead, they create a theory that is ahistorical, one that suggests art may transcend the very context out of which it emerges. If the work has an emotional life or content, this dimension is rooted entirely in itself. In other words, the art object – in its self-contained state – is sufficient, needing nothing beyond itself to create meaning. In 'Narcissus as Narcissus,' Allen Tate declares that 'in a manner of speaking, the poem is its own knower, neither poet nor reader knowing anything that the poem says apart from the words of the poem' (*Collected Essays* 595). The extremity of this assertion, of course, remains problematic, especially in the present moment when the idea that art might somehow be divorced from its context is met with great incredulity. Yet, as we examine the historical and cultural context for this desire to remove the art object from human limitations (cultural and historical influences) – a desire that leads to the act of close reading or the relentless call for an *explication de texte* – we can see clearly that this is at least in part a reaction to previous critical practice and cataclysmic cultural and historical change.

Moving from theory to practice: The legacy of I. A. Richards and Cleanth Brooks

As a psychologist and semanticist, I. A. Richards demonstrated a continued interest in the effect of poems on the reader. At first glance, such a statement might suggest that Richards does not belong in the company of other formalists. With his proclamation that a poem is the experience that the 'right kind of reader' has while reading, Richards seems more the progenitor of reader-response theory than an influential player in the transition from genetic forms of criticism to practical formalism. In his early books, however, Richards emphasizes both the poem's emotive function as well as its formal composition in an effort to mark clearly his rejection of not only genetic forms of criticism, but also any highly moralistic, message-based evaluation of literature. While most New Critics either ignored or dismissed Richards's allegiance to psychology and science, they acknowledged their tremendous debt to his theories concerning such signal concepts as 'tension,' 'balance,' 'irony,' 'pseudo-statement,' and 'emotive' and 'referential' language.

In *Principles of Literary Criticism* (1924), Richards posits that the critic must have balance in approaching a work of art, an attitude especially important to the study of tragedy but not exclusive to that form. 'This balanced poise, stable through its power of inclusion, not through the force of its exclusions,' Richards explains, 'is not peculiar to Tragedy. It is a general characteristic of all the most valuable experiences of the arts' (248). Five years later, Richards chronicled his experience examining the written responses of several hundred Cambridge University students to a selection of poems. In his introduction to *Practical Criticism* (1929), Richards maps the variety of difficulties students have in apprehending both the content and meaning of a poem, as well as in deciphering its structural or formal qualities. Richards creates ten descriptive categories that illustrate the elements of confusion or misreading that plague his students. First, many students have trouble 'making out the plain sense' of a poem, a failure 'to understand it, both as a statement and as an expression' (13). Second, the misapprehension of meter and rhythm often occurs. As Richards makes clear, there is a wide gap between the reader who 'naturally and immediately perceives this form and movement' and the reader who 'either ignores it or has to build it up laboriously with finger-counting, table-tapping, and the rest' (14).

Next, Richards names the 'pervasive influence of *mnemonic irrelevancies*' (15) as a consistent barrier to any apprehension of the poem. As a precursor to Wimsatt and Beardsley's affective fallacy, this desire on the part of the reader to introduce 'some personal scene or adventure, erratic associations, the interference of emotional reverberations from a past which may have nothing to do with the poem,' Richards contends, often interferes with the student's understanding of the poem. The remaining barriers that Richards extrapolates include 'misinterpretation of figurative language,' 'stock responses,' 'sentimentality,' 'inhibition,' 'doctrinal adhesions,' 'technical presuppositions,' and ' general critical preconceptions.' What many of these 'problems' have in common is an *a priori* theoretical perspective that Richards believes inhibits or restricts the student from seeing the poem for what it really is. Whether these barriers be personal experience – a new critical problem that both poets and critics of this movement attempted to squash in their allegiance to a poetics of impersonality – or the 'stock responses' provided by our culture at large, Richards's observations seem to point toward a disengagement of the student with his or her personal experience, as well as the oppressive theoretical baggage, of which the student likely is ignorant. What these moves lead to in terms of a 'practical criticism' is an emphasis upon the text and the act of 'close reading.'

Most literary historians point to the publication of William Empson's *Seven Types of Ambiguity* (1930) as a fundamental shift in literary criticism. As Richards's pupil, Empson carries forward Richards's own high regard for a criticism that is not merely appreciative but analytical, one that focuses its attention on the rhetorical approach to close reading. While his delineation of differing types of ambiguity in literary texts did not take hold, his rallying cry in the closing pages of *Seven Types of Ambiguity* for a kind of close reading that in some fashion uses techniques of analysis – not unlike those used by the scientific method – was met with open arms by a growing number of formalist critics in the United States. Empson also addresses, however, the tension or antinomies of a criticism that wishes to disconnect the art object from its human creator – from its cultural and historical contexts – in order to study the literary text under the microscope of close reading while continuing to insist that, as an art object, it belongs to what is most human and humane. Empson explains the double-bind in which he finds himself embroiled by examining the humanistic and the scientific elements of his approach:

> It would be tempting, then, to say I was concerned with science rather than with beauty; to treat poetry as a branch of applied psychology. But, so far as poetry can be regarded altogether dispassionately, so far as it is an external object for examination, it is dead poetry and not worth examining; further, so far as a critic has made himself dispassionate about it, so far as he has repressed sympathy in favor of curiosity, he has made himself incapable of examining it. (248)

Empson's answer to such a difficulty mirrors his teacher's own idea of a 'poised balance.' In some way, the critic must find a balance between the close, objective analysis of the art object and his or her more passionate appreciation or connection with it. But Empson contends that while such an idea may appear contradictory, perhaps even impossible, it remains clear that humans do, in fact, hold such antinomies within their person at once. 'Because the act of knowing is itself an act of sympathizing,' Empson asserts, then 'unless you are enjoying the poetry you cannot create it, as poetry, in your mind' (248). What Empson points to is the circularity inherent in the very act of criticism, its relational play between these two disparate points. His confession reflects the difficult, but rewarding dance that formalism rehearsed and performed for several decades as it used certain tools or skills of close analysis that suggested the craft or mechanical workings of a poem were of utmost importance, yet at the same time embraced the intangibly human elements that clearly were borne out of personal experience and cultural context.

In *The Well-Wrought Urn* (1947) – perhaps the single most important text for American formalism – Cleanth Brooks attends to the tension between formalism's focus upon structure and humanism's embrace of art as representative of humanity's range of emotional or spiritual life. Here, Brooks argues that formalism, as practiced by the New Critics, must always be seen as praxis, as an act that cannot be dissected or parsed into distinct theoretical categories without ceasing to be the act itself – in much the same way that a poem ceases to be a poem if the formalist critic merely attends to its mechanical workings. Perhaps the best way to describe Brooks's emphasis upon the practical implications of *doing* literary criticism is by way of analogy. When one uses a hammer to drive a nail into a board, it is difficult to break down into distinct or separate categories the many movements involved – the swing of the hammer; the way it rests in the hand of the carpenter; the manner in which it strikes the head of the nail; the success or failure as the nail either enters the wood or bends above it. In breaking down the various stages and movements involved in this work, we do harm to the whole, or as Wordsworth claims, 'We murder to dissect.' Brooks is ever mindful – in the act of criticism – that he must work toward an organic unity, a holistic act that attempts to embrace the poem at once – not in pieces. He does not wish to make of the poem something else – an example for his theoretical concerns – as the critic might do if he or she separated the swing of the hammer from the arc of the arm and the strike of the nail.

To this end, Brooks contends in 'Irony as a Principle of Structure' that the poet risks direct communication when using metaphor, yet the potential gains in the use of metaphor make such a risk more than justifiable. Brooks suggests that formalist criticism, while fraught with paradox, bridges the gap between the concrete, detailed workings of the poem and what the poem says in terms of content, opening a space for a different form of communication, as metaphor does in the making of a poem. 'The concrete particulars with which the poet loads himself,' Brooks asserts, 'seem to deny the universal to which he aspires. The poet wants to "say" something. Why, then, doesn't he say it directly and forthrightly? Why is he willing to say it only through his metaphors? Through his metaphors, he risks saying it partially and obscurely, and risks not saying it at all.' Yet Brooks insists that 'the risk must be taken, for direct statement leads to abstraction and threatens to take us out of poetry altogether' (799). For this reason Brooks fights adamantly against any notion that a literary text may be paraphrased. Unlike fellow formalist John Crowe Ransom, who argued that a poem has a 'paraphrasable core,' Brooks maintains that the 'being' of the poem rests in its formal structure, in its numerous parts that work in concert – not in some paraphrase ripped from the center of the poem. In 'The Heresy of Paraphrase,' Brooks describes the violence done to a poem in the act of abstraction: 'If we allow ourselves to be misled by the heresy of paraphrase, we run the risk of doing even more violence to the internal order of the poem itself. By taking the paraphrase as our point of stance, we misconceive the function of metaphor and meter. We demand logical coherences where they are sometimes irrelevant, and we fail frequently to see imaginative coherences on levels where they are highly relevant' (1036). Again, we return to the idea of formalist criticism as praxis, as a moment when poem and reader are fused, when the formal structure of the poem, as well as its relevance to the human condition, become clear, when the universal and the concrete are joined by metaphor and coalesce into something that may be described but never fully explained – and, of course, all of this returns us to the ambiguity and paradox that the New Critics not only embraced in the art they were drawn to, but also in their own criticism, in the very act of engagement with the art object. As Brooks notes, there are ways of thinking that move beyond the walls of logic. In his call for the reader to note the imaginative coherences, the asso-ciative ways of thinking that work outside of Western dualities and a sole reliance upon the logos, Brooks seems more a precursor to contemporary forms of criticism than one might anticipate, pointing to the radical nature of this kind of criticism given its place in history.[4]

Another way of knowing: Formalism as literary discourse

With philosophical ties to Kant and aesthetic connections to the English Romantic poets, formalists insist that literature offers a differ-ent way of knowing, a different mode of discourse than science or history, sociology or psychology. As an ontological form of criticism, formalist theory wishes to identify the unique knowledge that art may communicate. In *An Approach to Literature* (1964), Cleanth Brooks, John Purser, and Robert Penn Warren argue that 'literature gives us a picture of life – not the picture that science gives and not a picture that is actually (historically) true, but a picture that has its own kind of truth – a "truth" that includes important elements that science, from its very nature, is forced to leave out' (8). The most significant difference, according to Brooks, Purser, and Warren, involves science's desire to classify and in the process of classification move toward an exclusive use of conceptual and abstract language. Literature, and the criticism that attempts to illuminate it, conversely, relies upon the concrete, the particular, the individual. In concert with dramatic action, these elements 'allow us to experience imaginatively the "lived" meanings of a piece of life' (8).

Again, universalism enters formalist desire by way of the experience of literature. While most formalists continued to mouth the mantra of 'art for art's sake' and insisted that cultural context, biography, history, or a particular reader's response had no place in the workshop of the critic, they did not divorce their pursuit of the literary work from their own human concerns entirely. Rather, the end goal of a close formalist reading was to bring the critic experientially closer to what another human may have felt or encountered – arriving at the conceptual or abstract knowledge of the universe, that science purports to tell, by means of the particularity of art. William Carlos Williams's modernist mantra – 'No ideas but in things' – relates in this way to formalist criticism. It is through the concrete, specific, individual moment captured in a poem or a story that we connect with the universal, elemental core at the heart of all human experience. According to Williams and the New Critics who championed his work, we cannot know the universal through the abstract. The universal can only be experienced through the specific, the particular, the tangible. In *Understanding Poetry* (1938), Brooks and Warren suggest that 'poetry gives us knowledge. It is a knowledge of ourselves in relation to the world of experience, and to that world considered, not statistically, but in terms of human purposes and values' (xiii). Despite their critique of Aristotle's contention that literature is an imitation of life, in their practice the New Critics always return to art as representative of human life. Brooks makes this quite clear in *The Well-Wrought Urn* when he claims that the poem 'is a simulacrum of reality' because it is an experience itself, 'rather than any mere statement about experience' (213).

But how does one begin to differentiate between the experience of the art object and the experience that the art object seeks to represent? Formalist criticism walks a tightrope between these two poles, attempting to balance both concerns. 'The function of criticism,' Allen Tate explains, is 'to maintain and demonstrate the special, unique, and complete knowledge which the great forms of literature afford us. And I mean quite simply *knowledge,* not historical documentation and information' (*Collected Essays* 8). As the reader or critic experiences the poem, he or she gains a certain kind of knowledge – one based upon representation and formal structure. Yet this knowledge remains associated with human interaction in a world beyond the text. Despite Brook's assertion in 'The Formalist Critic' that 'form and content cannot be separated' because 'form is meaning' (72), modernist humanism resides at the heart of formalism. While form and content cannot be parsed from one another and clearly form has a direct impact upon meaning, nonetheless, formalist critics do not choose indiscriminately the forms they praise. Instead, humanist principles appear to direct the critic in the kinds of art studied and the elements praised. 'The whole story is the meaning,' Flannery O'Connor declares, 'because it is an experience, not an abstraction' (*Mystery and Manners* 73), and the experiences that formalist critics doggedly seek after tend to be those that carry the reader toward a contemplation of human struggles and triumphs, emotional toil and joy.

The limits of formalism: Universalism, eclecticism, and morality in the work of F. R. Leavis and Kenneth Burke

In *Literary Criticism: A Short History* (1978), Brooks and Wimsatt describe the distinction between art and science and the bridge criticism and poetry may offer in negotiating this chasm of difference:

> We can have our universals in the full conceptualized discourse of science and philosophy. We can have specific detail lavishly in the newspapers and in records of trials. . . . But it is only in metaphor, and hence it is *par excellence* in poetry, that we encounter the most radically and relevantly fused union of the detail and the universal idea. (479)

It is this grasping after the universal that inevitably led to the demise of formalism in general and New Criticism in particular. While during the first half of the twentieth century most did not condemn the desire of critics to find what might offer universal connection between humans and their cultures – a dominant modernist perspective – the critical practice that emerged from this desire became a tool for British and American dominance and an easy target of critique from more socially oriented forms of criticism like Marxism, feminism, and reader-response theory. Instead of a universalism that attempted to account for a plethora of cultural experiences, Anglo and American critics consistently forced their own narrow perspectives and values upon other cultures and subcultures, often ignoring or devaluing what was different from their own epistemologies and ontologies. For formalists of this ilk, the act of reading always involved both evaluation and explication, and it is in their evaluation of particular works of art that they demonstrated a bias that blinded them to many other formal structures in literary texts within their own and other cultures.

The wide-ranging and influential work of F. R. Leavis offers the best picture of the marriage of formalism and morality, as well as a serious example of the radically truncated picture of universalism shared by many in the academy. An important fixture at Cambridge, Leavis's role as critic cannot be divorced from his role as teacher, nor should his position as chief editor of the journal *Scrutiny*, which published most of his scholarship before it was collected in book form, be overlooked. As the journal's nomenclature suggests, for Leavis, 'scrutiny' is the critic's main concern. While many critics attack Leavis's lack of specificity in his practice of scrutinizing a given text – most notably René Wellek debated Leavis on this matter in the pages of *Scrutiny* in 1937 – little doubt remains that Leavis's demands for close reading, practical criticism, and a celebration of what he called *Life* left an indelible mark upon the ways literature was brought before the masses – both in school and in the generally educated public of England. Leavis's influence in the classroom may be seen most demonstrably in the texts selected for the curriculum of numerous schools and in the manner these texts were approached *vis-à-vis* a formalist close reading that in some slippery fashion transformed the texts into moral beacons of *Life* for an entire culture.

In *Literary Theory: An Introduction* (1983), Terry Eagleton describes Leavis's work with *Scrutiny* and his role as critic as 'nothing less than the last-ditch stand of liberal humanism, concerned, as Eliot and Pound were not, with the unique value of the individual and the creative realm of the interpersonal' (42). As have other critics, Eagleton rails against Leavis for his general and purposefully vague use of the term *Life* – a verbal signifier, Eagleton claims, that Leavis could use to point toward the virtuous elements of humanistic living. Eagleton explains that 'if you asked for some reasoned theoretical statement of their case, you had thereby demonstrated that you were in the outer darkness: either you felt *Life* or you did not' (42). Even more irksome for critics like Eagleton is Leavis's devotion to such writers as D. H. Lawrence. Eagleton claims that Leavis remakes Lawrence, altering – or more likely ignoring – what Eagleton sees as Lawrence's 'raging contempt for liberal and democratic values' and 'a slavish submission to impersonal authority' (42). Perhaps best remembered – notoriously by some, gratefully by others – for his proclamation and codification of the 'Great Tradition,' Leavis's example as a close-reader of noted skill should not be ignored. Leavis liked to compare the accomplished reader to an 'executant musician' who recreates faithfully what he or she divines the composer to have conceived. In this way, Leavis used close-reading and formalist acumen as tools that helped illuminate the work of the composer, that animated the black notes upon the page, leading the reader to a better feeling for *Life*. Yet Leavis could not divorce himself from his broader role in culture. It is for this reason that he lauds technical or formal originality in *The Great Tradition* (1948) only insofar as it leads to a 'reverent openness before life' (18). Leavis demands that the true focus of the creative artist and the critic alike must be the 'interests of life' (16), the moral or spiritual valuation of all human activity. Needless to say, it is in his desire to embrace *all* human activity that Leavis falls short. Just as his limited listing of writers that comprise the 'great tradition' radically truncates the kinds of human *greatness* that might exist in literature, Leavis's notion of human life represents only his own limited perception, not the true variegation of human community in all its radical and ever-changing diversity – a shortcoming for one of formalism's most celebrated and vocal proponents that allowed many opponents of the critical movement to critique and overturn its decades-long dominance.

In a similar fashion, the work of Kenneth Burke offers a fine example of the inevitable shifts formalism would make in order to survive in some evolved manner during the mid-twentieth century.

Unlike Leavis, Burke is seldom held up as the object of disdain – perhaps because he did not hold the political clout that Leavis or Eliot held at the height of their careers. Yet Burke offers a clear picture of the kinds of shifts and permutations that formalism experienced as it slowly rendered its role as the dominant and domineering critical methodology of the age to other more reader-oriented forms of criticism. Never a narrow formalist, Burke consistently flouted the 'rules' established by his more stringent and legalistic contemporaries. In fact, as latter day defender of 'pure' formalism, Murray Krieger dismisses Burke from the formalist roll call in *The New Apologists for Poetry* (1956) because, as Krieger notes, Burke's progressive turn toward other disciplines and his claims for the different ways of seeing and knowing offered by these disciplines in the reading of a literary text in some way polluted or diluted the power of the formalist paradigm. Burke's work does indeed encompass sociology, psychology, philosophy, biography, aesthetics, politics, ethics, religion, and anthropology in a manner that reveals how formal structure might relate to many other ways of thinking and perceiving. As he explains in 'Kinds of Criticism,' close reading 'sustains the intense contemplation of an object to the point where one begins to see not only more deeply into the object but beyond it, in the direction of generalizations about the kinds of art and artistic excellence, and even the principles of human thought and experience universally' (278).

This progressive shift from the work of art to what lies beyond the art object mirrors Burke's own critical divisions. Of utmost importance to Burke is the clear delineation between different modes of thought and critique, suggesting that like other formalists he believed matters of biography or history – when looked at in concert with formalist concerns – might lead the reader away from a better understanding of the art object. Instead of combining these varied concerns at once in the act of reading, Burke contends that a layered approach functions best to illuminate one's interpretation of the text. In this system, Burke links *Poetics* with *Grammar, Rhetoric,* and *Ethics,* while cautioning that each should be used distinctly, not in concert, during critical analysis. For Burke, Grammar relates to content, to literature as a source of information; Rhetoric focuses on response, or upon the power a given text may have to enact change; Poetics attends to the aesthetic, to the idea of what may be defined as beautiful; and, finally, Ethics involves moral value, the way a text may capture the ethical dimensions of a given life. In *Language as Symbolic Action: Essays on*

Life, Literature, and Method (1966), Burke's desire to separate these modes of analysis surfaces in a rather dramatic and straightforward fashion. 'With regard to Poetics in particular,' Burke asserts, 'I would propose to make rules in that dimension as strict as possible. Absolutely no biographical reference would be admissible. History itself would be admissible only in the sense that the meaning (and allusiveness) of a term will change throughout the centuries' (497). Burke's reason for this adamant turn from history or biography when contemplating what he called poetic action is grounded in the formalist's insistence that 'the material must stand or fall by reason of its role in the story, regardless of whether it arose in the course of the writing, or was lifted from a notebook, or was even stolen or borrowed from someone else' (497). But unlike his formalist kindred, when using his other critical modalities, Burke allowed for the critical consideration of more than just the formal success of a given work. In *Counter-Statement* (1931), Burke insists that we consider the emotion of the artist, as well as the structures the artist uses to stir emotion in his reader: 'The artist begins with his emotion, he translates this emotion into a mechanism for arousing emotion in others, and thus his interest in his own emotion transcends into his interest in the treatment' (55). Clearly, such statements placed Burke beyond the tight inner-circle of regimented formalists, but Burke nonetheless retained his formalist stripes by consistently returning to form, albeit not as ascetically as some would have liked. In *The Philosophy of Literary Form* (1941), Burke demonstrates most plainly the fluidity of his thought and its relation to form by insisting that the 'focus of critical analysis must be upon the structure of the given work itself,' but that an 'observation about structure is more relevant when you approach the work as the *functioning* of a structure' (74).

Burke's ability to transcend a single reading modality allows certain formalist concerns and techniques to survive to the present day. Clearly, many contemporary critics, regardless of their political stripes, engage formalist techniques to read works of literature through their own particular critical lenses. Burke's incorporation of a variety of disciplines, however, felt like a threatening gesture to many at the time. In strikingly similar fashion to the present cry that postmodern theories have overshadowed or even superseded the literary text, Randall Jarrell proclaimed in 1959 that 'critics are so much better armed than they used to be in the old days: they've got tanks and flame throwers now . . . it's harder to see past them to the work of art –

in fact, magnificent creatures that they are, it's hard to *want* to see past them' (85). And with Jarrell's worrisome words – representative of so many different schools of formalists – we come full circle to the true matter: the art object. Does literary art represent human rhetorical activity at a higher, more distinctive level? Should literature be privileged in some way beyond the more utilitarian texts of everyday life found in newspapers and magazines? Indeed, why are we drawn to the study of art in the first place, and how do formalist concerns help us to identify what we call 'art'? And, finally, what role in the contemporary setting should formalist ideals play in our desire to engage the art object?

The evolution of formalism: The case of Northrop Frye

By examining the influential work of Northrop Frye, we may find possible answers to some of these questions. Frye's work points in a direction that allows the critic to distinguish and accentuate the formal properties of a given artistic text, while remaining concerned with how that text speaks to our human experiences. By joining certain formalist techniques with a philosophy that emphasizes the interrelationship of human patterns of living and thinking, Frye helps move literary studies beyond a narrowly prescribed formalism without abandoning formalist thought altogether – an example that opens up the possibility of appending formalist techniques to other theoretical schools beyond Frye's own archetypal criticism.

The variety of archetypal criticism that Frye spent his career espousing – as a descendant of the psychological and anthropological work of theorists such as Jung – seems less dogmatic about the shared psyche of the entire human race and far more concerned with the way existing story patterns impact our shared human encounters. In the shift from pre-literary categories of ritual, myth, and folktale to the written artifacts of literary texts, archetypal criticism, as practiced by Frye, introduces issues of formal properties as vital to the study of story design. Similar to a formalist, Frye contends that 'in all literary verbal structures the final direction of meaning is inward' (*Anatomy* 74), and he assumes that literature inhabits language structures that differ from common speech and writing, that language in literary texts is elevated and manipulated in ways that transform it from the utilitarian tool of communication into the realm of art. For Frye, plot

motif, character type, image, and symbol are the tools of the literary
artist and the subject of investigation for the critic. When studying the
poem or fiction, the archetypal critic, like the formalist, assumes that
the art object represents a special space, one that is more or less self-
contained, and in some fashion outside the strictures of history or
personage. But Frye differs from some formalists in his understanding
of literature as permanent and universal, applicable to and connected
with human life throughout time. 'The true father or shaping spirit of
the poem is the form of the poem itself,' Frye explains in *Anatomy of
Criticism* (1957), 'and this form is a manifestation of the universal
spirit of poetry, the "onlie begetter" of Shakespeare's sonnets who was
not Shakespeare himself' (98). According to Frye, the form of the
poem shapes what it may say as well as how it will impact its readers.
Yet Frye oscillates between the formal structures of a given work and
its universal implications, between the connective tissue of design
and the particular understanding or way of knowing as it relates to all
humans – what Frye refers to as the 'universal spirit of poetry.'

In *Anatomy of Criticism*, Frye succinctly describes the difference
between literature and other forms of language use, a key to both his
work as a formalist and as a myth critic:

> In literature, questions of fact or truth are subordinated to the primary
> literary aim of producing a structure of words for its own sake, and the
> sign-values of symbols are subordinated to their importance as a
> structure of interconnected motifs. Wherever we have an autonomous
> verbal structure of this kind, we have literature. Wherever this
> autonomous structure is lacking we have language, words used
> instrumentally to help human consciousness do or understand some-
> thing else. Literature is a specialized form of language. (74)

Most critics today would not describe literature as 'a structure of
words for its own sake,' but this seems to be an argument of degree
not of complete disagreement. The texts that literary critics choose to
work with, as well as the *way* they work with them, reveals that Frye's
assertion that literature somehow is different – a structure of words
that revels in its own making as much as it revels in what it *says* –
continues to impact on the pragmatic decisions of most critics in the
academy. While some critics work with the popular narratives of a
given culture and time – for example, the Horatio Alger stories that
populated the late nineteenth- and early twentieth-century landscape

of the United States – these very same critics seldom, if ever, make an argument for the artistic merit or credibility of those narratives. Instead, it is assumed that these narratives tell us important information about gender or class or religion in America, but never about artistic integrity or success or, for that matter, about what lies at the core of human experience, what makes life worthy of attention and value. Unlike Frye, who plainly states that his preoccupation with archetypes does not do away with his concern for formal worthiness in his selection of texts, contemporary critics of all stripes often choose texts that clearly offer a level of artistic merit that other texts would not. Yet such critics will not admit to their predisposition for texts of literary and artistic merit.

In bridging the worlds of artistic worth and archetypal criticism – the former often associated with formalist criticism and the latter with myth criticism – Frye does not exclude the idea that literature has some relation to reality. Rather, he sees that relation as latent and ever-changing, as a place that does not offer the critic solid footholds. Rather than denying or banishing other critical concerns, Frye creates a hierarchy for those concerns, suggesting what the critic should pay most attention to first. An Aristotelian to the core, Frye wishes to study the art object in its complete and final unity. Yet he does not deny that literary texts have an impact upon the reader, that the experience of a given work might lead someone into ecstasy or despair, that such forms of art offer a kind of engagement with the range of human emotions. Such matters, however, seem less the province of the literary critic to Frye and more the domain of the common reader. Similarly, Frye has no patience for biographical criticism – despite the fact that he concentrated upon Romantic literature where such forms of criticism thrive.

Ultimately, Frye returns to the work itself. In the 'Polemical Introduction' to *Anatomy of Criticism*, he contends that 'critical principles cannot be taken over ready-made from theology, philosophy, politics, science, or any combination of these. To subordinate criticism to an externally derived critical attitude is to exaggerate the values in literature that can be related to the external source, whatever it is' (7). It is not that Frye does not see the value in theology, philosophy, politics, or science, but rather, that he believes in literary art as a special and separate realm – somehow distinct and independent from these other ways of knowing. This position echoes the ideological stances of many formalists, yet Frye's ability to move forward without the dogmatism and shaky insecurity that characterize most formalist rants against other disciplinary approaches to literature distinguishes him and his work. Because Frye's position incorporates a formalist aesthetic, but does not limit itself solely to the defense of that aesthetic, his criticism, while remaining distinct from other disciplines, does enter into conversation with those same disciplines. 'The moment we go from the individual work of art to the sense of the total form of the art,' Frye explains, 'the art becomes no longer an object of aesthetic contemplation but an ethical instrument, participating in the work of civilization' (*Anatomy* 349). In this way, Frye allows for the intersection of other disciplinary approaches to literature. The 'work of civilization' permits the critic to join with other scholars from other fields in an attempt to bridge the disciplinary boundaries that far too often restrict the kinds of conversations that lead to fruitful knowledge about who we are and how we build the structures that contain our knowledge and our daily patterns of living.[5] In *The Critical Path* (1971), Frye succinctly concludes that 'criticism will always have two aspects, one turned toward the structure of literature and one turned toward the other cultural phenomena that form the social environment of literature. Together, they balance each other' (25), and it is such a balance that brings vitality to Frye's own investigation.

Formalist concerns in the present

It would be naïve to suggest that with the shift in power from formalism to mythological criticism, psychoanalytic criticism, Marxist criticism, feminist criticism, and the many other forms of theory-driven reading that have dominated the second half of the twentieth century, we have altogether left behind formalist thought. The idea that formalism was in some way conquered and then vanquished from the kingdom of criticism makes use of a combative, competitive model of knowledge. It establishes a hierarchical form of thinking – as Harold Bloom's *Anxiety of Influence: A Theory of Poetry* (1973) set forth in terms of an Oedipal complex of critical proportion – that demands the critic kill his or her forbears, disregarding their accomplishments and their discoveries. Sadly, the world of literary criticism has continued to operate under a system of veiled silences or passive aggression in which scholars ignore or disdain the work of other scholars in order to further their interpretive causes.

Yet if postmodern theory has done anything at all, it has, at the very least, opened up space for the proliferation of critical voices. Rather than searching for a univocal reading of a literary text – an act championed by more than just the New Critics – postmodernism insists that there can be no single reading of a work, only endless multiplicities. Such freedom, however, does not necessarily lead to complete relativism; judgements of literary texts and literary criticism are still bound by discourse communities: there remain valid and invalid interpretations based upon the accepted framework of the given community. Of course, as the academy has grown in number and diversity, the kinds of communities involved in literary studies have radically changed, and the types of languages spoken by the literary critics who inhabit these communities often serve only to distance one community from another. Such distancing, at times, creates the very boundaries that postmodern theorists had hoped to destroy. Moreover, in the end, such ideological turf wars seem to do nothing more than confuse students and scholars alike as they search for an entry into the study of literature.

Rather than perpetuate a model of critical thought that may only operate through verbal violence – the silencing of other critical modes through attack and the obfuscation of position by over-publishing – we suggest that criticism at present be seen as an amalgamation of a variety of critical discourses. Far from vanquished, formalist concerns play a significant role in a wide range of critical modalities. While the question of aesthetic value is posed in radically different ways than it was 60 years ago – and answered by even more distinctive means – this does not suggest that the question has ceased to impinge upon the work of the critic. With the accretion of theoretical knowledge, a critic takes into account a number of issues as he or she examines a short story or a poem or a novel. Because the human activity of literary criticism is limited – finite in what it may examine and report – no critic may write about all of the elements of a given work: the aesthetic, the social, the psychological, the structural, the philosophical, and so on. But that does not mean the critic has not taken into consideration such formal concerns in the selection of the text or in the reading of that text. Like Burke or Frye, the critic wears scholarly lenses that cause certain elements of a literary work to rise from the page, similar to the shift that occurs when one views an image with 3-D glasses. And we can only hope that contemporary critics will be as magnanimous in their inclusion of other disciplines and epistemologies as Burke and Frye. At present, the glasses worn by most critics do not produce an image that focuses with any great intensity upon the formalist qualities of a given text. But, as Christopher Clausen has noted in 'Reading Closely Again,' critics as diverse as Stanley Fish, Frank Lentricchia, Richard Rorty, and Harold Bloom have all suggested that literature may, in fact, be different than other kinds of texts, that it may be read for pleasure and not as an illustration of something else.

2 Russian Formalism, Mikhail Bakhtin, Heteroglossia, and Carnival

> There can be neither a first nor last meaning; it always exists among other meanings as a link in the chain of meaning, which in its totality is the only thing that can be real. In historical life, this chain continues infinitely, and therefore each individual link in it is renewed again and again, as though it were reborn.
>
> (Mikhail M. Bakhtin, *Problems of Dostoevsky's Poetics*[1])

As with American and British variations of formalist criticism, the historical confluence of Russian Formalism, the Moscow Linguistics Circle, and the Prague Structuralists in the first three decades of the twentieth century acted as one of the most significant and formative influences upon the direction of literary theory and criticism during the latter half of the century. While it is difficult to pinpoint the precise impact of these movements upon American New Criticism or the advent of postmodernity, for example, their insights into narratology, linguistics, and literary interpretation provided later scholars with the intellectual foundations for the structuralism that would exist as the bedrock for an evolving theoretical project. Led by such figures as Victor Shklovsky, Boris Eichenbaum, Jan Mukarovsky, Yuri Tynyanov, and Roman Jakobson, among others, Russian Formalism resulted from the work of two groups of Russian literary critics and linguists, including the Moscow Linguistics Circle (founded in 1915) and the Society for the Study of Poetic Language (founded in St Petersburg in 1916). Russian formalists eschewed the notion that literature could best be understood in terms of such extra-literary matters as philosophy, history, sociology, biography, and autobiography. Initially, they employed formalism as a derogatory term for the analysis of literature's formal structures and technical patterns. As Russian Formalism's ideology became more refined, however, the concept began to assume more neutral connotations. Russian Formalists – as with the Prague Structuralists who would champion Russian Formalism's critique after their suppression by the Soviet government in the 1930s – argue that literature functions upon a series of unique features of language that allows it to afford the reader with a mode of experience unavailable via the auspices of ordinary language.

Russian Formalists refer to these special features of literature as *literaturnost*, or a particular work's 'literariness.' In a 1921 essay, Jakobson writes that 'the object of literary science is not literature but literariness, i.e., what makes a given work a literary work' (qtd. in Steiner, *Russian Formalism* 23). In addition to founding the Prague school of structural linguistics and phonology, his name would later become nearly synonymous with our universal concepts of structuralism as an intellectual movement of considerable influence upon the nature and direction of the twentieth-century theoretical project. For Jakobson, the concept of *literaturnost* underscores the distinctive features inherent in the various discourses and linguistic forms of literature. More specifically, the notion of literariness refers to the internal relations, within a given literary work, among the linguistic signs and signifiers that comprise such formal features of literary study. In *Russian Formalism: A Metapoetics* (1984), Peter Steiner writes: 'If all literary works were literary, but some at a given moment were more literary than others, it is not an unchangeable essence but a changeable *relationship* among works that constitute literariness' (114). In short, the concept of literariness resides within the relational spaces established by a text's capacity for utilizing literary or poetic language.[2]

Expositors of Russian Formalism often ascribe the relational aspects of the formalist critique to Kantian notions of unity, meaning, and the organic structure of art. The Russian symbolist Andrey Bely based his conception of symbolism on Kant's theories regarding the relationship between art and other modes of human experience. In 'The Symbolization of Meaning,' Bely profoundly influenced the course of the formalist methodology through his analyses of 'the unity of form and content' and 'the unity of cognition in the forms of experience' (qtd. in Thompson 60). While anti-symbolists such as Shklovsky challenged the arguments of Bely and the other progenitors of Russian Symbolism, Shklovsky recognized the interpretive value of understanding a given literary work's form in terms of its relationship with the notions of content and experience. Although terminological battles characterized much of early Russian Formalism, Shklovsky's 1916 essay, 'Art as Device,' provided formalists with a significant touchstone in their quest to establish their own form of intellectual and theoretical unity. Shklovsky's essay advanced a theory of narrative prose in which the author introduced the concept of *priem*, or 'device.' In addition to distinguishing between the aims of literary scholarship and the empirical sciences, the idea of the device afforded Shklovsky with the means for postulating the textual mechanism responsible for the literary structures and effects that distinguish literary modes of experience from the properties of ordinary language. As Jurij Striedter observes in *Literary Structure, Evolution, and Value: Russian Formalism and Czech Structuralism Reconsidered* (1989), Shklovsky's ground-breaking study of *priem* resulted in 'the thesis that art is nothing but the consistent application and effect of such devices' (23).

Shklovsky advanced Russian Formalism's differentiation between ordinary language and artistic discourse by highlighting art's ability to provide avenues of fresh perception that allow us to recognize new dimensions of reality and aesthetic value. Shklovsky contends that art accomplishes this end through its 'defamiliarization' of the world. In addition to revealing the artistic devices that account for artistic effect, Shklovsky hypothesized that this defamiliarizing concept of *ostranenie*, or the 'making strange' of things, finds its origins in literary, as opposed to ordinary, language. While Jakobson, among others, argued that *ostranenie* neglected to account for the artistic essence of poetic language, Shklovsky's analysis of estrangement acted as a defining moment for incipient Russian formalism because of the manner in which it imbued the movement with a significant and much needed sense of intellectual and artistic relevance. Simply put, *ostranenie* provided literary critics with a means for comprehending Russian Formalism's goals for understanding the origins of art's creative and transformative vitality. Shklovsky's concept of defamiliarization involves two distinct concepts, including the idea that estrangement challenges conventional notions of linguistic and social perception, thus forcing the perceiver to reconceive his or her relationship with the world. Secondly, *ostranenie* focuses the perceiver's attention upon the literary work, as well as its contingent possibilities for defamiliarization and for undermining the ordinariness inherent in the extra-textual world. As Striedter notes, the innovative and polemical nature of *ostranenie* is underscored by its ramifications in terms of the literary tradition and the concept of canonicity: 'If literature gains and maintains effectiveness only through defamiliarization, once the newly created forms become canonized and thereby automatic, they, too, must be made strange once again. The theory of defamiliarization,' Striedter adds, 'flows into a theory of literary evolution as a "tradition of breaking with tradition"' (24).

As with *ostranenie*, Shklovsky's explorations of *syuzhet* (plot) produced a variety of meaningful revelations regarding the role (or lack thereof) of plot in literary works. In a 1921 essay, 'Literature beyond Plot,' Shklovsky devotes particular emphasis to works of 'plot-less' literature. Shklovsky demonstrates that the dissolution of traditional plot conventions allows for a kind of literary evolution because of the manner in which it forces writers to experiment with new themes and devices. Shklovsky's article yields two significant conclusions in terms of Russian Formalism's methodological aims. First, Shklovsky underscores the various ways in which plot experimentation ultimately serves as a catalyst for a given genre's structural evolution – an important aspect of Russian Formalism, particularly in terms of the movement's interest in organicism. Second, Shklovsky challenges the boundaries inherent in our understanding of the concept of genre. Rather than functioning as a fixed canon that operates in terms of a set of firm rules and procedures, genre also exists in Shklovsky's schema as a constantly shifting and evolving mechanism. In his own discussions of plot and its structural role in literary works, Tynyanov takes issue with the latter conclusion, especially regarding Shklovsky's comprehension of literary parody, which he perceives as an automatic and comedic device. In his 1921 article, 'Dostoevsky and Gogol: Toward a Theory of Parody,' Tynyanov identifies parody as an organic force that – as with *syuzhet* – operates as an instrument for literary evolution because of the way in which parody simultaneously deconstructs its precursory texts as it constructs new forms of narrative.

As one of the most influential formalists of his era, Vladimir Propp also formulated a system for understanding the operation of literary works based upon a series of functional elements. Propp devoted particular attention to the role of surface detail, literary characters, and narratological elements in Russian fairy tales. Recognizing that previous efforts at analyzing fairy tales in terms of theme and plot had been intellectually fruitless, Propp opted instead to evaluate the tales via the series of character sequences and narrative tropes that characterize their construction. In *Morphology of the Folktale* (1928), Propp emphasizes the abstract structural elements and their textual function in terms of a given work's artistic and aesthetic whole. Propp's important work on behalf of Russian Formalism's critical aims cannot be emphasized enough. As Steiner writes: 'On the most abstract level, he conceived of the fairy tale as a narrative about actions performed by certain characters. And it is the actions, and not the interchangeable characters, that count' (*Russian Formalism* 84). By demonstrating the organic qualities of narrative, Propp succeeded in revealing the nature of the generic, structural components of story. Propp's attention, moreover, to the relational aspects of literature finally afford Russian Formalism with the capacity for establishing general laws regarding the conditions and nature of the structural elements associated with narrative. Propp's achievements in terms of Russian fairy tales also provide formalists with the critical means for articulating their programmatic goals and concerns to other schools and their proponents.

As with *ostranenie, syuzhet,* and Propp's elucidation of various structural elements, Eichenbaum's conception of *skaz* remains among Russian Formalism's most significant contributions to literary criticism. A richly textured narrative technique inherent in nineteenth- and twentieth-century Russian prose, *skaz* refers to literary works in which metaphor, theme, and point of view function according to the stylistic requirements of oral narration and folktales. In a 1918 essay, 'The Illusion of the *Skaz*,' Eichenbaum offers a detailed discussion of *skaz* as a literary phenomenon, as well as a vehicle for understanding the fundamental nature of plot as a structural element. In addition to defining plot as the 'interweaving of motifs by the aid of their motivations' (qtd. in Striedter 44), Eichenbaum examines the role of the narrator in establishing the tone of a given plot. In an essay on Nikolai Gogol's 'The Overcoat,' for example, Eichenbaum explores the ways in which the narrative serves to create distance between the reader and the plot, as well as between the narrator himself and the story's protagonist. The aesthetics of irony in the story demonstrate the manner in which *skaz*'s structural elements exist in a kind of interrelationship that impinges upon the nature of the reader's textual experience. Eichenbaum's postulation of *skaz* exists as a singular moment within the brief history of Russian Formalism precisely because of its illumination of the simultaneous roles of such structural elements as linguistics, stylistics, point of view, and plot in our consumption and understanding of narrative.

In one of Russian Formalism's most significant instances of narratological innovation, Mukarovsky proposed the concept of 'foregrounding,' or the act of placing an idea or element in sharp contrast with the other components of a given work of art. Clearly, estrangement or defamiliarization operates as a kind of foregrounding technique that allows readers to perceive the structural nature of literary language. Jakobson, Tynyanov, and other formalists accomplish a similar end in their analysis of such structural matters as meter, alliteration, and rhyme. As with such fundamental prose concepts as plot and genre, the notions of meter, alliteration, and rhyme function as the organic material via which poetry evolves as a literary tradition. In poetry, meter establishes a kind of progressive force that propels the verse, while alliteration and rhyme, on the other hand, serve as regressive elements because of their reliance upon sound repetition. In other words, formalists such as Tynyanov comprehend poetry in terms of these inherently contradictory forces – the former of which contributes to the organic, evolving nature of poetry as a literary tradition, while the latter operates as a constraining mechanism. Foregrounding various structural elements inherent in verse enables critics such as Tynyanov to isolate these narratological components and identify their role in poetry's textual construction. This process also reveals the unifying mechanisms that undergird works of literary art. For the Russian Formalists, unity clearly exists as one of the central principles of literary organization.

Signs, signifiers, and the Prague Linguistic Circle

As with the Russian Formalists, contemporary literary critics and linguists clearly owe a historical and intellectual debt to the efforts of the Prague Linguistic Circle, the group of scholars in the former Czechoslovakia who continued the work of the Russian Formalists after their suppression by the Soviet government during the 1930s. Led by such figures as Jakobson, Vilém Mathesius, Lucien Tesnière, and René Wellek, the Prague Structuralists explored the intersections between linguistics and literary theory. As a group, their examinations of language and other sign systems became more specialized and illuminating after they began to absorb the theories of Ferdinand de Saussure regarding the synchronic analysis of language and its semantic functions. In terms of linguistics, the Prague Structuralist's most important achievements include the liberation of phonology from phonetics, as well as Jakobson's work on semantics, Mathesius's revolutionary discoveries regarding syntax, and Wellek's theories about literary theory and aesthetics. The advent of the Second World War curtailed their activities, which came to a sudden and precipitous halt after the Nazis closed Czech universities in October 1939. Jakobson continued their work in the interim in the United States; the Prague Structuralists resumed their activities in Czechoslovakia in the 1950s, only to be interrupted by the pressures of Marxist dogmatism. They reformed during the latter half of the 1950s under the auspices of the Soviet-inspired Czechoslovak Academy of Sciences, an organization that witnessed many linguistic accomplishments in the tradition of the Prague Linguistic Circle, especially the discoveries of such figures as Bohumil Trnka and Josef Vachek, among others. The Prague Structuralists enjoyed a revival of sorts during the 1990s after the restoration of democracy in Czechoslovakia.

In an essay commemorating the Prague Structuralists' pioneering work in 'Phonology and Graphemics,' Vachek attributes one of the group's most enduring achievements to the Praguian conception of the phoneme, which has since become a standard phonological term. Jakobson defines the phoneme as 'a set of those concurrent sound properties which are used in the given language to distinguish words of unlike meaning' (14). By highlighting the nature and function of the basic unit of phonology, the Prague Structuralists were poised to emancipate the study of phonology from the more exclusive terrain of phonetics. Phonology involves the study of speech sounds of a given language and their operation within the sound system of that language. In the contemporary parlance of linguistics, the term refers not only to the field of phonemics, but also to the study of sound changes in the history of a given language, that is, diachronic phonology. The Prague Structuralists' innovative research on behalf of phonology resulted in new discoveries regarding the problems of written language and orthography, while also serving as a means for highlighting the interdisciplinary connections between linguistics and narratology. The group's work in the 1930s included similar accomplishments in terms of our larger understanding of semantics and syntax. Through his examination of the Russian case system,

Jakobson identified the presence of binary oppositions, a concept that would impact our understanding of morphological units, as well as the course of structuralism. Mathesius is often credited with having postulated the Prague Structuralists' sentence-pattern model of syntax, a morphological mechanism that allows for the analysis of the linguistic signs inherent in every communicative speech act.

While many literary historians acknowledge the Prague Structuralists' efforts on behalf of linguistic innovation, the group's significant contributions to our understanding of literature and aesthetics merit attention. Felix Vodichka's commentaries on the nature of the literary process and Wellek's attempts at formulating general principles of literary study exemplify this aspect of the Prague Structuralists' work. In 'The Concretization of the Literary Work: Problems of the Reception of Neruda's Works,' Vodichka discusses the role of readerly perception in the literary process, a system that he defines in terms of the authorial subject who generates the artistic text and yet another subjectified other, the reader. Recognizing that the socially produced artistic norms of a given era ultimately share in the construction of literary works, Vodichka demonstrates the ways in which readers perceive narratives based upon their own socially and historically contingent moments of being. A signal moment in the early history of reader-response and phenomenological criticism, Vodichka's study of perception theories reveals the manner in which the reading process is encoded by the conditions and structural components inherent in the literary experience. 'The higher structure of the artistic literary tradition is always present as a factor organizing the aesthetic effect of the work if it is to become an aesthetic object,' Vodichka writes. 'Therefore the work is understood as a sign whose meaning and aesthetic value are comprehensible only on the basis of the literary conventions of a specific period' (110).

Vodichka's study of readerly perception also established several important inroads into our conception of authorship and its place in the construction of literary works. 'Besides the literary work,' Vodichka observes, 'the "author" often becomes related to the developing literary structure. Here, we are concerned with the author not as psychophysical being but, in a metonymical sense, as the unity comprised of the works of a particular author in their entirety' (122). As with the Prague Structuralists' Russian Formalist precursors, Vodichka's conclusions about the interrelationships between authorship and narrative ultimately demonstrate the significant role of unity

in the artistic experience. In his various analyses of the general principles that govern literary study, Wellek acknowledges similar interconnections between a given work's structural elements and its capacity
for creating unity. 'The work of art is,' Wellek writes in *Theory of
Literature* (with Austin Warren, 1942), 'considered as a whole system
of signs, or structure of signs, serving a specific aesthetic purpose'
(141). By accenting the structural devices that characterize the literary
experience, the Russian Formalists' and Prague Structuralists' critique
of literature and language inevitably strives to highlight the roles of
linguistic signs, artistic unity, and literariness that produce our
conceptions of narrative. Their discoveries about the nature of
linguistics and literary criticism altered the course of twentieth-
century textual scholarship and ushered in a new era marked by an
interest in narratology and structuralism. The lingering effects of the
Russian Formalists and Prague Structuralists are evidenced, moreover, by the influential scholarly work of such later figures as Roland
Barthes, Mikhail M. Bakhtin, and Fredric Jameson, among a host of
others.

Bakhtin and the narratological revolution

Perhaps the most renowned Russian Formalist in the annals of
contemporary literary studies, Bakhtin revivified Saussure's theories
of linguistics in his approach to narrative and literary analysis. In his
vast critical corpus, Bakhtin differentiates between monologic, single-
voiced works in which a given culture's dominant ideology contra-
dicts subordinate textual voices and dialogic, multivoiced texts that
allow numerous voices to emerge and engage in dialogue with one
another. In 'Discourse in the Novel,' Bakhtin argues that 'form and
content in discourse are one, once we understand that verbal
discourse is a social phenomenon – social throughout its entire range
and in each and every of its factors, from the sound image to the
furthest reaches of abstract meaning' (259). Bakhtin's narratological
theories of heteroglossia and carnival continue to emerge as his most
significant contributions to literary criticism. Bakhtin's conception of
heteroglossia assists us, for example, in understanding the manner in
which literary works function on microlinguistic levels by intersecting
a wide variety of competing utterances and speech acts. In 'Discourse
in the Novel,' Bakhtin writes that heteroglossia involves 'specific

points of view of the world, forms for conceptualizing the world in words, specific world views, each characterized by its own objects, meanings, and values' (291-92). Heteroglossia refers to the centripetal (or official) and centrifugal (or unofficial) forces that permeate the rhythms of daily life, and these forces register our responses to the events that mark our workaday worlds. Our interaction with them, according to Bakhtin's astute expositors Gary Saul Morson and Caryl Emerson in *Mikhail Bakhtin: Creation of a Prosaics* (1990), subsequently reinscribes the nature of our cultural institutions, our various languages, and ourselves.[3]

Bakhtin's postulation of carnival as a narratological phenomenon finds its origins in *Rabelais and His World* (1968), which includes his analysis of various aspects of carnivalesque folk-culture in the Renaissance-era writings of French humanist François Rabelais. For Bakhtin, carnival refers to the celebratory period in which official hierarchies and texts become inverted by populist, utopian notions of society and festivity. In short, low culture replaces high culture as the primary determinant of social structure and language; exuberance, scatology, and excess trump decorum, etiquette, and restraint. In *Rabelais and His World*, Bakhtin writes: 'As opposed to the official feast, one might say that carnival celebrates temporary liberation from the prevailing truth and from the established order; it marked the suspension of all hierarchical rank, privileges, norms, and prohibitions'. 'Carnival was the true feast of time,' he adds, 'the feast of becoming, change, and renewal. It was hostile to all that was immortalized and completed' (10). Characterized by the suspension of hierarchical precedence, carnival establishes equality and elevates the roles of communication and experience in human interrelations. Carnival consists, moreover, of a 'continual shifting from top to bottom, from front to rear, of numerous parodies and travesties, humiliations, profanations, comic crownings and uncrownings,' Bakhtin writes. 'It is to a certain extent a parody of the extra-carnival life, a "world inside out"' (11). Carnival, in the Rabelaisian sense, devotes particular attention to the body's various experiences and transformations during the carnivalesque moment. How does the body assert itself among other bodies? How does it transgress official channels of communication and effect cultural, intellectual, and economic commerce with other, equally transgressive bodies?[4]

Bakhtin's conception of dialogism undergirds much of his philosophy of literary formalism, particularly in regard to his postulation of the carnivalesque. In *Problems of Dostoevsky's Poetics* (1929), Bakhtin differentiates between monologic and dialogic texts. In Bakhtin's terminology, monologic works are dominated by single, controlling voices or discourses. Although such texts may feature characters speaking from a diversity of viewpoints, monologic works typically represent the official ideological stance of the author's culture. Dialogic texts allow for the existence and convergence of a wide range of disparate voices and discourses. In contrast with monologic texts, dialogic works depict the voice (or voices) of a culture's dominant ideology in competition with the voices or discourses of the larger popular culture. For Bakhtin, moreover, no work can exist in a genuinely monologic vacuum. Bakhtin contends that narrators – despite what may be their ostensible intentions to represent only official ideologies and discourses – inevitably interact with the divergent voices that characterize the popular cultures of their fictive worlds. As Chip Rhodes astutely observes, 'The tremendous appeal of Mikhail Bakhtin's dialogic lies in its refusal of the old problematic of the relationship between the individual and society. By rejecting Saussure's distinction between *langue* and *parole*, Bakhtin effectively dissolves the facile dichotomy between subjects and social formations, thus opening up new ways to conceive of agency and social transformation' (760). Simply put, Bakhtin's conception of dialogism affords literary critics with the means for understanding society's peculiar, invariably competing and contradictory vocabularies of meaning.

Finally, Bakhtin's concept of the chronotope represents one of his most significant, albeit complex contributions to Russian Formalism.[5] Chronotope (literally 'time space') refers to the aesthetic or envisioning of the human subject as it is situated materially within a specific geotemporal location or spatial/temporal structure that determines the shape of a narrative. For this reason, the protagonists of epic narratives can be described as defined by, as well as inhabiting, particular chronotopic spaces. In 'Forms of Time and of the Chronotope in the Novel: Notes Toward a Historical Poetics,' Bakhtin explains the chronotopic phenomenon as the 'image of man.' With the chronotope, Bakhtin observes: 'Time, as it were, thickens, takes on flesh, becomes artistically visible; likewise, space becomes charged and responsive to the movements of time, plot, and history. This intersection of axes and fusion of indicators characterizes the artistic chronotope' (84). As Morson writes in *Narrative and Freedom: The Shadows of Time* (1994), Bakhtin's postulation of the chronotope irrevocably alters our understanding of time's formal properties and their impact on literary works: 'Once we recognize chronotopic multiplicity, we can no longer view time "naïvely," as if only one kind exists. Which one governs a particular part of natural or social life or best models social life as a whole cannot be presumed in advance' (107). By challenging the manner in which we conceive of narrative's various formal and communicative levels, Bakhtin's theories of chronotope, dialogism, heteroglossia, and carnival have not only influenced the direction of reader-response theory in recent decades, but have also participated in the advent of cultural studies and a revival of interest in the analysis of the formal properties of literary works.

3 Reader-Response Theory, the Theoretical Project, and Identity Politics

> The conspiracy of silence surrounding the supposed impersonality of critical reading is now gradually being unmasked.
>
> (Elizabeth Freund, *The Return of the Reader*)

> What makes one set of perceptual strategies or literary conventions win out over another? If the world is the product of interpretation, then who or what determines which interpretive system will prevail?
>
> (Jane P. Tompkins, *Reader-Response Criticism*)

Reader-response criticism devotes considerable attention to the act of reading itself, particularly in terms of the many different ways in which readers respond to literary texts. Reader-response criticism's theoretical apotheosis during the last three decades of the twentieth century exists as a signal moment in poststructuralism that shared in the establishment of the self-referential foundations of various postmodern critical paradigms and, perhaps most importantly, cultural studies. As a theoretical paradigm, reader-response criticism explores three principal questions: do our various responses to literary works produce the same (or similar) readings?; can literary texts genuinely enjoy as many meanings as readers are able to create?; are some readings essentially more valid and justifiable than others? Reader-response criticism also provides us with models for understanding the reading process itself, as well as with mechanisms for exploring the ways in which the construction of literary works shares in the production of meaning. Although literary historians often suggest that reader-response theory's critical heyday begins in the 1970s and continues in various formulations and reformulations into the present, the paradigm's conception finds its roots well before the twentieth century in the ancient Greek and Roman cultures that viewed literature as a rhetorical device for manipulating a given audience's reactions. The ancients intuitively recognized that a basic understanding of the rhetorical strategies inherent in literary works afforded them with the means for registering the impact of those texts upon their audience of 'readers.'

In many ways, reader-response criticism would *seem* to function as a response to, or redaction of, formalism, which focuses exclusively on the materiality of the text rather than on such external forces as biography, history, or audience. Yet, as Jane Tompkins astutely demonstrates in her important anthology, *Reader-Response Criticism: From Formalism to Poststructuralism* (1980), reader-response criticism finds its theoretical origins well within the boundaries of formalism and the New Criticism. By the 1950s, scholars such as Walker Gibson had begun to articulate new conceptions of formalist studies that reconceived the New Critical boundaries between the authorial production of texts and their literary consumers or readers. Of particular significance is Gibson's formulation of the 'mock reader,' the quasi-persona that the text invites the reader to assume via the language and rhetorical devices inherent in a given literary work. According to Gibson, the 'mock reader is an artifact, controlled, simplified, abstracted out of the chaos of day-to-day sensation' (2). The mock reader, moreover, functions as the mask that readers wear as they explore the mock possibilities available in the narrative. For Gibson, understanding the relationship between ourselves and the author allows readers to recognize the interconnections between the narrative's authorial voices and the fictive modifications or manifestations of ourselves in the text. Even more significantly, Gibson contends that distinguishing 'between the mock world of the literary experience and the real world of everyday experience' prepares us for comprehending that 'in the end our appeals for decisions of value are toward sanctions of society in a very real world indeed' (6).

Gibson's valuation of the reader's role in constructing literary meaning underscores a paradigm shift of sorts as the critic attempts to fashion a place for readerly attributes within the previously more confining spaces of the New Criticism. As Tompkins observes, 'the concept of the mock reader allows the critic to dramatize the social attitudes implicit in a text by reconstructing the kinds of understandings and complicities narrators and mock readers arrive at over the heads of the characters and quite apart from the manifest content of the prose' ('Introduction' xi). In short, the notion of the mock reader underscores formalism's evolution toward a more readerly oriented framework of literary interpretation. In many ways, the development of reader-response criticism via the auspices of the New Criticism finds its roots in the ground-breaking work of I. A. Richards in the 1920s and Louise M. Rosenblatt during the 1930s. Although he is generally regarded as one of formalism's theoretical progenitors, Richards also assisted in creating the firmament for new, readerly based theories of literary interpretation. In *Practical Criticism: A Study of Literary Judgment* (1929), Richards identifies the ways in which readers examine the authenticity of a given literary work through the narrative's effect on their own emotions and experiences. According to Richards, readers establish an 'attitude' about a narrative, 'some special direction, bias, or accentuation of interest towards it, some personal flavor or coloring of feeling; and we use language to *express* these feelings, this nuance of interest. Equally, when we pick it up, rightly or wrongly,' Richards adds, 'it seems inextricably part of what we receive' (175).

Transactional reading in the theories of Louise M. Rosenblatt and Wayne C. Booth

By registering the significant role of the reader in the interpretive process and in the construction of meaning, Richards created the foundation for Rosenblatt's landmark postulation of 'transactional' reading in such volumes as *Literature as Exploration* (1938) and – four decades later, at the zenith of the reader-response movement – *The Reader, the Text, the Poem: The Transactional Theory of the Literary Work* (1978). In the former volume, Rosenblatt demonstrates the existence of a reciprocal relationship between the reader and the text. Perhaps even more significantly, she challenges the New Critical dicta regarding critical objectivity. Interestingly, Rosenblatt describes this reader-intensive approach to literature as a 'new moral attitude' and contends that critics should be more 'humane' during the act of interpretation. 'Instead of simply approving or condemning, one might seek to understand,' Rosenblatt writes. 'Instead of being based on fixed rules of conduct unconditionally applied to all under all circumstances, judgment should be passed only after the motives of the behavior and the particular circumstances had been understood' (222). In addition to exploding the notions that literary study must be conducted via rigid systems of interpretation and by virtue of scientifically refined principles of observation, Rosenblatt argues that the act of reading provides us with the opportunities for 'vicarious experience' – indeed, for actively engaging in and responding to literary texts. 'From enhanced perceptions may flow a sense of the human and practical implications of the information that has been acquired,' she observes. 'This information is no longer words to be rattled off; the words now point toward actual human situations and feelings' (228).

In *Literature as Exploration*, Rosenblatt also seeks, rather boldly in retrospect, to recast the nature of the reading experience for a new generation of critics and readers. She argues that literary criticism's existing terminology – essentially the deliberately detached vocabulary of the New Criticism – serves only to 'obscure' the value and richness of the reading process. Hence, Rosenblatt posits that critics must differentiate between the text and the meaning that it evokes. 'In the past,' Rosenblatt writes, 'reading has too often been thought of as an interaction, the printed page impressing its meaning on the reader's mind or the reader extracting the meaning embedded in the text.' Attempting to reframe our conception of the reading experience, Rosenblatt contends that 'reading is a constructive, selective process over time in a particular context. The relation between reader and signs on the page proceeds in a to-and-fro spiral,' she adds, 'in which each is continually being affected by what the other has contributed' (26). By highlighting the synergistic relationship between reader and text, Rosenblatt explodes formalist notions of the reading process as a neutral event that occurs in an historical or cultural vacuum. Having established the foundations for new ways of thinking about the reading experience and its reciprocal nature, Rosenblatt underscores reading's inevitably personal and intrinsically human qualities. 'It is a kind of experience valuable in and for itself, and yet – or perhaps, therefore – it can also have a liberating and fortifying effect in the ongoing life of the reader,' Rosenblatt writes (277).

In *The Reader, the Text, the Poem*, Rosenblatt supplies reader-response critics with an interpretational matrix for explaining the motives of readers and their 'transactions' with literary texts.[1] Rosenblatt identifies two different types of reading strategies – aesthetic reading, in which the reader devotes particular attention to what occurs *during* the actual reading event, and nonaesthetic reading, a reading strategy in which the reader focuses attention upon the traces of knowledge and data that will remain *after* the event. Rosenblatt designates the latter strategy as a kind of 'efferent' reading in which readers primarily interest themselves in what will be derived materially from the experience (23–25).[2] Efferent readers reflect upon the verbal symbols in literature, 'what the symbols designate, what they may be contributing to the end result that [the reader] seeks – the information, the concepts, the guides to action, that will be left with [the reader] when the reading is over' (27). Rosenblatt describes the act of reading itself – whether aesthetic or nonaesthetic – as a transaction that derives from the peculiar array of experiences that define the reader's persona: 'Each reader brings to the transaction not only a specific past life and literary history, not only a repertory of internalized "codes," but also a very active present, with all its preoccupations, anxieties, questions, and aspirations,' she writes (144).

There is little question among literary historians that Rosenblatt was clearly well ahead of her time – particularly in terms of the publication of *Literature as Exploration*, which emerged during formalism's theoretical hegemony. The thrust of *The Reader, the Text, the Poem* finds its origins in a seminal 1969 essay, 'Towards a Transactional Theory of Reading,' a signal moment in the development of reader-response theory. During the 1960s, the New Criticism's influence had waned rather substantially under the weight of literary study's growing eclecticism and gestures toward interdisciplinarity. Recent advances in semantics, semiology, sociolinguistics, and psychoanalysis fueled the emergence of structuralism, and reader-response criticism – with its timely exploration of the reader's significant place in the literary experience – flowered soon thereafter at the intellectual cusp of poststructuralism. Any survey of reader-response criticism must, by virtue of the paradigm's multidisciplinary aspects, include attention to the movement's various forays into such critical modes as rhetoric, structuralism, history, psychology, and feminism. Stanley Fish's important work as one of reader-response theory's most visible proponents will be discussed below in concert with close analysis of the paradigm's phenomenological and epistemological manifestations.

As with Rosenblatt's postulation of the reading transaction, Wayne C. Booth's creation of a communicative model for understanding the reading process functions as a key moment in the evolution of reader-response criticism, especially in terms of its rhetorical aspects. Along with the work of French rhetorician Gérard Genette, Booth's conception of the synergistic relationship between the implied reader and the implied author affords us with a powerful means for recognizing reader-response theory's narratological value. In his classic volume, *The Rhetoric of Fiction* (1961), Booth identifies the roles of implied authors and readers in the reading process, as well as the ideological and ethical ramifications of our reading experiences. According to Booth, the implied author functions as the actual author's 'second self,' the persona that the reading process invariably constructs – or, perhaps more accurately, reconstitutes during the act of reading. Booth's implied author is responsible for the text's ultimate verbal meanings, as well as for the value systems that undergird those meanings. 'The author creates, in short, an image of himself and another image of his reader,' Booth writes in *The Rhetoric of Fiction.* 'He makes his reader, as he makes his second self, and the most successful reading is one in which the created selves, author and reader, can find complete agreement' (138).

For Booth, the idea of the implied reader exists as the most significant variable in the formulation of a successful and enjoyable reading experience. According to Booth, such an experience involves two principal factors: the correct identification of the implied reader's belief systems and the implied author's simultaneous attempt to seek agreement with that reader's values. In Booth's critical schema, the relationship between implied authors and readers takes on deliberate levels of moral significance. As Susan R. Suleiman perceptively observes: 'Any criticism that seeks to study the means whereby authors attempt to communicate certain intended meanings or to produce certain intended effects is both rhetorical and audience-oriented' (10). In his later work, Booth has devoted considerable attention to the ethical relationship that exists between the readerly audience and the text. In *The Company We Keep*, Booth describes this kind of reader-response theory as a form of ethical criticism that examines the interconnections between our lives and the literary works that we consume: 'We can no longer pretend that ethical criticism is passé,' he writes in *The Company We Keep.* 'It is practiced everywhere, often surreptitiously, often guiltily, and often badly, partly because it is the most difficult of all critical modes, but partly because we have so little serious talk about why it is important, what purposes it serves, and how it might be done well' (19).[3]

Booth argues that ethical criticism's theoretical or ideological opponents often misread the paradigm's intent as didactic in nature. Instead, Booth argues, 'ethical criticism attempts to describe the encounters of a storyteller's ethos with that of the reader or listener. Ethical critics need not begin with the intent to evaluate, but their descriptions will always entail appraisals of the value of what is being described.' As a form of avant-garde reader-response criticism, Booth's formulation of ethical criticism acknowledges the powerful factors of language and ideology in its textual assessments. 'There are no neutral ethical terms,' Booth writes, 'and a fully responsible ethical criticism will make explicit those appraisals that are implicit whenever a reader or listener reports on stories about human beings in action' (89). Booth defines these instances of appraisal – these practical applications of ethical criticism – as acts of 'coduction,' referential moments in which critics compare their reading experiences with the conclusions of others. Coduction, in Booth's schema, valorizes the reflexive relationship that develops between texts and their readers, as well as the equally reflexive manner in which texts postulate meaning. 'The question of whether value is in the poem or in the reader is radically and permanently ambiguous, requiring two answers,' Booth writes. 'Of course the value is not in there, *actually*, until it is actualized, by the reader. But of course it could not be actualized if it were not there, *in potential*, in the poem' (89).

Reader-response theory, narratology, and the structuralist imperative

Genette's theories regarding the nature of discourse also contribute meaningfully to our understanding of the act of reading as a rhetorical enterprise. In concert with such other critics as, perhaps most significantly, Gerald Prince, Genette has formulated the concept of the 'narratee' in an effort to account for the audience's role in the production of narrative.[4] Genette, for example, defines the narratee as the narrator's extra-textual counterpart and as the receiver of a given narrative. In *Narrative Discourse: An Essay in Method* (1980), Genette examines the various levels of narration that comprise the reading experience. Genette explains these different levels of narration and meaning, moreover, in terms of their relation to the 'diegesis' (or story). 'Any event a narrative recounts is at a diegetic level immediately higher than the level at which the narrating act producing this narrative is placed,' Genette writes in *Narrative Discourse* (228). At the first level of narration – the 'extradiegetic' level, in Genette's terminology – the recounted events exist within the narrative itself; hence, Genette also refers to these events as being 'intradiegetic' in nature. At the second or 'metadiegetic' level, the narrative itself exists within a series of other metanarratives. In terms of the narrative's implied reader, the first-level narratee functions as an inscribed reader of sorts who shares in the narrative's interpretation, and thus in its ultimate layers of meaning. The second-level narratee, then, refers to a given narrative's capacity for rendering additional qualities of meaning beyond the text.

Reader-response theory owes a particular debt to the advent of structuralism, which attempts to delineate the ways in which literature ultimately functions as a series of signs. Structuralism finds its roots in the efforts of such figures as Roman Jakobson, Claude Lévi-Strauss, and Roland Barthes. Structuralists perceive the world as the scientific or systematic fusion of arbitrary signs based upon various sets of language conventions or linguistic codes. The work of Barthes and Jonathan Culler is of particular interest because of the manner in which their theoretical conclusions intersect with reader-response criticism's various attempts at understanding the conditions that impinge upon the reading experience as both a performative and interpretive activity. Structuralists are significant, moreover, for their rejection of the term *work* in favor of *text* in order to demonstrate the ways in which literary study operates as a text-centered mode of interpretation. The concept of the text highlights its existence as a representation, of sorts, of various cultural codes, linguistic conventions, and social norms promulgated by a given author. Although structuralism's theoretical hegemony began to dissipate during the late 1960s as poststructuralists challenged its scientific approach to literary study, it nevertheless established one of reader-response theory's most important foundations for understanding the various ways in which we determine meaning during our textual encounters.

Barthes's contributions to our understanding of the reading process – particularly in terms of structuralism's *and* poststructuralism's valuation of the reading experience – continue to resound as signal moments in the world of literary criticism. In *S/Z* (1970), Barthes argues that 'the goal of literary work (of literature as work) is to make the reader no longer a consumer, but a producer of the text. Our literature is characterized by the pitiless divorce which the literary institution maintains between the producer of the text and its user, between its owner and its customer, between its author and its reader' (4). In addition to valorizing the reading experience as a reflexive process that involves a fusion of sorts between text and reader in the production of meaning, Barthes devotes particular attention in *S/Z* to making distinctions between 'readerly' and 'writerly' texts. Barthes employs the term *lisible* (readerly) in conjunction with literary texts that exist in a straightforward fashion and require little special effort on behalf of the reader in order to create meaning. *Scriptible* (writerly) texts, on the other hand, are more difficult to interpret because their meanings are not immediately evident to the reader. In Barthes's schema, a readerly text provides a series of easily identifiable characters and events, while writerly works function, rather self-consciously, via a fairly elaborate approach to language, plot, and character. Hence, writerly texts require readers to share in the process of meaning making as they seek to decode and decipher the cultural, ideological, and historical codes that inform their production. As Julian Wolfreys observes in *Readings: Acts of Close Reading in Literary Theory* (2000), 'Barthes operates a reading from within. This reading opens to us, and allows us to open, the "theoretical" or the "political" in those very places where such acts of reading have been discounted' (14).

In his important 1968 essay, 'The Death of the Author,' Barthes famously writes that the author 'enters into his own death' when 'writing begins' (*Image-Music-Text* 142). This metaphorical death finds its origins, of course, in the meaning-making process that emerges in the synergistic relationship that exists between writer and reader. In *S/Z*, Barthes identifies five codes of reading that provide a semantic model for the ways in which readers construct meaning. Barthes's proairetic code determines the reader's construction of the plot, while the hermeneutic code draws upon the logic of three binaries in its attempt to create meaning: question and answer, enigma and solution, suspense and peripeteia. Barthes's semic code affords the reader with frameworks for examining the semantic features concerning the construction of literary characters. The symbolic code governs the interrelationship between a given text's symbolic and thematic readings. Finally, the referential code devotes attention to the significance of the text's cultural context.[5] In *The Pleasure of the Text* (1973), Barthes defines the reading experience that results from his five codes in terms of its satisfying or potentially gratifying ramifications. Barthes emphasizes the quality of experience associated with 'applied' reading in which the text 'imposes a state of loss' and 'unsettles the reader's historical, cultural, psychological assumptions, the consistency of his tastes, values, memories, [which] brings to a crisis his relation with language' (14). In short, such reading experiences challenge our place in the world; they shift, often irrevocably, our cultural perspectives.

As with Barthes, Culler's structuralist imperatives include describing the nature of readers themselves, as well as their divergent approaches to the reading experience. Culler's conception of a 'competent' reader refers to the educated or literate reader who employs various interpretive conventions in his or her analysis of literary works such as poems or novels. 'Since literature is a second-order semiotic system which has language as its basis,' Culler writes in *Structuralist Poetics: Structuralism, Linguistics, and the Study of Literature* (1975), 'a knowledge of language will take on a certain distance in one's encounter with literary texts, and it may be difficult to specify precisely where understanding comes to depend on one's supplementary knowledge of literature' (114). In this manner, structuralists such as Culler examine literary works as the products of an inherently closed system – a system which requires that its readership possess the necessary culturally and institutionally inscribed tools for decoding or establishing meaning. For Culler, literary competence finds its origins in a set of conventions for interpreting literary texts. Culler describes the primary convention of reading as a 'rule of significance' in which the literary work is interpreted in terms of humankind's metaphorical relationship to the universe. Culler's second readerly convention involves the notion of 'metaphorical coherence' that dictates the fashion in which readers understand a given text's place in the larger historical-literary continuum, as well as its capacity for generating meaning on a personal level.[6]

In an effort to identify the precise nature of the reading experience, Culler isolates three principal modes of reading in terms of structuralism's linguistic-oriented aims. Culler argues that structuralism provides both a theoretical perspective and a critical framework for establishing a foundation that makes possible the accretion of literary competence. Culler maintains, moreover, that readers must re-orient themselves with the basic principles of the reading process in order to enjoy fully 'the revitalizing powers of a structuralist poetics' (128). In the first of his three modes of critical reading, Culler distinguishes between literary and nonliterary operations: 'we can say that genres are not special varieties of language but sets of expectations which allow sentences of a language to become signs of different kinds in a second-order literary system,' Culler writes. Thus, 'the same sentence can have a different meaning depending on the genre in which it appears' (129). In his second mode of critical reading, Culler contends that understanding literature as an institution provides readers with the means for comprehending what one *does* during the reading process. Readers respond differently to the literary signs and discourses of reading; hence, readers can produce a wide range of variant interpretations of a given literary work depending on their experiences both as readers of literature and as members of the larger human community. Finally, Culler's third mode of critical reading concerns the reader's willingness to comprehend literature as an institution unto itself that relies upon sets of signs and conventions in order to generate meaning. 'Literary effects depend on these conventions,' Culler writes, and 'literary evolution proceeds by displacement of old conventions of reading and the development of new [ones]' (130).

In his influential volume *The Implied Reader: Patterns of Communication in Prose Fiction from Bunyan to Beckett* (1972), Wolfgang Iser explores similar aspects about the ways in which readers construct meaning. Iser's phenomenological approach to theorizing reader response accounts for the text itself, as well as for the various activities involved in the act of critical interpretation. 'The convergence of text and reader brings the literary work into existence,' Iser writes, 'and this convergence can never be precisely pinpointed, but must always remain virtual, as it is not to be identified either with the reality of the text or with the individual disposition of the reader' (275). Iser contends that authors must fashion literary works that engage readers and establish an active and creative fusion between writer and reader. This synergy creates, in turn, what Iser refers to as *Konkretisation* – the realization (or comprehension) of the literary text by the reader. This process involves two poles: the artistic pole allows for the text created by the author; the aesthetic pole refers to the consumption and – perhaps more importantly – the realization of the text by the reader. 'From this polarity,' Iser observes, 'it follows that the literary work cannot be completely identical with the text, or with the realization of the text, but in fact must lie halfway between the two' (274). For Iser, this aspect of the reading experience constitutes the 'unwritten' nature of the reading process, the vague spaces of comprehension that result from the interaction between the text and the reader.

Reader-response theory's historical implications owe a particular debt to the work of Hans Robert Jauss, whose notion of reception theory finds its roots in structuralism's identification of the reading process's conventional elements of competing signs and discourses. In his landmark study *Aesthetic Experience and Literary Hermeneutics* (1982), Jauss devotes special attention to the senses of aesthetic pleasure that we derive from the reading experience itself. Jauss defines the notion of aesthetic pleasure as a moment in which 'the subject always enjoys more than itself. It experiences itself as it appropriates an experience of the meaning of the world which both its own productive activity and the reception of the experience of the other can disclose, and the assent of third parties can confirm. Aesthetic enjoyment that thus occurs in a state of balance between disinterested contemplation and testing participation,' he adds, 'is a mode of experiencing oneself in a possible being other than which the aesthetic attitude opens up' (32). In short, an individual's capacity for registering the benefits of aesthetic experience is directly related to the balance that Jauss ascribes to the degree of that person's levels of aesthetic contemplation and actual participation in the event itself. In his analysis of aesthetic experience and the twentieth-century novel, Jauss defines two principal modes of aesthetic experience, the language-critical and the cosmological function of aesthesis. In the language-critical mode, the precepts of language govern the reader's aesthetic enjoyment of literary texts; the reader remains fully cognizant, moreover, of the transparent, artificial nature of the reading experience. In the cosmological mode of aesthesis, the reader recognizes the literary work's larger place in cultural and intellectual history; further, the reader discovers a more expansive view of the text when he or she reads it within an approximation of that work's original historical context and cultural reception.

In his discussion of the efficacy of aesthetic experience, Jauss also makes valuable inroads into our understanding of aesthetic enjoyment's communicative power. Jauss attributes this form of aesthetic experience in *Aesthetic Experience and Literary Hermeneutics* to a kind of catharsis, or 'the enjoyment of affects as stirred by speech or poetry which can bring about both a change in belief and the liberation of [the] mind in the listener or spectator.' This 'definition' [of catharsis],

Jauss adds, 'presupposes the dialectical interplay or self-enjoyment through the enjoyment of what is other and makes the recipient an active participant in the constitution of the imaginary' (92). Drawing upon the insights of Aristotle and Montaigne, Jauss ascribes the reader's need for catharsis to his or her desire to experience the 'exemplary' aspects of the reading experience. Jauss defines the concept of the exemplary as the quality of reflection that the reader enjoys when contemplating the interaction between the aesthetic experience and the invariably shifting nature of the self. Perhaps even more importantly, Jauss's concept of the exemplary 'can bridge the gap between aesthetic judgment and moral praxis and make clear the transition from aesthetic to moral identification' (111). In this way, readers achieve more expansive senses of identification with the literary work itself, as well as with the experiences of the characters in its pages. The textual experience affords readers with moments of aesthetic pleasure via their increasing transition into states of self-reflection and self-awareness.

A subjectivist feast: Reader-response theory and psychological criticism

Reader-response theory's interconnections with the nature of the self necessitate at least a rudimentary understanding of the paradigm's significant psychological manifestations. A number of different theorists have shared in reader-response criticism's psychological inquiries because of the variety of primal, psychosocial forces that impinge upon the act of reading. As one of the proponents of reader-response criticism's 'subjectivist' modes of inquiry, Norman N. Holland posits that a given reader's responses to literary texts are often influenced by that individual's fundamental psychological needs. Holland coined the phrase 'identity theme' in an effort to account for the ways in which readers draw upon literary works in their quests for self-replication and interpersonal renewal. In his important essay, 'Unity, Identity, Text, Self,' Holland writes that readers 'use the literary work to symbolize and finally to replicate ourselves. We work out through the text our own characteristic patterns of desire and adaptation,' Holland adds. 'We interact with the work, making it part of our own psychic economy and making ourselves part of the literary work – as we interpret it' (124). Holland's identity theme – his mechanism for understanding the manner in which readers search for remnants of the self in literary texts – attempts to account for the systemic ways that humans interact with (and, indeed, respond to) the larger psychosocial worlds in which they live.

Holland describes these psychological processes of interaction and assimilation in 'Unity, Identity, Text, Self' as 'adaptive strategies' in which readers employ the fantastical elements inherent in the reading experience as a means for adhering to our relentless zeal for gratification. 'The fantasy content we conventionally locate in the literary work,' Holland observes, 'is really created by the reader from the literary work to express his own drives' (125). Holland's theories about the psychological aspects of the reading experience find their origins in his groundbreaking volume, *The Dynamics of Literary Response* (1968), in which Holland ascribes our collective yen for fantasy to the 'willing suspension of disbelief' that we generally apply during our reading experiences. Holland contends that we explore the core possibilities of the self in such fantastical moments. Our willing suspension of disbelief, Holland writes, 'is the *sine qua non*, the unvarying precondition for art's mass and stature, art's power to make us not just know but inwardly, richly, deeply experience moral, social, and intellectual meaning' (102-03). Drawing upon his own theory regarding the nature of our readerly suspension of disbelief, Holland argues that the psychoanalytic concept of affect exists at the core of our textual desires. Holland defines affect in *The Dynamics of Literary Response* as the 'subjective experience of emotion, in contrast to its behavioral signs' (361).

Holland's reader-response schema locates affect at the nexus of our anxieties, our desires for wish-fulfillment, and our drives for gratification and self-replication. Hence, affect remains the least understood and most complex psychological aspect of the reading experience. As one of the principal elements of human consciousness, though, affect plays a significant role in our understanding of individual approaches to the reading process. In his 1982 essay, 'Why This Is Transference, Nor Am I Out of It,' Holland observes that 'psychoanalysis has nothing, nothing whatsoever, to tell us about literature *per se*. But psychoanalysis, particularly in its theories of character, has a great deal to tell us about people engaged in literature, either writing it or reading it, or being portrayed in it' (31). Holland's theory of transactive criticism – his psychological model of the reading process –

involves a transaction of sorts between the formal elements of the text and what he deems the defensive aspects of the individual human consciousness. Hence, the literary transaction functions as a subjective experience. As Elizabeth Freund remarks, from Holland's 'psychoanalytic perspective literary meaning is constituted in the dynamic process of transforming an unconscious fantasy into intellectual terms' (119). Simply put, transactive criticism attempts to explain the peculiar psychological properties of the reading process by using the vocabulary of literary criticism. Holland's readerly transaction, moreover, reveals the ways in which individuals revivify themselves via a given literary text's social, moral, and intellectual reservoirs of meaning.

In *Subjective Criticism* (1978), David Bleich articulates his own subjectivist position regarding reader-response theory's burgeoning role in mapping the psychological terrain of the literary experience. Bleich identifies the individual feelings and personal associations of readers as the nucleus of the reading process, which he locates at the nexus of a wide range of issues impinging upon such allied disciplines as psychology, philosophy, and linguistics. In addition to challenging the hegemonies of various forms of literary interpretation, Bleich devotes attention to the prevailing conventions of Western pedagogy, which he views as flawed and ill-prepared for encountering readerly perceptions of literary works. Of particular interest to this study is Bleich's definition of knowledge, which presupposes the nature of an individual's reception of a given text, as well as the reader's participation in the construction of the text's meaning. For Bleich, knowledge exists as the product of extended negotiation between members of an interpretive community. Indeed, knowledge is ultimately subjective in its construction. As Bleich writes in *Subjective Criticism*: 'Even after a negotiation is completed, though, the final knowledge is only a judgment, whose authority may grow or diminish depending on how the judgment fares in ever-large communities' (151). In short, Bleich demonstrates that the process of making meaning occurs well beyond individual perspectives and exists in ever-widening discourse communities that continue to evolve long after the text's initial performance.

Bleich's contributions to the evolution of reader-response criticism's forays into psychology also involves his signal recognition of the paradigm's significant pedagogical imperatives. As the material of learning experiences as well as reading experiences, literary interpretation moves beyond spheres of subjectivity and into the more collaborative realms of intersubjectivity. Perhaps most importantly, though, Bleich views the task of meaning construction as an inherently social function that often belies the pedagogical needs and outcomes traditionally espoused in the classroom. In the latter setting, the concept of arriving at objective conclusions about literary interpretation often exists as an 'illusion,' in Bleich's words, as a kind of pedagogic sleight of hand. 'The salient motives are all subsumed under the prevailing pedagogical purpose of the classroom,' Bleich observes. 'Subjective criticism proposes that when the object of attention is symbolic, the attempt to explain that object is necessarily a subjective (and intersubjective) reconstruction of our own perceptions of the object. To construct a literary meaning is to explain a spontaneous perception and the means of understanding it in the same act' (237). Herein, of course, lies the crux of Bleich's critique of the psychological pressures inherent in the literature classroom's rage for producing collective notions of meaning. How, indeed, can such a setting – with its accent on literary study as the interpretation of an objectified text – produce genuinely collaborative meaning in discourse communities that lack subjective origins in the first place?

In many ways, the subjectivist perspectives revealed in the work of Robert Crosman attempt to answer this very question about the nature of literary criticism in general and the psychological prerogatives of reader-response theory in specific. In his essay 'Do Readers Make Meaning?' Crosman remarks that in the classroom 'the kind and extent of a teacher's authority in matters of interpretation hang on whether or not readers make literary meaning' (149). The very notion of meaning is itself a vexed proposition that literary critics inevitably confront during the business of interpretation. Verbal meaning refers, of course, to a particular combination of linguistic signs that allow for the meaning's conveyance. Yet, as reader-response criticism demonstrates, the construction of meaning ultimately resides in the auspices of readers, who approach literary texts from particularized vantage points – or perhaps more accurately, from their own subjectified perspectives. In other words, there is no single correct meaning that one can derive from a literary text, especially within the boundaries of a literature classroom brimming with divergent personalities and socially disparate points of view. 'Once we decide that readers *can* make meaning, and *ought* to be doing so, we begin to see it happening all around us – that is what reading is, after all. Meaning is made precisely as we *want* it to be made, and as usual we want different things,' Crosman writes in 'Do Readers Make Meaning?' 'Unanimity is neither possible nor desirable,' he adds, 'and reality is never unequivocal' (164).

As critics such as Holland, Bleich, and Crosman reveal, the psychological impact of Crosman's last remark is truly profound. In short, reader-response critics must contend – in dramatic contrast with some of their formalist precursors – that we can never derive an ultimate interpretation for any literary work, just as philosophers understand the absolute nonexistence of universal truth and textual critics must inevitably concede the fallacy of compiling a truly lasting, definitive, and authoritative edition of anything. In *Reading Paradise Lost* (1980), Crosman wrestles with the challenging issue regarding the psychological needs that humans quench via the reading process. As many have concluded before him, Crosman writes in *Reading Paradise Lost* that 'the act of reading is a process of self-discovery.' Yet the larger value of Crosman's various forays into reader-response theory lies in his recognition that readers – in opposition, in some instances, to the often more pedagogically driven desires of critics – seek to 'destroy aesthetic distance' (11). In other words, we want to establish as intimate and all-knowing a bond as humanly possible with the texts that we admire. This readerly imperative makes utter psychological sense, of course, because most readers, Crosman observes in *Reading Paradise Lost,* 'have an inevitable interest in certain basic human problems, such as love, death, immortality, and the fate of human desires and aspirations, among others.' We satiate these desires by consuming works of literary art whose authors generally attempt to communicate with all readers, regardless of historical or cultural context. 'The *purpose* of art is to address the basic human being' and his or her psychological makeup, Crosman writes in *Reading Paradise Lost,* to make him or her 'see and feel not simply the local issues of a particular time and place, but the underlying problems that repeat themselves in changing forms throughout human history' (15).

Steven Mailloux's influential contributions to the psychological manifestations of reader-response criticism include his resounding critique of prevailing psychological and social reading models, a framework for understanding the concept of authorial intention, and a typology of reading conventions. In *Interpretive Conventions: The Reader in the Study of American Fiction* (1982), Mailloux argues that

Holland's and Bleich's theoretical assertions regarding the psychological nature of reader-response study run 'counter to the dominant activities of American literary study' because they neglect, in Mailloux's estimation, to account for important aspects of authorial intention that impact the reading experience (38).[7] In other words, they over-emphasize the reader's role in the literary transaction and eschew any genuine contemplation of the writer's considerable input into the quality and shape of the reading process. Neither critic, according to Mailloux, evinces any regard for a truly communicative and reflexive model of reading. Mailloux devotes particular attention to Bleich's remarks about the significance of intersubjectivity, which Mailloux finds absent in the actual practice of Bleich's models of psychological reading. 'Without an intersubjective foundation or a communication model,' Mailloux contends in *Interpretive Conventions*, 'Holland and Bleich's psychological approach to reader-response criticism will have a very difficult time influencing the institutional study of literature' (39). In his analysis of existing social models of reading, Mailloux asserts that reader-response criticism must move beyond mere gestures and begin constructing a much-needed link between social frameworks of reading that address the manner in which meaning is ultimately created and forms of practical criticism that enable readers to understand the machinations of readerly interpretation.

In an effort to answer this critical aporia, Mailloux appropriates the scholarship of literary study's allied disciplines of bibliography and textual criticism in order to propose a framework for examining the role of authorial intention in reader-response criticism. The concept of intentionality continues to echo as one of literary *and* textual criticism's most controversial concepts. Critics enduringly debate what precisely constitutes authorial intention, and perhaps even more vexingly, whether or not we can, in fact, truly communicate with any certainty the degree of its existence in literary works. 'My theories of the text,' according to the esteemed textual critic D. C. Greetham, are 'theories of writing and reading, theories of intention and reception, theories of transmission and corruption, and theories of originary conception and of social consumption and variation.' Inevitably in the foreground of nearly every critical impasse, the text is 'not immune,' as Greetham usefully observes in *Theories of the Text* (1999), 'from the cultural conditions in which it operates' (1, 11). Greetham's remarks demonstrate textual criticism's contemporary understanding of reading (and, indeed, editing) as an invariably social transaction, a conclusion that finds its roots in a debate over intentionality that spanned nearly two decades.

Mailloux postulates a similar socially and culturally balanced position in *Interpretive Conventions*. His avant-garde schema for exploring the nature of intentionality includes three fundamental principles. As an 'inferred intention' of sorts, the first aspect of Mailloux's theory considers the conventions shared between an author and his or her readers. Mailloux recognizes that a series of linguistic and other communicative codes govern the reading experience, especially in terms of the author's ability to make his or her remarks (and more importantly, the author's sense of the text's larger meanings) intelligible to readers. Thus, the author's capacity for replicating the most effective speech acts often impinges upon his or her ability to infer intentionality. In the second aspect of his framework, Mailloux contends with the ways in which authors determine the range of their intended reader's response via shared conventions of literary communication. As Mailloux notes in *Interpretive Conventions*, 'an author can be said to intend something when that author understands himself to be performing acts (active intention) which will produce a certain response in a reader (operative intention) by virtue at least in part of the reader's recognition of the author's intention to invoke certain conventions (reflexive intention)' (104). In the third prong of his schema of authorial intention, Mailloux suggests that the reader act as an intentionalist critic who addresses both the author's intended meaning and the effects of that meaning. The reader's self-reflexive approach to intentionality will then confront the reader with the very real possibility of revising his or her earlier response to the literary work in question.

Mailloux's typology of reading conventions exists as the culmination of his critique of reader-response theory's psychological and social imperatives, as well as of his own forays into the vague auspices of authorial intention. Based upon a tripartite structure, Mailloux's typology begins with emphasis upon the traditional conventions of literary precedent. Predicated upon what Mailloux refers to as past 'regularities in action and belief,' these conventions involve customary and ritualistic representative terms that communicate, in an inter-subjective fashion, with similar elements within the reader's own social, cultural, and psychological makeup. The second aspect of Mailloux's typology discusses the regulative conventions of agreement or stipulation that guide the reader's response to the literary works and, ultimately, to the author's intentionality. These terms of representation prescribe or regulate the reader's capacity for registering the linguistic codes and speech acts that he or she encounters in the text. In the typology's third and final prong, Mailloux devotes attention to the author's constitutive conventions of meaning, which he locates in a series of descriptive systems that serve as communicative mechanisms between author and reader. Drawing upon his typology, Mailloux argues that literary interpretation invariably functions as a form of translation in which readers ascribe meaning to the literary conventions that they encounter in texts. It also affords him with the evidence for casting doubt on previous theories regarding the spurious nature of the implied reader and the actual reader, which Mailloux suggests are vague, potentially unknowable concepts in themselves. 'The portrayal of an actual reader's response is as much the result of a critical interpretation as the description of an ideal reader's experience,' Mailloux writes in *Interpretive Conventions* (205). In short, both concepts, as with the process of making meaning, are the direct result of reader response – in this instance, the response of literary critics to their readings of readers themselves.

Similar to Mailloux's encounters with the psychological complexities of reading are Peter J. Rabinowitz's various attempts to explain the fundamental aspects of the reading process and how they meet the interpersonal needs of the self. Of special interest to Rabinowitz are the ways in which literary interpretation inevitably impinges upon a given reader's (or readers') ideological motives. This concept exists at the core of his arguments about the nature of the reading experience. In *Before Reading: Narrative Conventions and the Politics of Interpretation* (1987), Rabinowitz discusses the manner 'in which any interpretive practice is always politically engaged.' 'Indeed,' Rabinowitz remarks, 'one of the functions of ideology – and literature helps in this function – is to naturalize these power relationships' (5). Rabinowitz reveals the ways in which the act of reading inevitably influences such politically and emotionally charged issues as class, race, and gender – formidable challenges to the coherent interpretation of literary works. In his discussion of canon formation and detective fiction, Rabinowitz notes that texts by female authors, for instance, often become marginalized because of a masculine language bias that, through its encoding, denies access to female writers and readers. Rabinowitz argues that only the alteration of our existing evaluative procedures can provide an effective remedy for such a dilemma: 'Another course of action suggests itself,' he writes, 'to teach ourselves to read in new ways . . . that are selfconscious about how interpretation itself can be ideological, and ways that can thus help us to make the most of the rich literary heritage that has been passed down to us' (230).

For this reason, Rabinowitz posits four conventions of reading, which he describes as the rules of notice, signification, configuration, and coherence. Rabinowitz's readerly conventions are predicated upon the concept of 'authorial reading.' Rabinowitz defines authorial reading in terms of the audience that an author imagines will function as the readership for his or her text. In short, the author speculates that the audience's knowledge and belief systems will likely coalesce favorably with the author's own commitments, biases, and general scope of life experiences. Authorial reading provides the foundation for Rabinowitz's four conventions of reading. Rabinowitz's rules of notice refer to the basic gestures of noticeability that authors employ in order to seek the attention of their authorial audience. These rules of notice, simply put, instruct readers about where and when to concentrate their attention during the reading experience. Rabinowitz defines his rules of signification in terms of the manner in which authors implicitly (and occasionally explicitly) ask readers to place more significance or literary weight on some instances in a given narrative than in others. 'The ease with which readers are able to make such determinations,' Rabinowitz writes, 'is one factor influencing the degree to which they find the book readable or comprehensible' (105). It also prefigures the extent to which readers are able to understand (or receive) the author's ideological message. Rabinowitz's rule of configuration explains the ways in which the structure of a literary work impacts the reader's ability to realize the narrative's possibility of outcomes – and perhaps most importantly, why the author chose to resolve the narrative in one direction instead of in another. In short, configuration determines the degree to which the author is able to construct a cogent sense of meaning for his or her readership to interpret. Finally, Rabinowitz defines the rules of coherence as the reader's capacity for recognizing the unity, fundamental patterns, and larger meanings inherent in a given narrative. Clearly, these aspects of the literary work affect the reader's ability to receive and contemplate the author's overarching message or ideology.

In recent years, reader-response theory's forays into psychological criticism include the emergence of family systems psychotherapy as a form of literary criticism. Both as a means of therapeutic treatment and as an interpretive methodology, family systems psychotherapy – in contrast with Freudian and other psychoanalytic approaches – maintains that the family presupposes the individual as the matrix of identity. In *The Theory and Technique of Family Therapy* (1979), Charles P. Barnard and Ramon Garrido Corrales observe that 'the members of one's family are one's significant others par excellence' (9). Proponents of family systems psychotherapy acknowledge that the family's most important role is fraught with difficulty: as an inherently open system, the family must at once provide support for its individual members' integration into a solid family unit, as well as their differentiation, or emotional and psychological separation, into relatively autonomous selves.[8] This mutual developmental process possesses the capacity for producing functional and dysfunctional families. In functional families, individual members evolve into fully realized selves that allow them to act, think, and feel for themselves. In dysfunctional families, however, family members develop pseudo-selves – often fostered by fear and anxiety within the system – and thus, such individuals frequently remain unable to maintain any real equilibrium between their inner feelings and their outward behavior (Barnard and Corrales 85-87). In addition to its therapeutic applications, family systems psychotherapy's clinical vocabulary affords literary scholars with a critical mode for investigating the role of the family in fictional narratives both as an agent of change, as well as a mechanism for maintaining stasis.[9]

Of particular interest to students of reader-response criticism is family systems psychotherapy's conception of a form of 'narrative therapy' in which readers employ literary texts in an effort to confront various psychological dilemmas. In *Narrative Means to Therapeutic Ends* (1990), Michael White and David Epston observe that 'in order to perceive change in one's life – to experience one's life as progressing – and in order to perceive oneself changing one's life, a person requires mechanisms that assist her to plot the events of her life within the context of coherent sequences across time – through the past, present, and future' (35). These mechanisms – works of narrative therapy – offer cogent methodologies that assist clients (or readers) in simultaneously identifying with and separating from the dilemmas that plague their lived experiences. Therapists such as White and Epston argue that the externalization of interpersonal problems through narrative therapy enables readers, then, to address their various issues via the liberating auspices of the imagination. Such stories encourage them 'to explore possibilities for establishing the conditions that might facilitate performance and circulation of their preferred stories and knowledges' (76). In short, the telling and retelling of stories furnishes readers with the capacity for transforming their lives through the therapeutic interpretation of their textual experiences.[10]

Searching for the gendered self: Reader-response theory and feminist criticism

Of particular significance is reader-response criticism's theoretical forays into the vital interconnections between the act of reading and feminist criticism's interpretive aims. In addition to highlighting the nature of reading communities and various aspects of female reader-ship, feminist approaches to reader-response theory include atten-tion to the differences between male and female reading processes, as well as to patriarchal resonances in literary works and to the notion of the impact of sexual preference upon the reading experience. In *Reading the Romance: Women, Patriarchy, and Popular Literature* (1984), Janice A. Radway makes powerful distinctions about the concept of reading communities, which, in her study, refers to the tightly knit community of (generally female) romance-novel readers. In her examination of female interest in these fictions, Radway attempts to create a schema for understanding female reading processes, which, in her estimation, differ significantly from mascu-line reading patterns. 'The act of romance reading must first involve any reader in a complex process of world construction through which the reader actively attributes sense to the words on a page,' she writes. 'In doing so, that reader adopts the text's language as her own and appears to gesture toward a world she in fact creates.' 'Because the process must necessarily draw more or less on the language she uses to refer to the real world,' Radway continues, 'the fictional world created in reading bears an important relationship to the world the reader ordinarily inhabits' (187). In short, the female reader in general (and of romance novels in specific) engages in a simultaneous process of repetition and reinforcement in which she constructs and rein-forces highly particularized worldviews.

In *Reading the Romance*, Radway demonstrates the ways in which the romance genre's readership believes that 'meaning is *in* the words only waiting to be found.' For them, 'reading is not a self-conscious, productive process in which they collaborate with the author, but an act of discovery during which they glean from her information about people, places, and events not themselves *in* the book' (190). Simply put, readers of romance novels assume that the language in the narrative is imbued with meaning before they even begin consuming the text in the first place. In her study of a group of female romance-novel readers, Radway explored the ways in which they accepted characters and events in romance narratives without questioning their veracity or accuracy. According to Radway, the romance genre's female readership chooses to link linguistic signifiers with appropriate meanings or with interpretations of their own making in order to satisfy the historical or cultural demands of the reading event itself. 'They rely on standard cultural codes correlating signifiers and signifieds that they accept as definitive,' Radway writes. 'When they encounter familiar words, epithets, and modes of designation in a book, they automatically attribute to these signs the sense they have always had for them previously, assuming all the while that this sense is natural, immutable, and unproblematic' (190–91).

While the readership of romance novels hardly begins to account for the taste and textual predilections of *all* (or perhaps even the majority of) female readers, it nevertheless underscores subtle differences between male and female reading (and writing) processes. A number of feminist critics have commented on this important issue regarding the nature of readerly responses to literary works. In her significant essay 'Reading Ourselves: Toward a Feminist Theory of Reading,' Patrocinio P. Schweickart identifies three distinguishing features of a feminist theory of reading. The first of Schweickart's aspects of reading involves the issue of *how* women read. For male readers, Schweickart argues, the text functions as a vital interconnection between the personal and the universal. In the literary experience, masculine readers enjoy easy senses of identification with texts – or, perhaps more accurately, works of androcentric (or male-centered) literature – because they generally validate and approximate the nature of male readers' range of life experiences. In short, the male reader already feels a sense of connection with the larger world in which he lives because of his privileged status of maleness. Conversely, female readers often find themselves confronted with the requirement of identifying with masculine points of view in their reading experiences. During the reading process, women readers are asked to accept male value systems as normal and legitimate perspectives of the world. Schweickart describes the result of this double-bind as a kind of 'immasculation' in which women become further oppressed by virtue of their reading experiences. 'Androcentric literature is all the more efficient as an instrument of sexual politics because it does not allow the woman reader to seek refuge in her difference,' Schweickart writes. 'Instead, it draws her into a process that uses her against herself. It solicits her complicity in the elevation of male difference into universality and, accordingly, the denigration of female difference into otherness without reciprocity' (42).

In the second prong of her theory, Schweickart asserts that feminist theory must imagine ways in which to establish a privileged status for the experiences and interests of women readers. This can be accomplished, she argues, by creating a community of women readers who draw upon their experiences, commitment, and training in an effort to influence and educate future generations. The androcentric canon works in a 'vicious cycle,' Schweickart observes, that succeeds in replicating the implementation of androcentric interpretive strategies, which, she reasons, logically ensure the canonization of androcentric texts and the marginalization of gynocentric literature. Finally, Schweickart contends that a feminist theory of reading must become conscious of any reading process' invariably political dimensions, as well as of the ideological aspects inherent in writing and in the concept of gender itself. She proposes two meaningful questions about the fundamental nature of reader-response theory: 'Does the text manipulate the reader, or does the reader manipulate the text to produce the meaning that suits her own interests?' and 'What is "in" the text?' (48). For feminist critics, the notion of gender and its textual inscription exists at the crux of these issues. How, indeed, do masculine-inscribed texts impact female readers? 'The reader can submit to the power of the text,' Schweickart suggests, 'or she can take control of the reading experience. The recognition of the existence of a choice suddenly makes visible the normative dimension of the feminist story: She *should* choose the second alternative' (49). Hence, the feminist reading model ultimately involves the necessity of establishing reading communities that ensure the construction and maintenance of readerly connections among women.

Elizabeth A. Flynn's feminist model of reading originates in a

reading process that assumes a confrontation of sorts between the self
and the other. In her model, the self (or reader) encounters the other
(or the text); the nature of this confrontation is predicated upon the
reader's background, as well as upon the text's cultural or sociological
history. The self and the other establish a form of coexistence, according to Flynn, although this relationship is inherently imbalanced and
contingent upon a number of issues, particularly in terms of the critical distance that exists between the reader and the text. During the
reading experience itself, the reader engages in dialogue with the text;
the degree of interaction between the self and the textual other relates
to the degree of actual communication occurring between the reader
and the text. Readers who dominate the text during the reading
process typically become bored or unaffected by the experience,
while readers who submit themselves to the text during the dialogue
frequently become overly involved in its textual details and thus suffer
from a lack of essential critical distance. Hence, more productive
reading experiences often involve a balance – impossible as it may be
to establish – between the reader and the text.

During her research while constructing a feminist model of reading,
Flynn found that her male students frequently seemed to dominate
(and, in some cases, remain detached from) the text and pass judgment on its characters. Female readers, according to Flynn's research,
achieve very different sorts of balances between detachment and
involvement in the text. They typically reserve passing judgment,
sympathize with the text's characters, and seem willing to submit to
the text, rather than attempt to dominate it. The degree to which
readers become either detached or involved in the text quite obviously informs the degree of critical distance between the self and the
other. Perhaps even more significantly, Flynn's work revealed a peculiar discrepancy between women's expressions of their reading experiences in the classroom versus their written responses to literary
works. Flynn's female students evinced a genuine sense of engagement with the text in their written statements, while often becoming
reticent and somewhat tentative during classroom discussions about
the very same works of literature. Flynn ascribes this to the fact that
reading consists of a largely silent and private activity for many
readers; hence, it affords women with a sense of protection unavailable in the classroom. In her essay 'Gender and Reading,' Flynn
suggests that the solution to this gendered issue might be the
construction of a feminist model that relies on interpretive strategies

that teach women readers how to remain receptive to the text while simultaneously enhancing their levels of critical assessment. 'A willingness to listen, a sensitivity to emotional nuance, an ability to empathize with and yet judge,' Flynn writes, 'may be disadvantages in speech but advantages in reading. We may come to discover that women have interpretive powers that have not been sufficiently appreciated' (286).

Judith Fetterley's work on behalf of feminist criticism and reader-response theory evinces a similar argument about the ways in which women encounter literary texts. In *The Resisting Reader: A Feminist Approach to American Fiction* (1978), Fetterly identifies the paradox that develops when female readers become estranged from the reading experience because literary texts often function from the point of view of masculine writerly and readerly perspectives. Only feminist criticism, Fetterly argues, can begin to assuage the gender gap established by male-dominated curricula. 'To expose and question that complex of ideas and mythologies about women and men which exist in our society and are confirmed in our literature,' Fetterly writes, 'is to make the system of power embodied in the literature open not only to discussion but even to change.' Because of the weight of social and literary history, Fetterly adds, 'such a closed system cannot be opened up from within but only from without. It must be entered into from a point of view which questions its values and assumptions and which has its investment in making available to consciousness precisely that which the literature seeks to keep hidden' (xx). Fetterley asserts that readers – female and male alike – must act as 'resisting' readers in order to question the gendered value systems that often characterize our literary texts. Only then, she maintains, can we inaugurate the important work of rethinking the direction of our textual lives.

Nancy K. Miller's insightful theories about the act of reading itself offer a valuable corollary to the observations of critics such as Schweickart, Flynn, and Fetterley. In *Subject to Change: Reading Feminist Writing* (1988), Miller contends that female readers must engage in simultaneous processes of under- and overreading. Underreading occurs, Miller argues, when readers intentionally skim the text because of an inherent restlessness caused by the experience of encountering a familiar text. Underreading succeeds in unsettling the text by loosening its linguistic and cultural signifiers. By subsequently overreading a given text, Miller suggests, female readers can construct a new, more enhanced reading object. Overreading involves reading the text 'not "as if it had already been read," but as if it had never been read' and was being read '*as if* for the first time.' Such a process, according to Miller, 'thematizes explicitly the conditions of text production under the classical sex/gender arrangements of Western culture,' which naturally contain their own 'coded signatures' of male- and femaleness (83). In this manner, the interrelated mechanisms of under- and overreading function as revolutionary acts that afford readers with the opportunity for undermining the cultural power of gendered texts.[11] For Miller, the dilemmas that exist between gender and the act of reading essentially find their roots in the notion of agency, particularly regarding the ways in which readers contend with the inherently gendered aspects of existing critical and institutional ideologies.

In her important work on gender, lesbian studies, and reading, Monique Wittig addresses the notion of a 'feminine writing,' which she challenges as an unfounded expression that refers to the politically unstable concept of 'woman.' Wittig's observations about writing in *The Straight Mind and Other Essays* (1992) impinge upon our understanding of the reading experience because they directly relate to the ongoing debates about the ways in which men and women approach texts. Wittig argues that '"feminine writing" is the naturalized metaphor of the brutal fact of the domination of women, and as such it enlarges the apparatus under which "femininity" presents itself: that is, Difference, Specificity, Female Body/Nature' (59–60). In contrast, Wittig suggests that there are only two forms of writing – 'feminine' and 'general,' with the latter referring to the larger masculinized culture that succeeds in establishing a context of 'estrangement' that serves to delimit female textual voices, as well as the ways in which women encounter texts themselves. Wittig describes her ideological stance as a materialist-feminist approach that endeavors to account for the manner in which women have been naturalized into various spheres of oppression, which include, as a matter of course, the worlds of reading and writing. As Wittig demonstrates, the act of naturalizing or attempting to normalize women as members of a select social group within the confines of a patriarchal culture ultimately distorts notions of individuality and selfhood, thus ensuring the continuation of female oppression.

Luce Irigaray grapples with largely similar issues in her classic work of literary criticism, *An Ethics of Sexual Difference* (1993), a volume in which she maintains that genuine notions of sexual difference between the masculine and the feminine – as well as between their highly contingent outlooks and perspectives – will only occur after the advent of an ethical revolution in which men no longer control the nature of discourse and speech acts. Only then, Irigaray writes, will everyone, male as well as female, have equal 'access to transcendence' (217). As with the divergent textual ideologies regarding the reading experience itself, structuralism's literary imperatives, and the competing discourses of psychological criticism, gender studies, and feminist criticism continue to engage in the brand of identity politics that will surely dominate the horizon of literary theory for the foreseeable future. Reader-response theory's seemingly endless fecundity will likewise surely impact on the ways in which we think about reading as a communal and ideological act that necessarily involves the interaction between the reader's perspectives and the cultural power of the page.

4 Stanley Fish, Self-Consuming Artifacts, and the Professionalization of Literary Studies

Reading is an activity, something *you do*.
(Stanley Fish, *Is There a Text in This Class?*)

It is difficult to account for Stanley Fish's allegedly significant influence upon reader-response theory in specific and literary criticism in general at this juncture. It is simply too early to ascertain precisely how literary historians may yet judge his impact upon letters during the last quarter of the twentieth century. For some, he exists as a kind of professor cum critical pioneer who shared in the theoretical project's intellectual apotheosis, as well as being the progenitor of a form of academic professionalization that has reshaped the ways in which we view ourselves both as thinkers and as professorial commodities. For others, he represents a far more sinister force, literally embodying the character of Morris Zapp, that fictive paragon of self-interested poststructuralism for whom Fish ostensibly serves as the model in the academic novels of David Lodge. A shrewd textual combination of killer zeal and knowing egotism, Zapp plans to embark upon an ambitious critical project in Lodge's *Changing Places: A Tale of Two Campuses* (1975) that would treat each of Jane Austen's novels from every conceivable hermeneutic perspective: 'historical, biographical, rhetorical, mythical, Freudian, Jungian, existentialist, Marxist, structuralist, Christian-allegorical, ethical, exponential, linguistic, phenomenological, archetypal, you name it.' In this way, Zapp plans to exhaust Austen's canon of novels for future critical study. 'There would be simply *nothing further to say*,' Lodge writes, 'periodicals would fall silent, famous English Departments [would] be left deserted like ghost towns' (44–45).

While Lodge's characterization of his all-too-human subject is clearly and understandably overdrawn – the heart of academic fictions resides, of course, in the acerbic world of satire – Fish's well-publicized activities in the humanities have branded him as a rather notorious figure in academe, particularly for his role in establishing a star-studded English department at Duke University during the 1980s and for his subsequent departure, in the late 1990s, for the University of Illinois at Chicago, where he seems bent on assembling yet another coterie of academic heavyweights. Much of his success in the frequently bashful world of literary studies finds its roots in his eclectic and colorful persona. Larissa MacFarquhar portrays him as a

> loudmouth, a showoff, a mediocre tennis player, and a scourge of Western civilization as we know it. He likes to humiliate people in public for the fun of it and is, not surprisingly, widely loathed. He is greedy, neurotic, controlling, and short. He has appalling posture, and because he can't deal with tight belts his pants are always falling down in a way that does not suit a man of his age. . . . His own wife [Jane Tompkins] has described him as a 'slightly pudgy person, who sometimes looked cross-eyed and occasionally wore something that resembled a leisure suit.' He is, in other words, a surpassingly delightful human being. (62)

Despite his own, carefully fashioned cult of personality, Fish will very likely be remembered principally for his signal place as an advocate of the reader-response movement. The luster of his caustic persona will hardly outlive him, but his intellectual insights will surely survive to emerge in some distant – or perhaps not so distant – battleground of ideas. Literary historians often locate reader-response theory's emergence within Fish's early work, particularly in *Self-Consuming Artifacts: The Experience of Seventeenth-Century Literature* (1972), a volume in which Fish problematizes the concept of reading objectively without concern for issues extrinsic to the text. It is important to remember, though, that Stephen Booth's influential study, *An Essay on Shakespeare's Sonnets* (1969), makes significant strides in our understanding of the reading process as an inherently convoluted and intensely personalized experience. In Booth's estimation, the Sonnets are a decidedly readerly oriented enterprise: 'The reader has to cope with the multitudinous organizations of a Shakespeare sonnet,' Booth writes. The reader, moreover, must become 'engaged and active' because 'the sonnets are above all else artificial, humanly ordered' (187). This conception of the reading process as a fundamentally fragmented experience underscores one of reader-response criticism's primary assertions that the reader's struggle to produce meaning is an issue of scholarly significance in itself.

'Meaning as an event': The evolution of Stanley Fish's reader-response theory

In his own work, Fish broadens reader-response theory conceptually in an effort to provide the movement with a vocabulary for engendering further debate about the symbiotic nature of the reading process. In *Self-Consuming Artifacts*, Fish discusses the manner in which readers must invariably labor to evoke meaning. Fish identifies two kinds of literary presentation, including what he deems, respectively, as rhetorical presentation and dialectical presentation. Rhetorical presentation refers to the kind of literary works that mirror and reinforce readers' existing interpretations. Conversely, texts that evince dialectical presentation techniques challenge readers to establish their own meanings for literary works. These latter texts – 'self-consuming artifacts,' in Fish's terminology – often feature contradictory elements that countermand the aspects of unity and symmetry extolled by the New Critics. Rather than attempting to locate coherence and truth in Fish's self-consuming artifacts, reader-response critics seek to explain how readers contend with the complications presented by dialectical texts.

In his own ruminations on the nature of readerly functions, Fish describes the reader as an 'actively mediating presence' (*Self-Consuming Artifacts* 384). In his effort to revivify our understanding of the reading process as a cumulative experience, Fish frames his conception of reader-response theory via the idea of '*meaning as an event*, something that is happening between the words and in the reader's mind, something not visible to the naked eye, but which can be made visible (or at least palpable) by the regular introduction of a "searching" question (what does this do?)' (389). Fish argues that we accomplish this end by substituting our immediate, linguistically grounded experiences with our more abstract interpretations of the text and its impact upon our comprehension of its various meaning events. Fish maintains, moreover, that this process produces a kind of 'forgetting' in which our reading experiences merge with one another and coalesce into larger planes of meaning, rather than individual instances of emphasis and significance. In *Self-Consuming Artifacts*, Fish devotes particular attention to formulating his well-known concept of the informed (or 'intended') reader. In Fish's postulation, the informed reader possesses a ready knowledge of the various properties of literary discourse, especially in terms of such devices as figures of speech and the divergent qualities inherent in different literary genres. Fish's informed reader also draws upon a degree of semantic knowledge that affords him or her with the power to author particularized interpretations of the literary work at hand.[1]

In many ways, Fish's influential arguments in *Self-Consuming Artifacts* find their origins in his previous volume, *Surprised by Sin: The Reader in Paradise Lost* (1971). In his reading of Milton's epic poem, Fish asserts that *Paradise Lost*'s 'uniqueness' emerges from the reader's simultaneous participation in the poem's action and as a self-reflective critic of his or her own interpretive performance. Fish argues that Milton draws upon the precepts of reader-response theory in his construction of his epic poem. First, Milton recognizes that the reading experience takes place within the confines of linear time – that is, we read one word after another. Second, Milton intuits what Fish refers to as the reader's 'childish habit of moving the eyes along a page and back again,' a readerly phenomenon, which, in maturity, 'is more mental than physical' and which 'defies measurement.' Finally, Milton understands that the human mind – when confronted with 'a succession of rapidly given bits of detail (mental or physical),' in Fish's words – 'seizes on the simplest scheme of organization which offers itself' (23). In short, Milton deftly comprehends the rhythms of the reading transaction in relation to the textual performance of *Paradise Lost*. In *Surprised by Sin*, Fish demonstrates the ways in which the reader fashions an image based upon the readerly components inherent in Milton's poem. The resulting interpretation, then, exists as a product both of Milton's writerly imagination and of the mind of the reader, who brings, presumably, an informed intelligence and a bevy of life experiences to the reading process.

Through his careful, detailed reading of *Paradise Lost*, Fish's postulation of an informed reader whose knowledge contributes to the production of meaning begins to take shape. Fish argues that the experience of reading Milton's long poem reveals the fusion that exists between writers and readers throughout the reading process. A synergy emerges that finds its roots in the writer's use of language, organization, and narrative, as well as in the textual and extra-textual matter that the reader brings to the reading experience. 'There is a pattern,' Fish writes, 'into which the experiences of all successful readers fall (although there are as many variations within it as there are readers)' (352). Fish contends that during a reading of *Paradise Lost* readers are forced to refine their moral and spiritual value systems in response to vastly similar 'essences' inherent in Milton's poem. Second, Milton challenges readers to assess their progress based upon the abstract nature of their interpretations throughout the textual duration of *Paradise Lost.* Finally, Milton's construction of the epic asks readers to work toward the moment in which their experience of reading *Paradise Lost* unites the author's textual imperatives with the reader's knowledge and education. This mergence between writer and reader is the *sine qua non* of reader-response theory, as well as the foundation for the production of a form of truth that only exists within the abstract boundaries of a given reading experience.

In his essay, 'What Is Stylistics and Why Are They Saying Such Terrible Things About It?' (1973), Fish advances the rudimentary reader-response theory of *Surprised by Sin* and *Self-Consuming Artifacts* in an effort to incorporate aesthetics and stylistics into the readerly equation. Arguing in response to the work of stylisticians and grammarians, Fish contends that such aspects of a given text only accrue meaning in regard to the 'shape of the reader's experience.' In other words, only readers can confer meaning upon a particular text, and – perhaps even more significantly – such meanings cannot arise 'independently of human transactions' (131). Fish's influential essay crucially redacts previous disciplinary assumptions that fixed and arbitrary signs and signifiers produce the same meanings amongst readers from a wide range of perspectives, ethnicities, and social groups. In short, Fish's essay underscores the manner in which circumstance and happenstance invariably share in the readerly construction of meaning. As Fish observes: 'Meaning is not the property of a timeless formalism, but something acquired in the context of an activity' (140). Fish identifies reading as an interpretive act, moreover, in which readers decode a given text in terms of their own particularized contexts and circumstances. Simply put, reading is an ineffably human enterprise. Stylisticians and grammarians may explain the ways in which writers attempt to evoke meaning in their texts, but only readerly performance ultimately shapes the nature of meaning.

In many ways, Fish's widely cited and important volume, *Is There a Text in This Class?: The Authority of Interpretive Communities* (1980), exists at the zenith of his contributions to literary studies. Essentially a collection of Fish's most influential essays, *Is There a Text in This Class?* highlights the manner in which Fish shed various formalist assumptions in order to postulate an even more rigorous incarnation of reader-response theory. 'The act of recognizing literature,' Fish writes, 'is not constrained by something in the text, nor does it issue from an independent and arbitrary will; rather, it proceeds from a collective decision as to what will count as literature, a decision that will be in force only so long as a community of readers or believers continues to abide by it' (11). Fish's more enlightened view of the reading process emerges from his reflections upon two potential avenues for self-actualization. In the first model of self-actualization, the self becomes constituted via conventional ways of thinking about literature. In the second model, an autonomous self explores conventional ways of thinking about literature and chooses a methodology that suits the self's needs and perspectives. Simply put, Fish finds himself in the awkward position, at times, of advocating the inalienable rights of the reader to adopt interpretive stances that may provoke disagreement from divergent communities of readers. Fish's pronouncements regarding the rights of readers underscores the instability inherent in texts, as well as their shifting nature across time and amongst different readerly cohorts.

Fish's conception of interpretive communities functions at the ideological core of *Is There a Text in This Class?* A controversial issue in its own right,[2] Fish's notion of interpretive communities accounts for those readers 'who share interpretive strategies not for reading (in the conventional sense) but for writing texts, for constituting their properties and assigning their intentions. In other words,' Fish continues, 'these strategies exist prior to the act of reading and therefore determine the shape of what is read rather than, as is usually assumed, the other way around' (171). Textual instability, then, finds its origins in the growth and decline of interpretive communities, as well as through individuals shifting from one group to another. Hence, like the texts themselves, interpretive communities are equally unstable bodies that shift over time. Fish asserts that texts do not change because of different ways of reading, but rather, because they are being written differently across the temporal spectrum. As a decidedly 'chancy affair,' in Fish's words, the act of communication (which, regarding literary texts, obviously includes both writing and reading) is inevitably in a state of flux. Writers do, indeed, encode meaning – but they do so for a world of independent thinkers who align themselves with a wide range of different reading communities. Authors merely invite their readers to adopt a set of textual strategies; what happens next is up to a host of interpretive communities that, in many cases, the writer can scarcely begin to imagine.

In an effort to underscore the nature of reader-response theory's place in poststructuralism's critical continuum, Fish identifies two models of critical activity. Fish's demonstration model produces critical interpretations that 'are either confirmed or disconfirmed by facts that are independently specified.' This model's interpretive activity is ultimately controlled by free-standing objects of which either adequate or inadequate accounts have been proffered. In regard to his second model – the model of persuasion – Fish argues that 'the facts that one cites are available only because an interpretation (at least in general and broad outlines) has already been assumed.' In this instance, critical activity is 'constitutive of its object' (365). Simply put, the interrelationship between the self and the object under the critical lens reveals the inherent differences between the demonstration and persuasion models of critical activity. In the former instance, the self eschews prejudices and presuppositions in order to view literary texts without the weight of critical bias. In the case of the latter model, the self embraces an independent, prejudicial perspective in an effort to propound subjective (and potentially new) critical stances about a given text. This persuasive model of critical thinking closely resembles the ideological aims of Fish's reader-response theory, a critical mechanism that recognizes textual instability as a virtue, rather than as a theoretical constraint. The critical stakes for the persuasive reader remain inevitably high, Fish writes, because the persuasive critic functions both as the 'maker and unmaker of rules' (367).

'Reading' critical theory, professionalization, and the lingering problem of intentionality

In *Doing What Comes Naturally: Change, Rhetoric, and the Practice of Theory in Literary and Legal Studies* (1989), Fish inaugurates the three principal threads of intellectual thought that pervade the latter years of his career, including his musings on the state of the theoretical project, his forays into the law and literature movement, and his commentary on his considerable role in assessing the ethics of the professionalization of literary studies. Fish devotes particular attention in *Doing What Comes Naturally* to 'reading' paradigmatic events in the recent history of critical theory. Fish's responses to postmodernist criticism's much-vaunted place in contemporary scholarship illustrates the esteemed (albeit perennially controversial) critic in the very act of interpreting the evolving text of the theoretical project. The overarching politicization of literary studies, Fish contends in *Doing What Comes Naturally*, demonstrates that the 'abandonment of formalism – of the derivation of meaning from mechanically enumerable features – is always and already occurred' (7). Fish astutely establishes a linkage between critical theory's prevailing identity politics and its genuine ability (or lack thereof) to put into practice many of its stated truth-claims. Fish writes: 'This is what I mean when I say that theory cannot have the consequences of its claim – the claim to provide a perspective to the side of practice from the vantage of which practice might be guided or reformed – but that it can have any and all of the contingent consequences of a vocabulary that already commands attention and can therefore be invoked in the confidence that it will be an ornament to one's position' (23)

In many ways, it is critical theory's prolixity, Fish argues, that prevents it from asserting itself in the larger, more immediate worlds beyond the academy. In short, the theoretical project's penchant for language games undermines its capacity for exerting its influence in any forum outside of the narrow interpretive communities of scholarship. In *Doing What Comes Naturally*, Fish addresses the 'notorious difficulty' of reading such contemporary thinkers as Jacques Derrida and J. L. Austin, who are 'alike in writing a prose that complicates its initial assertions and obfuscates the oppositions on which it supposedly turns; and they are alike in the use to which prose is put, a simultaneous proffering and withdrawing of procedural tests for determining the force and significance of utterances.' Austin, in particular, fashions a writing style that 'is not a mannerism at all but a self-consciously employed strategy that is intended to produce, among other things, impatience and irritation' (63). While Fish admires the work of both theorists, he nevertheless registers a larger critique of the academy's capacity for self-actualization beyond the university's sacred groves – especially when its language games render it unintelligible for an audience of nonacademic readers. How, indeed, will such readers respond to critical theory's arcane and convoluted activities? Perhaps even more significantly, how will such readers see them as worthy of their time and energies? The theoretical project must be able to 'sustain a challenge to its usefulness,' Fish writes in *Professional Correctness: Literary Studies and Political Change* (1995). 'It is a requirement for the respectability of an enterprise,' he adds, 'that it be, or at least be able to present itself as, *distinctive*' (16–17).

Fish's commentary regarding the law and literature movement similarly explores critical theory's problematic discrepancy between theory and practice.[3] In *Doing What Comes Naturally*, Fish reminds us that 'one cannot read *or* reread independently of intention, independently, that is, of the assumption that one is dealing with marks or sounds produced by an intentional being, a being situated in some enterprise in relation to which [the reader] has a purpose or a point of view' (99–100). Fish takes particular issue in *Doing What Comes Naturally* with jurist cum literary critic Richard Posner's theories about the reading process. Quite obviously, both legal and literary studies share an important reader-response component that intersects Fish's own, well-known forays into the nature of the reading experience. Posner's flawed reading schema identifies two reading strategies, one of which highlights authorial intention and another that requires the interpreter to assign a coherent meaning or set of meanings to a given text. Fish remarks that, in Posner's view, 'those who ignore intention, either because they are bad jurists or good literary critics, cut themselves loose from contextual constraints; while those who defer to intention allow contextual constraints to limit the scope of their interpretive activity' (294–95). In his blistering rejoinder, Fish rightly notes that intentionality – whether from the interpretive vantage point of legal studies or literary scholarship – never constrains the scope or effectuality of interpretation because meaning ultimately emerges under the larger conditions of intelligibility and within the context of the interpretive community (or communities) at hand.

Interestingly, the notion of intentionality resonates in Fish's important work, in recent years, regarding the professionalization of literary studies in specific and academic life in general. In *There's No Such Thing as Free Speech, and It's a Good Thing, Too* (1994), Fish discusses an increasing yen for professionalization, which denotes a given scholar's desire for specializing in a particular field, establishing credentials, and attempting to foment a national or potentially international reputation in that area of study. Fish's advocacy of professionalism exists in sharp contrast with the view of his opponents, the anti-professionalists, who value interdisciplinarity and less specialization as the foundations of higher education's pedagogical and research practices. Fish contends in *There's No Such Thing as Free Speech* that the problem with interdisciplinary study originates within its 'strategy of self-consciousness,' which requires its practitioners, 'while performing within a discipline, to keep at least one eye on the larger conditions that make the performance possible' (239). Fish's efforts on behalf of professionalization find their roots in his larger interest in reinvigorating the academy's ethical norms and intellectual rigor. As Fish observes in *There's No Such Thing as Free Speech*, our critiques must have force, 'even if it is the nature of things for the force of those critiques to be as vulnerable and transient as the conditions that give them form' (242).

Yet in *Professional Correctness* (1995), Fish also questions the efficacy of the academic drive for professionalism. Because academics largely produce their discoveries within the shadows of their respective institutions, Fish reasons, they remain virtually unable to impact the lives of anyone but their equally isolated colleagues. Such a scholarly vacuum, according to Fish, diminishes the professoriate's capacity for producing what he calls 'public intellectuals,' or those individuals who 'reach out to the inhabitants of other public spaces' beyond the university (117). As his commentary in *Professional Correctness* demonstrates, Fish clearly plans to continue championing the rights of individuals to postulate their own critiques within the particularized confines of their interpretive communities. Fish's work on behalf of readers in recent decades may register an even greater impact, though, upon the ways in which we think about literary texts and their possibilities for illuminating our condition – whatever that condition may be.

Part II

Readings in Formalist Criticism and Reader-Response Theory

5 Travelling through the Valley of Ashes: Symbolic Unity in F. Scott Fitzgerald's *The Great Gatsby*

> For a transitory enchanted moment man must have held his breath in the presence of this continent, compelled into an aesthetic contemplation he neither understood nor desired, face to face for the last time in history with something commensurate to his capacity for wonder.
>
> (F. Scott Fitzgerald, *The Great Gatsby*)

> Critical inquiries are not settled by consulting the oracle.
>
> (W. K. Wimsatt and Monroe C. Beardsley, *The Verbal Icon*)

> The emotion of art is impersonal. And the poet cannot reach his impersonality without surrendering himself wholly to the work to be done. And he is not likely to know what is to be done unless he lives in what is not merely the present, but the present moment of the past, unless he is conscious; not of what is dead, but of what is already living.
>
> (T. S. Eliot, 'Tradition and the Individual Talent')

As the subject of innumerable biographies,[1] F. Scott Fitzgerald's work may seem an unlikely choice for a formalist reading. Indeed, how does one hold at arm's length the ever-present intrusion of readers who clamor for exposés about the emotional instability of Fitzgerald's wife Zelda and their stormy relationship, about his soured friendship and competitive battles with Hemingway, about his own desperate attempts to stay afloat financially in order to put on a good front for the paparazzi of the East and West coast? Surely, no one should be surprised when *The Great Gatsby* is introduced by high school teachers and college professors alike as a novel that mirrors Fitzgerald's own movement from innocence to experience. We live in an age when our desire for 'real' experience, for factual grounding, has surpassed our understanding of truth and its various manifestations, that the 'truth' found in fiction or poetry does not necessarily have to draw its strength from fleshly sources as its counterparts on reality television seemingly do. And so it is that *The Great Gatsby* stands as one of the truly superior examples of formal lyricism in the twentieth-century American novel, pointing toward the truth that fiction and the formal structure that undergirds its making may offer a far more enduring truth than any number of factual occurrences. *The Great Gatsby*'s compelling play between symbolic unity and the historical and cultural milieu it so finely represents demands a critical act that holds formalism and biography in tension, that joins the examination of technique and cultural ephemera in a judicious dance of insight, producing an understanding and appreciation of the work that could not be achieved without both.

In 1924, Fitzgerald wrote to his editor Maxwell Perkins that the manuscript for *The Great Gatsby* 'will be a consciously artistic achievement and must depend on that as the first books did not' (*Letters* 163).[2] Here, Fitzgerald acknowledges that much of his earlier work was written without serious attention to formal detail and aesthetic intricacy because of the pressures for financial success and the supposed security it would bring. During this period of his writing career, Fitzgerald produced little that pleased him in terms of literary artfulness, and he was determined that his next book would focus less on its potential popular audience and more upon Fitzgerald's idea of aesthetic integrity. As he explains in a letter to Perkins, 'I've gotten in dozens of bad habits that I'm trying to get rid of' – habits that seemed to dissipate as he worked on *Gatsby*. 'I feel I have an enormous power in me now, more than I've ever had in a way,' he says triumphantly. 'Please believe me when I say that now I'm doing the best I can' (163). While Fitzgerald's own words point to a conscious, self-motivated decision to write a book that attends to design, to the formal scaffolding that will bring about a profound effect in the artful reader, is it necessary for the formalist critic to have evidence that the author of a given work *intended* to make such a design? Or can the formalist critic proceed with the assumption that all writers concentrate on matters of craft to some degree and that the search for design need not be sanctioned or condoned by the artist? Most formalists would contend that even if Fitzgerald's letters were lost or, more to the point, never written, we would have no less a mandate to examine *The Great Gatsby* in terms of form and structure than we do with Fitzgerald's reference to such matters in his correspondence. Unlike certain formalists, however, we do not believe that we should ignore Fitzgerald's comments about his own novel altogether. Instead, by reading Fitzgerald's correspondence, we are offered an entry into the work without being controlled by it – a small distinction, albeit one that helps to illuminate how certain forms of criticism coalesce with one another.[3]

Many critics continue to demonstrate how Fitzgerald's own life intersects with *The Great Gatsby* and how outside forces help shape prominent symbols in the text. As with the novel's narrator Nick Carraway, Fitzgerald grew up in the Midwest, attending school in Minnesota until he was 15, and, like Nick, Fitzgerald appears to have felt out of place at times in the East as he mingled with the literati and attempted to learn the cultural customs in this urban setting. Having said that, Fitzgerald engages with Eliot's notion of the objective correlative far more than he does with mere personal experience. It would be a mistake to characterize Fitzgerald's work in *The Great Gatsby* as the simple transcription of a personal encounter with a few fictional elements thrown in for good measure. Far from a fictional-ized autobiography, *The Great Gatsby* is a work that stands on its own merit as a text that is carefully structured and crafted, moving beyond its author's 'real life' experiences. Throughout the novel, Fitzgerald works arduously to find appropriate symbols to express the seductive nature of dreams, their ultimate failure, and the manner in which such sirens' calls resonate in the historical and cultural context of the United States in the early twentieth century.

In 'Hamlet and His Problems,' Eliot argues that the writer must find a way of expressing an emotion or idea by creating an objective correlative. 'A set of objects, a situation, a chain of events,' Eliot explains, 'shall be the formula of that *particular* emotion' (789). Making use of this technique, Fitzgerald builds a foundation for the novel upon the idea of loss and how loss is at all times wed to our hopes of something better, a life transformed. In this manner, *The Great Gatsby* develops slowly and deliberately, converging around certain images that are 'communicated to you by a skillful accumulation of imagined sensory impressions' (*Hamlet and His Problems* 789). One way to think about Fitzgerald's slow accretion of detailed images and their function within the text is by way of analogy. If we can imagine that each image is contained inside a domino and that the author slowly draws a more complete picture by using these dominos, we can better see that as Fitzgerald moves us toward the novel's epiphany, the dominoes will inevitably fall, one knocking over the other, creating an effect that is far larger, far more profound, than any single domino might achieve individually. The objective correlative exists and functions because of the range and strength of the individual sensory impressions and their total cumulative effect when they are experienced at once and together, an aggregate of sensory detail rushing over the reader. As a novel that attempts to chronicle both the carelessness of the Jazz Age and one man's hope for a more pure, more lasting relationship than that offered by parties preoccupied with gin, the latest dance steps, and chance encounters, *The Great Gatsby* erects its story upon three primary images or objective correlatives: the desolation created by the expansion of industrial America, the façade of idealized love, and the buoyant hope promised by the supposedly teeming fecundity of the North American continent.

Nick Carraway's narrative of hope and wonder

Similar to Melville's Ishmael, Fitzgerald begins his novel by having its narrator, Nick Carraway, reveal his motivation for telling Gatsby's story. Because Fitzgerald does not want Nick's own *Bildungsroman* to dominate the narrative – rather, he hopes it will offer only an echo to Gatsby's story of innocence and experience – he has Nick assure the reader that impartiality and a reservation of judgment are qualities he strives after. 'I'm inclined to reserve all judgments,' Nick explains, because 'reserving judgments is a matter of infinite hope' (1). In the end, of course, it is this capacity for an infinite hope that Fitzgerald wishes to communicate to his reader. Yet ambivalence about such hope consistently unsettles the novel, assuring that this fiction will not become another Horatio Alger story. Instead, Fitzgerald weaves images of hope and despair throughout, establishing an interesting cadence that demonstrates how one might move back and forth between these two poles. After introducing the reader to Tom and Daisy Buchanan, as well as to Jordan Baker, Fitzgerald closes the first chapter by describing Nick's initial disillusionment with urban life and its citizens: 'It made me uneasy, as though the whole evening had been a trick of some sort to exact a contributory emotion from me' (18), Nick explains after Daisy stops talking about her supposed urbane sophistication. While this passage refers to Nick's reaction to Daisy's reverie, it might as easily refer to the idea of the objective correlative or, more simply, the use of metaphor. Was it a trick, a sleight of hand, designed merely to elicit an emotion from Nick, as well as the reader, or was there something more to it? As a writer Fitzgerald loves the magic that such linguistic maneuvers create, and while Nick momentarily feels betrayed, he cannot help but be engaged by the hope and wonder that Gatsby evokes at the close of the chapter – nor can we as readers.

At the conclusion of the first chapter, after arriving home from his escapade with Tom, Daisy, and Jordan, Nick encounters Gatsby, 'hands in his pockets regarding the silver pepper of the stars.' Nick describes Gatsby's movements toward the dark water as a kind of reaching outward, a trembling of sorts, that causes Nick to look seaward toward 'a single green light, minute and faraway, that might have been the end of a dock' (22). Of course, as the novel proceeds we learn, along with Nick, that the green light that flashes across the bay rests at the end of the Buchanans' dock, a symbol of the hope that Gatsby feels about his love for Daisy and her pure goodness. Fitzgerald wisely shifts from this first allusion of hope and wonder to the unsettling and integral desolation that serves as the counterforce in the narrative. *The Great Gatsby* would not hold any of the strength that has made it one of the most celebrated novels of the twentieth century if it blindly and naïvely embraced hope without the concurrent shadow of despair.

Appropriately, then, the second chapter of the novel begins with a detailed description of the industrial complex and dumping ground that lies between West Egg and New York. Describing it as a valley of ashes – 'a fantastic farm where ashes grow like wheat into ridges and hills and grotesque gardens; where ashes take the forms of houses and chimneys and rising smoke and, finally, with a transcendent effort, of men who move dimly and already crumbling through the powdery air' (23) – Fitzgerald seems to play not only with Eliot's idea of the objective correlative in this passage, but with Eliot's own notion of the modern landscape as a waste land. Here, in the midst of despoiled plains, the ill-conceived fruit of industry blossoms and takes form, and like Eliot's Prufrock – or later his hollow men – 'ash-gray men swarm up with leaden spades and stir up an impenetrable cloud, which screens their obscure operations from your sight' (23). The similarity to Eliot's own conception of modernist desolation is not serendipitous. To the contrary, as Robert Sklar explains in *F. Scott Fitzgerald: The Last Laocoön* (1967), the critic Edmund Wilson was instrumental in introducing the work of Eliot and James Joyce to Fitzgerald, as well as for shaping Fitzgerald's views of such work with reviews published in *The New Republic* and *The Dial*. 'Fitzgerald was only one among many whose ideas about literature were drastically revised,' writes Sklar, 'because Wilson had guided them to the meanings in *Ulysses* and *The Waste Land*' (155). Eliot himself praised Fitzgerald's conception of the modern void when he wrote to Fitzgerald about *The Great Gatsby*. 'It has interested me and excited me more than any other new novel I have seen, either English or American, for a number of years,' Eliot wrote. 'In fact it seems to me to be the first step that American fiction has taken since Henry James' (qtd. in Fitzgerald, *The Crack-Up* 310).

Wilson's influence upon Fitzgerald's reading of major modernist texts, as well as Eliot's praise of *The Great Gatsby* after the fact, meant a great deal to Fitzgerald's development as a writer. But the work itself remains – as does Fitzgerald's uncanny and foreboding descriptions of the cost of industrialization – despite such extraneous facts. At the center of the novel looms the valley of ashes, a symbol of such power that nothing in the book remains untouched by the potential despair and desecration of Gatsby's wondrous dream. And presiding over that valley of ashes, the eyes of Dr T. J. Eckleburg see everything, like some ancient god who has become impotent and can do nothing to change the course of the many modern tragedies that happen with the regularity and numbing frequency that mark the lives of those who dwell there, lost in the anguish of despondency. In *F. Scott Fitzgerald and His Contemporaries* (1963), William Goldhurst argues that 'Eckleburg broods, not only over the valley of ashes with its quasi-human figures and fantastic shapes, but also over the actions of Tom and Daisy Buchanan, Jordan Baker, and George and Myrtle Wilson – each of whom, in his own way, demonstrates an indifference to ethical standards of conduct.' Goldhurst concludes that 'in these respects, Eckleburg is pervasive, integral, and significant – an organic part of the intricate metaphorical texture of *The Great Gatsby*' (39). The movement or pattern of the novel ensures that the valley of ashes – as well as its foreboding intimations that all of the integrity and the ethical codes that help sustain it have been lost – remain at the fore of the reader's mind. Because Fitzgerald places the valley of ashes between West Egg and New York, the characters must travel through it continuously, and by situating Myrtle Wilson and her husband's shop in the midst of the valley, Fitzgerald further implicates and damns the characters who pretend to pass unscathed through this industrial waste land. Even when the characters are in other settings than the valley of ashes, Fitzgerald wishes for the symbolic significance of it to continue to function. Therefore, he creates a character whose physical description resonates with that of Eckleburg, the advertising optometrist who serves as the waste land's deity.

While clearly not one of the main characters in the novel, as many critics have suggested, the character referred to by Nick as 'Owl-Eyes' serves to reconnect the reader with the image of Eckleburg, reminding us that the façade of New York City or West Egg or East Egg is simply that, a façade. Behind all façades there is something else, and Fitzgerald proposes that behind the mask of urbane modernism, behind the indulgent parties of the Jazz Age, only disappointment and despair may be found. At one of Gatsby's parties, Nick and Jordan encounter 'a stout, middle-aged man, with enormous owl-eyed spectacles,' drunk and sitting in the library of Gatsby's home. Owl-Eyes is astounded by his rather simple and obvious discovery about the books in the library. 'Absolutely real – have pages and everything. I thought they'd be a nice durable cardboard. Matter of fact, they're absolutely real,' he says (45–46). Like so much in this landscape, Owl-Eyes expects that nothing exists behind the mask, that only the emptiness of deception fills the space behind the illusion. Surely, if God is no more than the image of some haunting optometrist placed upon a billboard, if Gatsby's own life represents nothing but the loosely fabricated story of some drifter, it would follow that the books in this library must be made of durable cardboard and nothing more. With this seemingly offhand observation – that the books are absolutely real – made by a man who has clearly had too much to drink, the novel turns. In a world where virtually everything is a lie, a matter of convenience based on no solid footing, then why should these books be real? Like the image of the deified optometrist who can do little else than watch the comings and goings of criminals, of men like Tom Buchanan who cheat on their wives with women like Myrtle Wilson, Owl-Eyes is stunned by the revelation that there is something real, albeit seemingly insignificant, in this world. The guests who flood

Gatsby's parties offer no genuine affections or connections to Gatsby, nor do the criminals like Meyer Wolfsheim who use and are used by Gatsby to further their own empty desires for material gain. But the possibility that something real, even pure, might remain in objects as apparently irrelevant as books in a library establishes a tension in the novel that is fulfilled in certain ways by Gatsby's sincere devotion to his conception of love and the object of his affection – Daisy.

By structuring portions of *The Great Gatsby* around the idealized image of Daisy, Fitzgerald raises the question about the purity of one's dreams – and by association, the dreams of a nation. Are such dreams worthy of the sacrifice and the anguish that often greets the devoted at the end of the journey? At what point does such devotion cross the line into obsession, a ruinous state that injures all involved? Such questions are ever-present for the reader of *The Great Gatsby* because of Fitzgerald's judicious use of first-person narration, which establishes Nick's retrospective queries as the book's focus. Was Gatsby a good man? Did his sacrifice for Daisy – keeping the truth about who drove the car that struck Myrtle Wilson from the authorities – redeem his other criminal activities? And, ultimately, was it Daisy whom Gatsby longed for, or something that was larger than Daisy, larger than a love for any one person could ever be? Although Fitzgerald chooses to use a woman as the embodiment of Gatsby's dream, it would be a mistake to read such a decision as merely the result of the patriarchy's influence upon one of its artists. Admittedly, the unflattering light that Fitzgerald uses to capture Daisy functions within the clearly identifiable boundaries of a traditionally masculinist narrative. Daisy's convergence with the text's other symbols, however, appears to undercut a simplistic critique based upon a culturally bound male/female dualism. Instead, Fitzgerald works to create a picture of a new nation that holds nothing but endless possibilities, a place where one's past no longer matters and where one's hopes direct the course of action. In so doing, Fitzgerald alludes to one of the most important literary texts in American history – Ben Franklin's *Autobiography* (1789), a book that supplanted the sales of the epic Puritan poem 'The Day of Doom' in the eighteenth century and helped establish the idea that anyone might prosper in America if only he or she would be faithful and industrious. Late in the novel, after Gatsby's death, Nick is shown Gatsby's chart for self-improvement, which blatantly mirrors Franklin's own chart for eliminating his life's errata in *The Autobiography*. With this clue, Fitzgerald suggests that Gatsby, like so many Americans, understands issues of self-improvement and social mobility as products of self-determination, an idea that Fitzgerald both critiques and embraces. This conflation of Gatsby's life with the dreams of a nation and the way that such dreams continue to help us see ourselves as something more than we are shifts the impetus of the novel away from the critique of woman as the root of some evil and toward the idea that what we long for must always be somewhere just beyond our grasp.

Fitzgerald stresses the ephemeral quality of our aspirations by building the novel's climax upon the reunion of Gatsby and Daisy. Although in many ways Gatsby has already confirmed that his vision of Daisy can never match the corporeal truth of her existence, the fact that he cannot have her because she is married to another seems to offer him some hope for what Fitzgerald refers to as his 'grail,' a pilgrimage for romance that in the end may be nothing more than the ever-allusive images of his own desire. Recounting their meeting five years earlier in Louisville, Nick describes Gatsby's struggle with his solitary journey toward his dreams and the earthly tug of Daisy's beauty and affection as one that desperately needs a miracle of sorts for any kind of resolution; the possibilities of an incarnation that might join his heavenly desires with her fleshly splendor seem slim at best. 'Out of the corner of his eye Gatsby saw that the blocks of the sidewalks really formed a ladder and mounted to a secret place above the trees,' Nick tells us. 'He could climb to it, if he climbed alone, and once there he could suck on the pap of life, gulp down the incomparable milk of wonder' (112). The very milk of wonder that Gatsby so longs for, however, seems to be spawned by Daisy's exquisiteness, her place in the elite social order, and it is this paradox that frustrates Gatsby's very real desires. Nick explains that Gatsby 'knew that when he kissed this girl, and forever wed his unutterable visions to her perishable breath, his mind would never romp again like the mind of God. So he waited, listening for a moment longer to the tuning-fork that had been struck upon a star. Then he kissed her. At his lips' touch she blossomed for him like a flower and the incarnation was complete' (112). In this way, Fitzgerald reconciles for a moment the struggle that remains at the root of Gatsby's desire. Gatsby's mind, Fitzgerald asserts, will 'never romp again like the mind of God,' yet when he kisses Daisy, she blossoms in an act of incarnation. When Gatsby's conception of God's mind joins with the flesh of this woman, something is lost, just as Gatsby had feared. But something also is gained: a new creation steps forward out of this magical wedding of flesh and spirit. What Gatsby perceives as the mind of God becomes something different and beautiful when placed within Daisy's body, and with this event, Gatsby is given a vision that will sustain him for the next five years, a vision that will lead him to acquire a home across the bay from Daisy, to throw lavish parties in hopes of an encounter with her, to stare endlessly at the green light that shines in a rhythmic pattern at the end of her dock. When Gatsby kisses Daisy, in that moment, he may lose the ability to 'suck on the pap of life' like some modern-day Trimalchio, but he also discovers the very thing that will sustain him until his death.

As Kenneth Eble contends, the construction of narrative events in *The Great Gatsby* – far more than character or theme – remains the most crucial element in the novel's success. 'The static center of the novel – that moment when Gatsby is alone with Daisy and can hold past and present together,' Eble explains, 'extends itself on into Chapter Seven. The story of the Gatsby who sprang from his Platonic conception of himself is placed precisely where it will make its greatest impact: between that moment of suspended time at the end of Chapter Five and Gatsby's beginning to be aware of the vanity of his own dreams in the party scene of Chapter Six' (92), Eble concludes. In the space between Gatsby's meeting with Daisy, arranged by Nick, and the following days of re-envisioning what Daisy's presence means in his own life, the novel begins its movement downward. More to the point, the actual meeting with Daisy is the structural climax of the tale; it is not Gatsby's death that matters most in this narrative, but the disillusionment of his dream, which begins after he is brought face to face with the earthly vessel that he thinks carries his desires. After Gatsby's afternoon with Daisy, Nick observes that 'I saw that the expression of bewilderment had come back into Gatsby's face, as though a faint doubt had occurred to him as to the quality of his present happiness' (97). After devoting himself for so long to his vision of Daisy as the incarnation of the mind of God with his own desires, Gatsby cannot reconcile his dreams with the reality of what lay before him. 'There must have been moments even that afternoon when Daisy tumbled short of his dreams,' Nick writes, 'not through her own fault, but because of the colossal vitality of his illusion. It had gone beyond her, beyond everything' (97). What draws Gatsby to Daisy also confounds him: he is haunted by her voice, a siren's lament that 'couldn't be over-dreamed' because it is a 'deathless song.' And

Fitzgerald judiciously uses Daisy's voice as the catalyst that will make Gatsby question his own faithfulness to her. In many ways, he begins to believe that he has not been faithful to Daisy at all, but rather to his own idea of her, leading to his regimen of acquisition. He sees that the young James Gatz was led astray when he saw 'all the beauty and glamour in the world' (100–01) in the yacht that towered over his small boat, that such splendor does not lead to Daisy's affections, only to the idea of possession. Such an intricate and well-placed reversal, of course, creates a potential motive for Gatsby's sacrifice: he protects Daisy by taking the blame for the accidental death of Myrtle Wilson because he no longer wishes to play the game that he learned in his youth. With this moment of self-realization, Fitzgerald offers a way out for Nick and the reader: they can still admire Gatsby because Gatsby has come to understand that his way of life is based upon a lie, a selfish and narcissistic reverie that may be redeemed by some real act of sacrifice.

The Great Gatsby, the romantic tradition, and narrative transcendence

At the beginning of the sixth chapter, our narrator makes a dramatic declaration, changing the tone of the book, as well as our sympathies. While we have been prepared for this shift by the crumbling façade of Gatsby's illusion, Nick's revelation still shocks with its bluntness: Jay Gatsby represents nothing more than the invention of a 17-year-old whose devotion was to a 'vast, vulgar, and meretricious beauty' and whose heart 'was in a constant, turbulent riot,' haunted by the 'most grotesque and fantastic conceits' (99). The falling action of the novel echoes perfectly Nick's realization that his own perception of Gatsby has been flawed. Yet as a romantic novel that ultimately embraces the idea of transcendence, Fitzgerald must move his readers toward a final symbol that acknowledges both the ashes of the waste land and the green light of human yearning. Nick describes Gatsby's disenchantment as he comes to know more truly who Daisy is in terms of the light at the end of her dock. 'Possibly it had occurred to him that the colossal significance of that light had now vanished forever,' Nick says. 'Compared to the great distance that had separated him from Daisy it had seemed very near to her, almost touching her. It had seemed as close as a star to the moon. Now it was again a green light on a dock. His count of enchanted objects had diminished by one' (94). Nick's disenchantment with Gatsby parallels Gatsby's own disillusionment with his idea of Daisy, as well as of himself, and the position in the world that she would share with him. Later, when Gatsby confronts Daisy, asking her to admit that she never loved Tom, Nick tells us that with 'every word she was drawing further and further into herself, so he gave that up, and only the dead dream fought on as the afternoon slipped away, trying to touch what was no longer tangible, struggling unhappily, undespairingly, toward that lost voice across the room' (135). The lost voice brings both Gatsby and Nick to the depths of modernism's angst. 'I was thirty,' Nick explains. 'Before me stretched the portentous, menacing road of a new decade' (136). And with the resignation that the weight of such irony forces upon its victims, Nick states that 'we drove on toward death through the cooling twilight' (137).

As a novel in the romantic tradition, *The Great Gatsby*'s narrative cannot conclude with Gatsby's murder and subsequent funeral. Instead, Fitzgerald imitates the pattern of many mythic tales by taking the reader deeper into death, suggesting that before any creature may fly from the ashes that lie beneath the pyre we must confront the waste land, the darkness that resides in each of us. At the funeral, Nick encounters Owl-Eyes for the last time, establishing yet again the tension between the despair in the valley of ashes and the hopeful possibilities of the new world. As the rain falls upon the internment of Gatsby's body, 'someone murmurs "Blessed are the dead that the rain falls on"' (176), positing the possibility for the renewal that rain brings. The façade of Gatsby's life has crumbled absolutely, and nothing remains except a handful of people – mostly servants, his father, Owl-Eyes, and Nick – who see something worth paying homage to in the wreckage of this lost life. Nick's subsequent decision to leave New York and journey back to the Midwest does, indeed, involve his rejection of the city and its residents. He describes them in his dream as 'four solemn men in dress suits' walking along a sidewalk with 'a stretcher on which lies a drunken woman in a white evening dress. Her hand, which dangles over the side, sparkles cold with jewels. Gravely the men turn in at a house – the wrong house. But no one knows the woman's name, and no one cares' (178). Nick clearly finds the crass neglect of these people, their obliviousness to morality, to the sanctity of life, repulsive.

But this is not the only reason Nick must leave. It is at this point that Fitzgerald erects a bridge back toward transcendence. In the same dream of the drunken woman and the negligent men, Nick imagines, as in some surreal painting by El Greco, that the homes have multiplied, that this space has been invaded and used up. 'I see it as a night scene by El Greco,' says Nick. 'A hundred houses, at once conventional and grotesque, crouching under a sullen, overhanging sky and a lusterless moon' (178). With these images of the bizarre, lurking domiciles that consume the landscape, the endless possibility that is at the root of transcendence is erased; there can be no hope for a new world or a new way of life when the very space needed for such rebirth has been paved over and built upon with the vacuous maze of modernism's urban terrain. On the last night before he leaves, Nick walks over to what he describes as Gatsby's 'huge incoherent failure of a house' (181), and there he has an epiphany that heals not only himself but the reader as well. As he moves out on to the beach and looks across the water – which is dark at this time of the year because the wealthy have closed their summer homes for the season – he experiences that moment of transcendence that connects him to Gatsby, that heals some of the wounds of experience:

> I became aware of the old island here that flowered once for Dutch sailors' eyes – a fresh, green breast of the new world. Its vanished trees, the trees that had made way for Gatsby's house, had once pandered in whispers to the last and greatest of all human dreams; for a transitory enchanted moment man must have held his breath in the presence of this continent, compelled into an aesthetic contemplation he neither understood nor desired, face to face for the last time in history with something commensurate to his capacity for wonder. (182)

This vision of a world so vast and open that it might match one's capacity for wonder propels Nick to confront Gatsby's loss, the fact that 'Gatsby believed in the green light, the orgiastic future that year by year recedes before us' (182). Here, the tension that Fitzgerald constructs the novel upon – the desire for something akin to our ability to dream and the reality of the ashes that fall upon the frail mortality that we cling to – coalesces beautifully in a lyrical dénouement. 'It eluded us then,' says Nick. 'But that's no matter – tomorrow we will run faster, stretch out our arms farther. . . . And one fine morning – ' (182); Nick cannot finish the sentence. The possibilities of transcendence are struck speechless by the definiteness of the waste land, and we are left only with an image of endurance. Like Melville's Ishmael, another narrator in the romance tradition who must endure, Nick tells us that all that is left for us is to ' beat on, boats against the current, borne back ceaselessly into the past' (182).

6 Charlotte Brontë and Frye's *Secular Scripture*: The Structure of Romance in *Jane Eyre*

> I hold myself supremely blest – blest beyond what language can express; because I am my husband's life as fully as he is mine. No woman was ever nearer to her mate than I am; ever more absolutely bone of his bone, and flesh of his flesh.
>
> (Charlotte Brontë, *Jane Eyre*)

Romance and its contexts: The archetypal play of form and feeling

As Kathleen Tillotson contends, *Jane Eyre* (1847) is 'a love-story, a Cinderella fable, a Bluebeard mystery, an autobiography from forlorn childhood to happy marriage.' Yet Tillotson ultimately argues for the novel's greatness as an 'appeal first and last to "the unchanging human heart"' (258). While we do not wish to deny the fact that Charlotte Brontë does indeed appeal to the human heart – who can ignore Jane's sorrow when she discovers the other woman locked in the attic or the power of the scene in which the blind Rochester at last finds love and forgiveness in the arms of Jane? – the question as to how Brontë appeals to the human heart, the manner in which she effectively moves us to the empathetic place where we commiserate with her characters, must be addressed. Surely, we have all read books that attempt to tug at our heart's strings, but just as likely we have dismissed many such books as sentimental or nostalgic or melodramatic.[1] How does one 'earn' the reader's tears; how might the author move the reader in a way that more closely mirrors our emotional lives beyond the text, without in some way denigrating the experience?

The most common critique of the romance novel concerns its manipulative and formulaic designs upon the reader. Those novels churned out by the hundreds each year – whose plot devices, characterizations, and themes are chosen from the well-maintained stock of myriad publishing companies – are seldom considered seriously, outside of an assessment of their sociological or psychological impact. *Jane Eyre*, however, represents one of the finest examples of a novel that is at once an artfully constructed narrative, whose complexity and range of themes demonstrates the archetypal power of romance, as well as a story whose romantic goal differs little from its lesser cousin. Ultimately, both forms of storytelling wish to have a cathartic impact upon the reader by relating tales of love and loss. But how should the critic differentiate between the two? In contrast with those critics who focus solely upon formal matters, psychological issues, historical concerns, or an array of other theoretical considerations that dominate the story instead of interacting with it, Northrop Frye's balanced and judicious approach to the romance genre accounts for a wider range of these concerns. As previously discussed, Frye's strength as a critic rests in his ability to move formalism out from behind its cloistered walls, joining it in conversation with history and culture. The application of the principles that he outlines in *The Secular Scripture: A Study of the Structure of Romance* (1976) reveals how the emotional power of *Jane Eyre* emerges from its formal structure, demonstrating once again the symbiotic nature of form and meaning in the production of narrative.

In *The Secular Scripture*, Frye divides romance into the naïve and the sentimental (3). Naïve romances focus on folk tales, as with those found in *Grimms' Fairy Tales*, while sentimental romance, which will be the main concern of our reading of *Jane Eyre*, concentrates on the 'more extended and literary development of the formulas of naïve romance' (3). Hence, Frye suggests that we look at 'fiction as a total verbal order, with the outlines of an imaginative universe also in it' (15); by doing so, we begin to understand better the power that a given narrative possesses and the reasons for that particular story's continued role in a culture's socialization processes. As the novel developed, Frye explains, romance also evolved, taking on a pivotal role. 'Romance is the structural core of all fiction,' he remarks. 'Being directly descended from folktale, it brings us closer than any other aspect of literature to the sense of fiction, considered as a whole, as the epic of the creature, man's vision of his own life as a quest' (15). In

her creation of Jane Eyre, Charlotte Brontë establishes a clearly delineated quest pattern over the course of the novel. Jane's search for the
will of God in her own life – one that leads her in cyclical patterns of
descent and ascent – brings into clear relief the structure that Frye
suggests rests at the root of this narrative archetype.

According to Frye, the secular scripture, or sentimental romance,
borrows archetypal patterns from classical and Biblical mythology and
employs them to help establish plots and characters. 'A writer who
creates original plots and characters, only borrowing from mythology,'
he writes, 'is working in the fabulous, not mythical. But it should be
noted, the mythical and the fabulous do not differ in structure, only
authority and social function' (8–9). As a sentimental romance, *Jane
Eyre* works in the fabulous, not the mythical world. Brontë creates characters and develops her plot using typical romance patterns derived
from various mythic archetypes, but she does not use them to support a
mythological or religious cultural component. Rather, they function as
a rejoinder to a range of cultural assumptions, gaining their authority
not from some mythological or religious system, but from the common
activities and experiences of men and women during the nineteenth
century. Over the course of the novel, she includes patterns that range
from the idea of a mysterious or unfortunate birth to ocular prophecies
about the future – from foster parents or guardians to adventures of
misfortune. Brontë even manages to allude to such archetypal patterns
as the narrow escape from death, the recognition of the true identity of
a hero or heroine, and the eventual marriage of the heroine. Brontë's
use of these patterns imbues her narrative with a power that it would
otherwise not have; connecting her story with this tradition assures that
it will resonate with her readers. Frye explains that as a narrative form,
romance works across the ages and is not the product of a particular
literary movement. 'The conventions of prose romance show little
change over the course of centuries' (4), Frye observes, and it should
come as no surprise, then, that in order to meet the expectations of her
readers, Brontë would opt to borrow from this tradition.

By using the conventions of the prose romance, Brontë allows herself
to cross certain cultural boundaries, assuring a wider readership and a
greater influence. In the romance genre, often bourgeois and proletar-
ian elements come together through the interaction of a hero and
heroine. Early in *Jane Eyre*, Brontë follows this model, but by the
novel's end she will create a reversal that allows her at once to subvert
and fulfill generic expectations. Clearly, as the novel begins, Rochester

represents the proletariat in his position as a land holder and master of the house, while Jane, in her role as governess, symbolizes the bourgeois class. Frye argues that such social elements are never fully satisfied in the romance, 'and in fact the incarnations [of these elements] themselves indicate that no matter how great a change may take place in society, romance will turn up again, as hungry as ever, looking for new hopes and desires to feed on' (186). As social positions continue to change, our readings of *Jane Eyre* must also evolve. Certainly, the rigidity of the social hierarchy that existed at the time the novel was written impacted the first readers of the story in radically different ways than those subsequent readers who lived – or, indeed, live – under the prevailing strictures of very different social expectations.

Frye claims that another important factor in building a unified story within the boundaries of romance depends upon the concept of displacement, which he defines as an adjustment of 'formulaic structures to a roughly credible context' (36). Although there are many mythic archetypes in *Jane Eyre*, the plot and characters remain more credible than fantastic, and their actions seem to jibe with our own notions about how one might behave in a similar situation. Brontë moves the reader between what Frye calls the realistic tendency and the romantic tendency. 'The realistic tendency,' Frye writes, 'focuses more on the representational, and the romantic tendency focuses more on the myth and metaphor' (37). He further explains that 'the novel, as it was established in the eighteenth century, was a realistic displacement of romance' (39). This would suggest that *Jane Eyre* uses the same general structure in order to satisfy a demand for greater conformity to ordinary experience. Brontë's characters are believable, perhaps more so than the caricatures used by other writers working in this period. This credibility seems to be a direct result of her concentration on Rochester and Jane to the exclusion of others. For example, Dickens populates his novels with a wide array of characters and cannot take the time to make each one 'believable'; as a result, he must depend upon character-types or stock-characters to advance some of the action, assuming that by giving his reader certain signals, the reader will understand the function of that character. In such instances, the realistic nature of a given character does not hold the level of importance that it does for Brontë in her creation of Jane and Rochester. In Brontë's novel, Jane and Rochester are rather enigmatic, continuously flouting our expectations regarding what characters in romances do in certain situations. Of course, this is what drives us to delve further into the story: Jane and Rochester are not stock-charac-ters, although they are based upon the general character-types who populate such novels, and their desires and pasts drive them toward destinies that we cannot imagine yet hope to witness.

Brontë's decision to use first-person narration plays a crucial role in accommodating our wish to peer behind the enigmatic mask of Jane and Rochester's love. Jane's voice places us in contact with her inte-rior human struggle and demands that we see her, as well as Rochester, as fully realized characters, not mere caricatures. The nature and quality of their remarks give the reader clues to who Jane and Rochester are. Clearly, this movement from the inside out is in sharp contrast to the more 'exterior' plots of many of Brontë's contemporaries, yet even with this shift toward a greater intimacy through the relating of Jane's ordinary experience, there remains a need to return to certain generic expectations for romance. In this case, Brontë makes use of coincidence and a happy ending to satisfy her readers. For a narrative to fit within the structure of romance, adjustments or accommodations must be made. Frye sees such adjustments as the unification of form and content. 'All the adjust-ments are made with great skill,' he explains, 'but the very skill shows that form and content are not quite the same thing: they are two things that have to be unified' (40). By unifying form and content, Brontë's own work points the critic in a more balanced direction.

According to Frye, the use of coincidence is the 'key to romance's vertical perspective' (49). A vertical perspective within a given narra-tive allows the reader to see clearly delineated differences in people, place, and action. Quite often, the vertical perspective is used in mythic and religious texts to distinguish more easily the forces of good and evil. In contrast, realism moves the plot forward by using causal-ity: it tries to progress logically – as in a science experiment, a notion that Émile Zola will champion with the rise of Naturalism – and by basing the ensuing actions of the characters upon their positive and negative characteristics. Realism seldom offers a vertical perspective, preferring to present its characters as compromised, at once composed of both good and evil elements. Romance also differs from realism in the ways in which it moves its stories forward, using sensa-tional and dynamic plot shifts that pay little heed to logic. In romance, discontinuous episodes are juxtaposed, Frye explains, and they describe the action by using comparison and contrast, not reason (47). Thus, Jane's rejection and subsequent flight from Rochester and his proposed, albeit previously hidden, bigamous relationship lands Jane – by coincidence or good fortune – with a family who needs her and, in turn, whom she needs. While such a coincidence does not rise to a fabulistic or mythic level, it does represent a rather convenient and radically different locale for our heroine as we wait for her ultimate reunion with Rochester. The vertical perspective created by such a sensational movement, Frye explains, results in the polarization of characters and the avoidance of ambiguity (50). 'The characterization of romance is really a feature of its mental landscape,' Frye writes. 'Its heroes and villains exist primarily to symbolize a contrast between two worlds, one above the level of ordinary experience, the other below it' (53). Such an observation is true of *Jane Eyre* to a point; many characters are polarized and categorized as either heroes or villains. But this seems to be the case only for those characters in the novel who do not play a significant part. Blanche Ingram, Mrs Reed, Mr Brocklehurst, Bertha Rochester, and other characters with smaller roles are easy to define and categorize, but Rochester, Jane, and even St John Rivers cannot be labeled so facilely. Instead, they gain their power through the ambiguity and turmoil that ensnares them. Their lives are tangled and complicated, and we are drawn to them, at least in part, by our desire to see how they might work their ways through such complications. The worlds above and below ordinary experience, of course, are the places where such complications are resolved in romance, providing a framework for the descents and ascents of the heroes and heroines. The world that exists above the level of ordinary experience is characterized or associated with happiness, security, and peace. The world below is associated with separation, pain, loneliness, and humiliation. While both worlds are represented in *Jane Eyre*, Frye claims that 'we are usually carried directly from one to the other' (53). Despite the enigmatic quality of both Jane and Rochester, in the end Brontë moves us vertically from world to world in a series of shifts that are designed to bring greater relief and readerly satisfaction when their marriage is at last consummated and we are returned to the idyllic world above ordinary experience.

Romantic expectations: Heroes, heroines, and their quests

Generic boundaries create a set of expectations for the reader. Working within a specific genre establishes certain parameters that readers rely upon as a guide through the reading experience. If one is reading a detective novel, for instance, one assumes with a great degree of confidence that the crime upon which the novel focuses will be solved in the final few pages of the book. If this is not the outcome, the reader's critique of the book will likely have little to do with the quality of the work and much more to do with the profound disappointment that he or she feels. Has a hoax of sorts been carried out at the expense of the reader? Shouldn't a writer, just as an athlete, be expected to play by the formal rules of the game? When an author decides to test or experiment with such boundaries, the author must be aware that as the work deviates from the formal expectations of the reader, there is the chance that the reader will lose interest or dismiss the work as something outside the genre. In *Jane Eyre*, Brontë tests her readers by creating characters with a greater degree of moral ambiguity than those normally associated with the romance genre. For example, although Jane remains a committed, if not a devout Christian, her understanding of Christianity departs from the conventional religiosity represented by several rather undesirable and unsympathetic characters whom she encounters over the course of the novel. Jane's notions of God and one's path to God's will are far less clear for Jane than one might expect from a heroine of her time.[2] Another illustration of this strained depiction of good and evil is present in Brontë's creation of Rochester, who appears to be a brooding and menacing figure throughout most of the novel. At times, though, Brontë offers glimpses to her reader of a more tender and caring man who feels like his life is at cross purposes and who cannot seem to see any easy moral resolution to his dilemma. Because Brontë wishes for us to empathize with Jane – and, in turn, with Rochester – we, too, cannot see any facile way of defining the morality of Rochester's actions, nor of deciding what course Jane should take in dealing with such a devastating revelation as the existence of Bertha Mason. Yet despite Brontë's creative and influential deviations, *Jane Eyre* must fulfill a certain number of formal tenets in order to continue to function as a romance.

Frye contends that the hero and heroine of a romance are often consumed with some form of *froda* – a term from Dante's *Inferno* that literally means fraud and 'is often wielded, or symbolized, by a treacherous woman' (68). Frye explains that such an encounter usually leads them into a set of circumstances well beyond their control. In *Jane Eyre*, Bertha Mason functions as the symbol of *froda*. While Jean Rhys rewrites or establishes an alternate narrative for Bertha Mason in *Wide Sargasso Sea* (1966), in Brontë's novel Bertha represents the possibility of a bigamous fraud. In her depiction of Bertha, Brontë implies that she is an evil mirror of Jane herself and perhaps represents what Jane could become if she should give into the plans of Rochester and her own passions. This standard romance pattern of a double identity, or *doppelgänger*, combines with the concept of *froda* to develop or to initiate the main quest pattern that undergirds the novel. As Jane strives toward the idyllic world above experience, she has her passions blocked by the presence of Bertha. Powerless over the fraud, Jane can do nothing to bring about the realization of her quest until Bertha's death allows her to wed Rochester. Yet Brontë makes it quite clear that Jane must remain true to her self; she cannot ignore her religious faith nor its injunctions against bigamy. No set of circumstances can do away with such rules and her decision not to follow would mark the triumph of *froda* and the destruction of all that awaits her at the end of the quest.

Associated with Jane's decision to flee Rochester after the discovery that Bertha is his wife is the tenuous element of virginity. While ideas about virginity shifted radically in the second half of the twentieth century, sexual purity continues to function within the genre of romance. Frye contends, especially in texts written before the 1950s, that virginity serves as a symbol of a woman's honor (73). More specifically, Frye argues that virginity is 'the symbol of the heroine's sturdy, middle-class independence' (76), and to lose one's virginity meant a shift toward dependence.[3] As the orphaned daughter of a poor parson, Jane completes her education at Lowood and subsequently seeks employment as a governess. While compared to contemporary standards of independence Jane's position may not seem liberated; for her cultural context Jane's freedom as an educated, unmarried woman affords her with a number of options not available to those who may be less educated or married. Of course, her freedom is threatened at Thornfield Hall as she becomes romantically involved with Rochester. He appears to have the power and the magnetism to win Jane's love, and she reveals her willingness to relinquish her virginity to him in the bond of marriage. But Brontë chooses to preempt their union with the discovery of his first wife. Thinking Rochester still desires her as a mistress, Jane flees Thornfield Hall in an effort to protect her virginity from his ruling passion and her injured love. In Brontë's tale, virginity is not strictly a matter of middle-class independence or female honor; rather, it involves her relationship to God and the potential harm that might come to that relationship if she acquiesces to Rochester's desires. In this way, the quest pattern in *Jane Eyre* is built upon two merging ideas: Jane's desire to find and do God's will and her desire to fulfill her relationship with Rochester in marriage. Brontë presents these two ideas most profoundly and forcefully when Jane refutes Rochester. 'Do as I do: trust in God and yourself. Believe in heaven. Hope to meet again there,' she says. Jane makes clear, in a moment Frye might refer to as a scene with a vertical perspective, that she will not compromise her morality, even for a love of which she has dreamt. 'I will keep the law given by God; sanctioned by man,' she continues. 'I will hold to the principles received by me when I was sane, and not mad – as I am now' (278–79). And with her reference to sanity, Jane once again reconnects her quest to the *froda* carried upon the back of Bertha Mason. Jane turns away from her *doppelgänger* because she sees in her fleshly mirror what she might become if she follows the wrong road in her pilgrimage.

The virginal quality of the heroine in romance is also directly related to the heroine's role as a healer. Frye explains that the virgin may 'exert a certain redemptive quality by her innocence and goodness' (87), and in *Jane Eyre*, Brontë literally has Jane play the role of healer and redeemer. While this pattern of healing begins with the developing relationship between Jane and Rochester, it is temporarily broken when Jane must flee to Moore House. Brontë later has Jane called back, however, through an act that supersedes the laws of realism. As she wanders the moors with St John Rivers, many miles from Thornfield, Jane hears a voice and recognizes it as Rochester's; this prompts her to journey to Thornfield, and, upon finding Rochester at Ferndean House, she relates to him the story of the disembodied voice. He confirms that at the same hour he had involuntarily called her name. With this supernatural revelation, Jane recommits herself to the role of Rochester's redeemer and healer, and Rochester recovers much of his physical ability and grows spiritually in ways never imagined. Brontë makes it clear that Jane is willing to give up her own desires for Rochester in order to be his nurse. 'I will think what you like, sir,' she says. 'I am content to be only your nurse, if you think it better' (383). Frye explains that the movement to a higher world through the redemptive powers of a lover underlies the Eros myth and often surfaces in romance (90). Clearly, Rochester draws closer to a 'higher world' through Jane's efforts on his behalf. Her humility and sacrificial love transform Rochester from an angry and violent man into a man who says with great sincerity a prayer that will make possible his union with Jane: 'I thank my Maker that in the midst of judgement He has remembered mercy. I humbly entreat my Redeemer to give me strength to lead henceforth a purer life than I have done hitherto!' (395). The movement from lover to healer and finally back to lover suggests a cyclic pattern that serves as a foundation in romance. This movement from higher world to lower world and back to higher world also is represented in romance by the different cycles found in nature.

Frye contends that romance archetypes represent the equivalent cyclic movements observed in nature. The seasonal cycle, for example, frequently serves as associative imagery linked to the hero or heroine. 'The heroine who becomes a bride,' Frye explains, 'and eventually, one assumes, a mother, on the last page of a romance, has accommodated herself to the cyclical movement: by her marriage, or whatever it is, she completes the cycle and passes out of the story' (80). In Brontë's story, Jane first meets Rochester in January. Their romantic relationship develops through the spring and is to culminate with their marriage in summer. With her wedding in ruins, Jane flees in the early autumn to Moore House where she weathers the winter season, thinking her love has died. The cycle reaches completion with her return to Rochester at Ferndean House and their marriage in June. Such seasonal imagery serves to enhance the shifting moods and the emotional struggle of Jane and should be associated with the converging ideas of the quest. In the end, Jane travels through the entire cycle and fulfills the romance structure that culminates in her marriage and the subsequent birth of her son.

Finally, Jane's quest mirrors other romances in its use of the reversal archetype. For the heroine, the romance structure normally includes some form of secrecy and reversal that will lead to a discovery about her identity (Frye 74–75). Usually, this revelation about identity concludes with a dramatic shift in her fortunes. Throughout Brontë's novel, Jane's identity remains obscured. We know little of her past and assume that, with the death of her father, all contact with her kin has been lost. Even her relationship with Rochester is hidden from her surrogate family when she says to them that 'the name of the place where, and of the person with whom, I lived is my secret' (305). Such secrecy plagues Jane. To whom can she confide, and will the weight of her past that she works to conceal drag her down to the grave? Because of his love for her, St John Rivers works to discover Jane's true identity. When he unearths the truth about Jane, as Frye suggests, her life is marked by a radical and dramatic change. She inherits both a family and wealth, and with her secret no longer hidden, she is able to contemplate joining Rochester. Her movement back toward Rochester is typified by an act of reconciliation made possible by the reversal. Bertha's death, of course, releases Rochester from his chains, and with Jane as the catalyst for his remarkable spiritual and physical healing, the stage is set for the two lovers' final ascent.

Descent and ascent: The structural movements of Jane and Rochester

According to Frye, four primary narrative movements exist in literature. 'These movements consist of, first, a descent downward from a higher world: second, a descent to a lower world: third, an ascent from a lower world: and fourth, the ascent to a higher world,' he writes. To understand these shifts, we must acknowledge an implicit mythological universe consisting of four levels. The first and highest level is heaven – what Frye refers to as 'the place of the presence of God.' The second level is some form of earthly paradise, usually represented in the Judeo-Christian tradition as the Garden of Eden where sin has not yet entered. The world of ordinary experience, commonly referred to as *reality*, represents the third level, and, finally, the fourth level consists of a demonic world, a form of hell that can be symbolic or literal (Frye 97–98).

In Frye's structural schema, there is often a sharp descent at the beginning of a romance. Such a descent may be characterized by a change in social status and typically involves the loss of riches or privilege, leading to a struggle for survival for which the hero or heroine has not been prepared. As *Jane Eyre* begins, Jane is already in a world of loss: her parents dead and her care entrusted to an aunt who seems to detest her, Jane's resistance appears futile; her fate is sealed. At this point in the narrative, Jane is positioned somewhere between the level of ordinary experience and the symbolic level of the demonic world. She does have some privilege and status living with her aunt, but this is placed in the context of her aunt's oppressive cruelty. While at Gateshead Hall she is punished so severely that she becomes quite ill; her illness corresponds with the motif of survival in a lower world. Soon after her illness she is taken from the oppressive world of Gateshead to Lowood, a boarding school for orphaned girls. Paradoxically, this shift, although a descent downward in social status and privilege, signifies a move toward something far better; at least in this space there is the possibility for growth. Frye describes these kinds of shifts as the structural core for understanding individual loss or confusion. Such a 'break in the continuity of identity . . . has analogies to falling asleep and entering a dream world,' he explains (104). Brontë utilizes Jane's break from her past identity to offer the reader hope. Although Jane's existence seems to be little more than the grueling and cruel unreality of dreams, Lowood may yet prove to be something better. Appropriately, Jane's travel from Gateshead to Lowood is marked by rain, wind, and darkness. She even sleeps in the carriage – perhaps dreaming a bewildering dream – as the driver ushers her into a precarious and as yet undetermined new life.

The dream-like state that holds the heroine – serving as an entrance into romance – is related to the archetypal patterns surrounding mirror images. Frye contends that the 'pictures, tapestries, and statues which so often turn up near the beginning of a romance [seem] to indicate the threshold of the romance world' (109). As Jane enters the world of Thornfield Hall, Mrs Fairfax gives her a tour of the house. 'All these relics gave to the third story of Thornfield Hall an aspect of a home of the past,' Jane remarks. 'With wrought old-English hangings crusted with thick work, portraying effigies of strange flowers, and stranger birds, and strangest human beings, – all which would have looked strange, indeed, by the pallid gleam of moonlight,' she says in a state of wonder and possible foreboding, '[I] by no means coveted a night's repose' in this place (92). Ironically, Jane enters the world of romance that will be contained by the walls of Thornfield Hall through the third story where the tapestries foreshadow Bertha's presence. Jane's prescient comment about the 'strangest human beings' suggests that there is more to this place than mere bricks and mortar, than the fine hand-work of the tapestries. As if to emphasize this point, Brontë includes a passage very early in this section about Jane's own painting, an important detail because Jane's need for artistic expression will eventually lead to the discovery of her true identity by St John Rivers, providing for the possibility of her return to Rochester.

Frye asserts that while the heroine is in the lower world – seemingly trapped in a dream-like state – she must face both supernatural and natural powers (116). For Jane, these powers appear to work in tandem, threatening her chances to succeed in moving to a higher world. It is never clear to Jane if the powers are supernatural or natural, and this adds to the confusion she encounters in her descent. At Lowood she faces the specter of death in the natural form of disease that claims the life of her friend Helen Burns, leaving Jane bereft and all alone. Before Helen dies she speaks with Jane about coming into the presence of God; Jane questions Helen about the true existence and nature of God, but later, perhaps because of Helen's death, she changes her mind about God's presence and the reality of the supernatural. Jane's decision to accept the presence and relevance of the supernatural prepares us for Jane's own interpretation of Bertha Mason and Grace Poole. At Thornfield, Jane's dreams are comprised of several different levels of experience, even descending into the underworld where the future and her dreams cannot be easily divided. The night before she is to wed Rochester she dreams that Thornfield Hall 'was a dreary ruin, the retreat of bats and owls. I thought that of all the stately front nothing remained but a shell-like wall, very high and very fragile-looking' (248). Her 'dream' is a vision of the future. Brontë includes a number of such dreams in the novel, implying that they are in fact supernatural visions, that Jane is in some way prescient. The atmosphere at Thornfield is so fully imbued with both the natural and supernatural – due in large part to Brontë's flirtation with the Gothic tradition – that Jane even interprets 'natural' behavior in supernatural terms. After Bertha enters her room, removing her bridal veil and tearing it in two, Jane describes her as purple and swollen, with dark lips, bloodshot eyes, a furrowed brow, and raised black eyebrows. Jane calls her a 'foul German spectre – the Vampyre' (250). While later in the novel we understand that Bertha is Rochester's natural wife, we are never assured completely that Bertha is not a demon of supernatural origin. In fact, Rochester reinforces the potential for Bertha's supernatural presence by referring to her as a demon living in hell. '"That is my wife," said he. "Such is the sole conjugal embrace I am ever to know – such are the endearments which are to solace my leisure hours! And this is what I wished to have" (laying his hand on my shoulder: "this young girl, who stands so grave and quiet at the mouth of hell, looking collectedly at the gambols of a demon"' (258).

According to Frye, loneliness and alienation comprise the lower world of romance. Following the archetype of the fall, isolation and separation ensue as the heroine journeys further into the lower world. Her journey quite often culminates in what Frye calls an 'unjust trial' (115). Jane's life might be categorized as a series of moves from isolation and alienation toward union and friendship. Brontë structures these moves around Gateshead Hall, Lowood, Thornfield Hall, Moor House, and Ferndean Manor. At Gateshead Hall, Jane is completely isolated and never truly finds any union with her cousins or aunt; the exception at Gateshead Hall might be Bessie Lee, the servant who cares for Jane, but her acts of kindness are not overly significant or influential. Soon, Jane leaves to travel to Lowood, which provides her with two new companions, affording her brief respites from the lower world. Helen Burns and Miss Temple alleviate Jane's isolation for a time, but their fortunes ultimately return Jane to the lower world: Helen dies in the arms of Jane, while Miss Temple marries Reverend Nasmyth. At Thornfield Hall, Jane becomes part of a surrogate family, and we are tempted to think her time outside the garden has been served. Jane enjoys a mother-figure in Mrs Fairfax, a child in Adele, and a husband in Rochester, yet this tranquil household will be destroyed by Rochester's trial on their wedding day. The wedding itself represents Jane's final test before her ascension to an earthly paradise. The mark of Rochester's sin intervenes, however, and Jane, as does the reader, loses all hope. Her trial – the decision to leave Rochester after the awful revelation about his past marriage – seems unjust. What has Jane done to bring about her sorrow? Why has she been afflicted because of someone else's actions? But we must note that this trial is as much Rochester's as Jane's. Yes, the trial for Jane is unjust and undeserved; her suffering corresponds with Frye's schema, making her an even more sympathetic figure. But Brontë does not suggest that Rochester's trial concerning his marriage to Bertha is unjust. Instead, we are given sufficient background to understand his actions and forgive him as Jane does. From her depths of despair and loss, Jane is taken to Moore House where, again, she begins to ascend toward a higher world. Brontë continues to move Jane back and forth between the two worlds, generating a narrative tension that seemingly cannot be satisfied. For instance, although the discovery of her true identity affords Jane with the knowledge of her real family, a short time later the advances and denial of St John Rivers force her back into a world alienated from her hope for love.

Because in the end romance must conclude with a final ascent toward the upper world, this particular form of narrative is inevitably tied to the happy ending. Frye describes the most common images associated with this final ascent as escape and discovery (129). 'The conventional happy ending of romance may seem to us faked, manipulated, or thrown in as a contemptuous concession to a weak-minded reader,' Frye explains. 'But if the conception is genuinely romantic and comic, the traditional happy ending is usually the one that fits' (134). Brontë effectively moves the reader in patterns of ascent so that the traditional happy ending feels earned. Rather than moving the reader linearly through the plot – from the lower world to the upper world – Brontë wisely advances the plot through patterns of descent and ascent, making use of what Frye claims is the basis for romance narratives. 'Romance,' Frye contends, 'is truly about the unending and irrational human impulse to struggle, survive, and if possible, escape' (136). Thus, when Jane does finally 'escape' into the arms of Rochester, the reader identifies his or her own struggles with Jane's and is given hope by her success.

The discovery of Jane's true identity by St John Rivers and the realization of her inheritance initiates the final ascension that culminates in an earthly paradise. Not only is Jane's true identity discovered, however, but also the true identity or intentions of St John Rivers and subsequently, Rochester. Jane perceives that Rivers is full of Christian ambition and that to succumb to his offer of marriage would be a form of *froda* on her part. If Jane were to accept his proposal, the quest would go unfulfilled. Frye notes that the 'standard escape device of romance is that of escape through a shift of identity' (136), and while Jane's own identity has already been revealed, the identity of St John Rivers, rooted in his intention to take Jane as his bride and fellow missionary, serves as the vehicle that will send Jane back to Ferndean Manor, where Rochester's affliction will reveal the state of his heart.

As romance moves closer to a world of original identity, images associated with some form of paradise tend to appear. Frye claims that 'the social setting [is] reduced to the love of individual men and women within an order of nature,' and that 'this is closely related to the Eros theme in which a lover is driven by his or her love to ascend to a higher world' (149–51). Ferndean Manor rests deep in the woods far from any village. Its isolated location implies a removal from the fallen world of ordinary experience, and here both Rochester and Jane know their greatest happiness. Jane's presence transforms Rochester's isolation and alienation, changing Ferndean Manor into an Eden where Rochester begins to strive toward God and the life that faith will bring. 'Jane! You think me, I daresay, an irreligious dog,' Rochester declares in a speech that identifies his most radical transformation. 'But my heart swells with gratitude to the beneficent God of this earth just now' (393). With Jane's love as an agent of redemption and healing, Rochester miraculously ascends into this earthly paradise. The upward quest of sentimental romance depicted by Brontë in *Jane Eyre* represents, according to Frye, 'a sexual quest ending in marriage' (152). This differs from traditional romance, which Frye describes as 'the upward journey of a creature returning to its creator' (157). Brontë seems to fulfill both structures, however. Jane and Rochester end the upward quest of sentimental romance when they marry and later have a child. Yet they also fulfill, to a certain extent, the upward journey of the creature returning to its creator. Jane continually searches for the will of God in her life; she holds fast to the precepts laid forth by her understanding of Christianity; and it is through her that Rochester is healed spiritually. While Jane and Rochester do not move into the highest world, the world above Eden, they do acknowledge and seek after God, fulfilling the ultimate quest in sentimental romance.

7 'Telle us som myrie tale, by youre fey!': Exploring the Reading Transaction and Narrative Structure in Chaucer's *Clerk's Tale* and *Troilus and Criseyde*

> We currently use the word *narrative* without paying attention to, even at times without noticing, its ambiguity, and some of the difficulties of narratology are perhaps due to this confusion.
>
> (Gérard Genette, *Narrative Discourse*)

The deeply woven narrative textures inherent in Chaucer's corpus afford us with useful exemplars for exploring the wide-ranging interpretive possibilities of reader-response theory, especially in terms of its potential for revealing the narratological elements that impinge upon the transactions that take place between writers and readers. In the Prologue to the *Clerk's Tale*, the Host, Harry Bailly, encourages the Clerk to recite his tale for the pilgrims' storytelling contest – not a tale that will 'make us nat to slepe,' but a tale of 'som murie thyng of aventures' with 'youre termes, youre colours, and youre figures' (14-16). In the tale that follows, the Clerk imbues his story with a variety of narratological figures and patterns, thus forging what John M. Ganim aptly describes as a 'discourse marked by its grotesque, highly personalized, exuberant, and often satirical qualities' (113). Chaucer's fictionalized Clerk accomplishes such a discursive end by his careful appropriation of the rhetorical tropes that shape his narrative. A trained rhetorician and Oxford scholar, Chaucer's Clerk would surely be cognizant of the fictive value of tropological patterns and narrative designs, and moreover, as Ganim notes, the Clerk 'embodies one of the characteristic intellectual vices – the impulse to impose abstract order on experience' (121). The Clerk's authorial maneuvers in the tale indeed reveal such an ordered and intentional narrative structure, and a closer narratological reading of his tale divulges the manner in which these tropes operate together to produce the calculated and tightly woven poetic discourse that defines the *Clerk's Tale* for centuries of readers.

   In *Narrative Discourse: An Essay in Method*, Gérard Genette examines the elements of narratology that drive narrative movements within a literary work, in Genette's case, Proust's *À la recherche du temps perdu*. These narrative movements – specifically, summary, ellipsis, descriptive pause, and scene – illustrate the temporal foundations that produce the overall impression that a given narrative evokes. Such movements establish a tempo within a literary work, and their efficacy can be measured by the effects they create within that narrative. It is our intention in this chapter, then, to apply Genette's narrative principles to the *Clerk's Tale* in an effort to explain the overall impressions of authorial design and order that his tale produces, while at the same time examining the role of the Clerk's ironic oral discourse in the narratological presentation of his text, particularly in the case of the Envoy that concludes the tale.

Chaucer, narrative discourse, and the *Clerk's Tale*

Genette defines summary, in terms of his larger narratological schema, as those moments in a narrative that provide the background or history for later scenes. In fact, says Genette, 'summary remained, up to the end of the nineteenth century, the most usual transition between two scenes, the "background" against which scenes stand out, and thus the connective tissue *par excellence* of novelistic narrative' (97). Likewise, Chaucer – guised in the fictive authorial veil of the Clerk[1] – employs summary often in this tale, reducing scenes to brief stanzas of dialogue surrounded by lengthy historical digressions and character descriptions. Chaucer inaugurates the *Clerk's Tale* with precisely such a summary, and in the following instance, locates his tale in the 'noble contree' of Saluzzo, nestled at the foot of Mount Viso in Northern Italy:

> Ther is, at the west syde of Ytaille,
> Doun at the roote of Vesulus the colde,
> A lusty playn, habundant of vitaille,
> Where many a tour and toun thou mayst biholde,
> That founded were in tyme of fadres olde,
> And many another delitable sighte,
> And Saluces this noble contree highte. (57–63)

In this manner, Chaucer introduces his readers to the tale's principal locale, while at the same time indulging in a rhetorical figure not unlike the *descriptio* – what K. P. Wentersdorf describes as a 'passage setting forth a person's appearance and character traits, or the season of the year, or a particular landscape' (318). Chaucer employs summary in his initial descriptions of Griselda as well: 'But for to speke of vertuous beautee,/ Thanne was she oon the faireste under sonne;/ For povreliche yfostred up was she,/ No likerous lust was thurgh hire herte yronne' (211–14). In this instance, as in Chaucer's earlier descriptions of Saluzzo and its landscape, he uses summary to introduce the reader to one of the tale's principal characters, and at the same time, begins to ensure his audience's incipient sympathy for her.

Likewise, Chaucer frequently employs ellipses in the *Clerk's Tale* to denote the passage of time, and Genette defines such devices by their degree of distinction within the narrative. Explicit ellipses clearly indicate a lapse of time, according to Genette, while implicit ellipses suggest a more indefinite time-lapse and can only be inferred by the reader based on a gap in a given narrative's continuity (106–09). Chaucer utilizes ellipses often in the tale's fourth part, a section of the narrative that comprises one of the greatest periods of temporal flux in the *Clerk's Tale*. For example, the fourth section of the tale unfolds with an explicit ellipsis that suggests the passage of time by defining the years that have elapsed since Griselda surrendered her first child:

> In this estaat ther passed been foure yeer
> Er she with childe was, but, as God wolde,
> A knave child she bar by this Walter,
> Ful gracious and fair for to biholde.
> And whan that folk it to his fader tolde,
> Nat oonly he but al his contree merye
> Was for this child, and God they thanke and herye. (610–16)[2]

Similarly, Chaucer employs an implicit ellipsis earlier in the second part of the tale to register the changes in Griselda's character from her initial appearance in the story to her emergence as a beloved figure in Walter's kingdom. In the following example, Chaucer includes implicit referents within the stanza to signal a temporal change to readers:

> For though that evere vertuous was she,
> She was encressed in swich excellence
> Of thewes goode, yset in heigh bountee,
> And so discreet and fair of eloquence,
> So benigne and so digne of reverence,
> And koude so the peples herte embrace,
> That ech hire lovede that looked on hir face. (407–13)

By noting that Griselda 'was encressed in swich excellence/ Of thewes goode' – and further, by describing the reaction of the kingdom's denizens to her considerable personal charm and lovely countenance – Chaucer offers his readers implicit signals that a significant time shift has occurred without otherwise offering specific indicators to that effect.[3] The presence of ellipses – either explicit or implicit – is loaded with meaning in a narratological sense, and in the *Clerk's Tale* they are vital cues that signal temporal shifts to the reader, and in this instance, they identify the personal and public changes that have marked Griselda's character.

Chaucer also relies heavily on descriptive pauses in the construction of his narratological schema in the *Clerk's Tale*. According to Genette, these pauses occur when the author withdraws from the diegesis[4] to describe a scene that the reader and the other characters in the passage are not currently viewing (99–102). Chaucer's description of Griselda's dismissal from Walter's court in the fifth section of the *Clerk's Tale* exemplifies this notion. Here, Chaucer describes the forlorn figure of Griselda as she silently returns to the home of her father, wearing only her 'smok, with heed and foot al bare' (895):

> The folk hir folwe, wepynge in hir weye,
> And Fortune ay they cursen as they goon;
> But she fro wepyng kepte hire eyen dreye,
> Ne in this tyme word ne spak she noon.
> Hir fader, that this tidynge herde anoon,

Curseth the day and tyme that Nature
Shoop hym to been a lyves creature. (897–903)

Descriptive moments such as these allow readers to enjoy an ironic distance from the narrative, thus producing one of the tale's most attractive narratological features. As Anne Middleton notes, 'the value and pleasure of the tale lies precisely in that difference or distance from us: the effort required to close that distance, though variously described, seems to reveal the moral benefit of the fable' (121).

As with descriptive pauses, Chaucer utilizes mimetic scenes often in his narrative, and for this reason, scenes represent the most dramatic of the four narrative movements featured in the *Clerk's Tale*. A scene most often occurs in dialogue, says Genette, and 'realizes conventionally the equality of time between narrative and story' (94). Some of the most dramatic energy in Chaucer's narrative is concentrated in two scenes involving Walter's initial marriage bargain with Griselda, and later, when Walter reveals the truth about his test of Griselda's love. The first scene occurs in the second part of the *Clerk's Tale*, as Walter demands Griselda's steadfast allegiance as part of his marriage proposal. The narrative effect of this simple scene only reveals itself much later in the tale's closing stanzas, however:

I seye this: be ye redy with good herte
To al my lust, and that I frely may,
As me thynketh, do yow laughe or smerte,
And nevere ye to grucche it, nyght ne day?
And eek whan I sey 'ye,' ne sey nat 'nay,'
Neither by word ne frownyng contenance?
Swere this, and heere I swere oure alliance. (351–57)

The bargain forged in this passage truly underscores the definition of marriage in the *Clerk's Tale* according to Derek Pearsall, who describes it as 'a literally and uniquely accurate way of representing truthfully the exercise of absolute power over a powerless subject' (255).[5] In the dramatically charged mimetic scene that appears in the tale's closing stanzas, Walter reveals his motives for striking such a matrimonial bargain, as well as his motives for testing the bounds of Griselda's love for him: 'I have thy feith and thy benyngnytee,/ As wel as evere woman was, assayed,/ In greet estaat and povreliche arrayed./ Now knowe I, dere wyf, thy stedfastnesse' (1053–56). The true measure of the dramatic power of these two scenes lies, of course, in the irony of distance that Chaucer's narrative creates between Walter's initial bargain and the great lengths that he traverses in order to test Griselda's love. Chaucer's deliberate narrative design throughout the tale allows for the effects of that irony to reach fruition – an irony of distance that Chaucer secures for his audience initially when Walter finally reunites Griselda with her long-lost children and her crown, as well as an irony that the Clerk reiterates later in the tale's Envoy, Chaucer's 'literary defense,' according to Charles Muscatine (197).

As Muscatine further notes, 'Rhetoric was the common property of the literate,' and moreover, 'It could and did serve, in the hands of the same clerkly class of poets, every other kind of writing that pretended to more than plain speech' (173). Nowhere are the rhetorical properties and narratological figures of the *Clerk's Tale* more relevant than in the Envoy, itself a trope not unlike the summary in Genette's theory of narrative discourse.[6] In the Envoy, the Clerk recites the tale's fundamental moral conclusions, while also offering an ironic and often thoroughly comical reading of the ways in which the tale might be misunderstood by the other pilgrims, particularly the Wife of Bath:

> If thou be fair, ther folk been in presence,
> Shewe thou thy visage and thyn apparaille;
> If thou be foul, be fre of thy dispence;
> To gete thee freendes ay do thy travaille;
> Be ay of chiere as light as leef on lynde,
> And lat hym care, and wepe, and wrynge, and waille! (1207–12)

By proffering such an ironic coda to his narrative, the Clerk continues to confound the wishes of the Host and his other fellow travelers – thus satisfying the motive that has governed his self-conscious narratological maneuvers throughout the implicitly oral construction of his tale. As Wentersdorf notes: 'while the Clerk may appear to have agreed with the Host's blanket condemnation of rhetorical ornaments, his own style throughout the tale is studded decorously with many of the prescribed [narrative] devices. . . . Hence his implied rejection of such embroidery can only be interpreted as ironic' (316).

Such a self-conscious rhetorical strategy truly underscores the value of the Envoy to the overall effect of the Clerk's narrative – an effect that owes its efficacy to Chaucer's knowing infusion of narratological constructs into the *Clerk's Tale*. Indeed, by carefully weaving together diegetic scenes, summaries, descriptive pauses, and elliptical passages, Chaucer creates a consistent tempo and structure in the *Clerk's Tale*. Further, the consideration of Chaucer's narratological schema in terms of Genette's four narrative movements allows readers to impinge on – in Genette's words – 'the aesthetic consciousness of an artist' (264). This surely must be the greatest value of studying narrative discourse, and with the *Clerk's Tale*, Genette's narratology affords readers the opportunity of observing the machinery that evokes the tale's impressions of order and irony of distance, while at the same time offering readers the opportunity to acknowledge the ironic discourse that drives the Envoy at the tale's conclusion.

Chaucer and the transactional possibilities of literary parody

Chaucer's parody of Boccaccio's *Il Filostrato* in *Troilus and Criseyde* also demonstrates the ways in which he self-consciously engages his audience in a reading transaction. Medieval scholars have long acknowledged the source-texts for Chaucer's late fourteenth-century poem, *Troilus and Criseyde*, as Benoît de Sainte-Maure's *Roman de Troie*, Guido de Columni's *Historia Destructionis Troiae*, and Giovanni Boccaccio's *Il Filostrato*, among others. As Chaucer's principal narratological source, Boccaccio's poem remains the text upon which Chaucer both forged and expanded his vision for *Troilus and Criseyde* – thus fostering an original version of a tale already well known to fourteenth-century readers. As Charles Muscatine warns, however, 'the nature of his originality cannot be fully understood by subtracting, as it were, one poem from the other' (124). Indeed, an informed understanding of the *Troilus* requires a careful analysis of the narratological machinery that Chaucer appropriates from Boccaccio's earlier work, and moreover, such a study demands an equally careful examination of Chaucer's primary motives for his revision of *Il Filostrato*'s characterization schema and narrative structure.

While the narratological similarities between the *Troilus* and *Il Filostrato* might appear to suggest an intertextual relationship, Roland Barthes's definition of intertextuality warns otherwise: 'The intertextual in which every text is held, it itself being the text-between of another text, is not to be confused with some origin of the text: to try to find the "sources," the "influences" of a work, is to fall in with the myth of filiation' (*Image-Music-Text* 160). Because textual scholars have clearly revealed Boccaccio's poem as both a source for and powerful influence upon Chaucer's work, Barthes's definition of intertextuality implies that the relationship between the two poems is not an intertextual one. Robert A. Pratt reminds us, however, that Chaucer's poem is not a mere translation of *Il Filostrato*, but rather, 'a new creation; and in details as well as in the large, he goes his own way' (512).[7] As Stephen A. Barney adds, in the *Troilus*, Chaucer 'freely alters [the poems of his predecessors], augmenting and contracting his sources so much that the poems are essentially new' (471).

For this reason, then, Linda Hutcheon's theory of parody seems far more relevant to an analysis of Chaucer's appropriation of Boccaccio's earlier poem. 'Parody,' says Hutcheon, 'is repetition . . . that includes difference' (37). Further, notes Hutcheon, 'When we speak of parody, we do not just mean two texts that interrelate in a certain way. We also imply an intention to parody another work (or set of conventions) and both a recognition of that intent and an ability to find and interpret the backgrounded text in its relation to that parody' (22). With the *Troilus*, Chaucer clearly borrows from Boccaccio's modes of characterization and narrative structure, and thus self-consciously reinterprets Boccaccio's earlier poem while producing an original literary work. Such parodic moments in the *Troilus*, particularly Chaucer's characterization of the poem's principal figures, underscore the poet's primary motives for embarking on a parody of *Il Filostrato* – motives that find their origins in Chaucer's desire to satirize the romantic conventions of an earlier age for an informed audience of fourteenth-century readers.

In the *Troilus*, Chaucer replicates Boccaccio's fundamental characterization strategies for his poem's central characters, although at the same time, Chaucer alters subtly the manner in which these characters function within his narrative. In Chaucer's poem, these figures – Troilus, Pandarus, and Criseyde, respectively – are differentiated from their counterparts in *Il Filostrato* by the ways in which they respond to the constructs of the courtly love tradition, itself a matter of enduring debate among Chaucerian and medieval scholars alike. In Boccaccio's poem, Muscatine acknowledges the operation of a courtly love theme with a 'sensuality and a sauce of cynicism' in its romantic and idealistic dialogue – paradigmatic elements of the courtly love tradition and its elevated nobility as well as its overtly spiritual notion of romance.[8] In the *Troilus*, however, these same elements are exaggerated by Chaucer in an effort to provide a satiric commentary on the precepts of courtly love, and the characters of Troilus, Pandarus, and Criseyde function as vehicles for Chaucer's satiric motives.

In *Il Filostrato*, the character of Troilus indeed represents what Muscatine calls the 'courtly, idealistic view of experience' (133), and in Boccaccio's poem, he evinces the same form of protracted love-sickness that Chaucer later describes in the *Troilus*. In Boccaccio's narrative, Troilus weeps and swoons with the torment of his new and painfully unrequited love for the young widow, Criseida:

> Ah, Love, come to my aid! And thou, for whom I weep, captive as man never was before, ah, have a little pity on him who loves thee much more than his own life! . . . If thou dost this, lady, I shall renew my life like a flower in a fresh meadow in spring. . . . And, if this is grievous to thee, ah, cruel one, do thou at least cry to me, who am ready to do thy every pleasure: 'Kill thyself'; and indeed I will do it, thinking to please thee by that act.[9]

Chaucer likewise characterizes Troilus in a remarkably similar fashion, transforming 'this fierse and proude knyght' (I.225) into a woeful figure resembling the narrator's own lamentable prophecy, revealed shortly before Troilus first gazes upon Criseyde:

> As proude Bayard bynneth for to skippe
> Out of the weye, so pryketh hym his corn,
> Til he a lasshe have of the longe whippe –
> Than thynketh he, 'Though I praunce al byforn
> First in the trays, ful fat and newe shorn,
> Yet am I but an hors, and horses lawe
> I moot endure, and with my feres drawe' – (I.218–24)

As with the horse in Chaucer's description, Troilus lives to become controlled and helpless at the hands of love – the force that both sustains and dominates him. Troilus, later fully realizing his emotional incapacitation, remarks: 'O fool, now artow in the snare,/ That whilom japedest at loves peyne' (I.507–08).

Although Chaucer's characterization of Troilus is notably similar to Boccaccio's rendering of him in *Il Filostrato*, in the *Troilus*, Chaucer exaggerates the character's swoon in the face of love, and at the same time he subverts and humorizes the conventions of the courtly love tradition. As Muscatine notes: 'The fact is, that as medieval romance goes, as the "code" goes, Troilus is *too* perfect a courtly lover' (137). The manner in which Troilus embarks upon epic interludes of weeping and painful songs of love indeed appears to underscore such an argument. Moreover, Troilus's complete physical and emotional collapse in the face of his romantic response to Criseyde also seems to suggest that Chaucer's Troilus is '*too* perfect' a courtly lover – a conclusion that in turn argues for Chaucer's apparent satire regarding the elevated and exaggerated conventions of courtly love. Again, Chaucer's satirical approach to courtly love becomes increasingly evident when the narratological machinery of his parody is exposed.

Likewise, in his parody of Pandarus, Chaucer reveals his self-conscious attempt both to reiterate and yet differentiate the characterization strategies of his precursors, in this case, the narratological strategies of Boccaccio. In *Il Filostrato*, Boccaccio's Pandarus functions as an intermediary in the love affair between Troilus and Criseida, and, as Muscatine explains, the character of Pandarus is remarkably qualified for such an office, as he is 'both a devotee of courtly love and a practical realist' (138). Thus, in Boccaccio's poem – as Troilus struggles with his incipient infatuation with Criseida – Pandarus arrives to comfort and advise his troubled comrade:

> Wherefore, my friend, put thy trust in me and tell me who makes thy life so grievous and hard; and fear not lest I blame thee for loving, for sages of old declared in their wise discourse that love could not be taken from the heart unless it freed itself through long lapse of time. Leave thy anguish, leave thy sighs, and lessen thy grief through speech. Do thus and thy torments will pass, and greatly too does ardour slacken when he who loves sees companions with like desires. And I, as thou knowest, love against my will, nor can I do away nor add to my grief. (*G* 40)

In *Il Filostrato*, Troilus is genuinely consoled by Pandarus's friendly words, and remarks, 'thou knowest all that is needed to end my struggle' (*G* 43). While the character of Pandarus is replicated similarly in the *Troilus*, Chaucer again parodies Boccaccio's creation and forges an exaggerated version of Boccaccio's Pandarus.

In the *Troilus*, Chaucer produces a character who transcends the role of the intermediary, and instead acts as a calculating manipulator capable of extended, although often deliberately vague, circumlocutions. For example, in the following instance, Pandarus exhorts Criseyde to meet with Troilus, although in the process he employs a kind of double logic that preys upon both her romantic instincts as well as upon her fears:

> Now, nece myn, the kynges deer sone,
> The goode, wise, worthi, fresshe, and free,
> Which alwey for to don wel is his wone,
> The noble Troilus, so loveth the,
> That, but ye helpe, it wol his bane be.
> Lo, here is al! What sholde I moore seye?
> Doth what yow lest to make hym lyve or deye. (II.316–22)

This same gifted tactician – whom Muscatine appropriately describes as a 'doer' and a 'fixer' in a 'ponderable, manipulable world' (138) – is further parodied by Chaucer when he finally brings Troilus and Criseyde together to consummate their affair. In *Il Filostrato*, Pandarus is notably absent from their love scenes, while remarkably, in the *Troilus*, he remains present during the poem's most intimate moment. Pandarus's intrusion into such a private scene underscores Chaucer's parody of the character of Pandarus, as well as his attempt to satirize the role of the intermediary in the literature of the courtly love tradition.

Chaucer completes his parody of Boccaccio's poem through his deliberately vague characterization of Criseyde – thus effecting a kind of 'controlled ambiguity,' in the words of Muscatine (155). Indeed, while many of the details regarding her character remain the same in Chaucer's version of the poem, in the *Troilus*, many of these same narratological details are nevertheless skillfully veiled by Chaucer in a fog of ambiguity. For example, in Boccaccio's poem, she is clearly childless, though in the *Troilus*, Chaucer carefully conceals her maternal status: 'But wheither that she children hadde or noon,/ I rede it naught, therfore I late it goon' (I.132–33). In this manner, Chaucer parodies the more static characterization of Criseida in *Il Filostrato*.

Chaucer further enhances his parody of Criseyde's character in the *Troilus* by depicting her as a detached and fickle lover destined to betray the love-struck Troilus, and Chaucer produces such a characterization by altering the narrative distance previously established in Boccaccio's poem. Criseyde's literary reputation among fourteenth-century readers truly appears to advance this conclusion, because, as

Gretchen Mieszkowski notes, Chaucer's readers 'would have recognized Criseyde as a standard example of an unfaithful woman' (71), for her story and her duplicitous character were well-known to readers from the earlier works of Boccaccio and de Sainte-Maure.[10] Chaucer's appropriation of narrative distance in scenes involving Criseyde becomes particularly evident when she responds to Troilus's desperate letter in the tale's waning passages.

For example, in *Il Filostrato*, Boccaccio presents this emotionally charged scene entirely in the voice of his narrator, thus maintaining a substantial measure of narrative distance between the action of his poem and his audience:

> Criseida had written to him and made it clear that she loved him more than ever; and she had put forth many feigned excuses for delaying so long and not returning, and had asked for still more time ere her return – which was never to take place – and he had granted it to her, hoping to see her again, but he knew not when. (*G* 120)

In the *Troilus*, however, Chaucer depicts this same instance in his poem by offering the entire text of Criseyde's missive for his audience, and likewise decreasing the distance between the audience and the action of the poem. Perhaps more importantly, Chaucer tightly focuses the already biased attention of a fourteenth-century readership upon a character previously known for her abject betrayal of Troilus:

> Youre lettres ful, the papir al ypleynted,
> Conceyved hath myn hertes pietee.
> I have ek seyn with teris al depeynted
> Youre lettre, and how that ye requeren me
> To come ayeyn, which yet ne may nat be;
> But whi, lest that this lettre founden were,
> No mencioun ne make I now, for feere. (V.1597–1603)

By portraying this scene with such an intense narratological focus – and moreover, by offering a letter filled with the strangely disparate emotions of pity and detachment – Chaucer reinterprets the character of Criseyde for an audience already prejudiced regarding her character's duplicity.

Chaucer's reconfiguration of Criseyde thus reveals the depth of his parody of her character in Boccaccio's poem, while also underscoring his satirical approach to the conventions of courtly love – conventions clearly satirized in the *Troilus* when Criseyde unabashedly betrays her unusually tormented and often comically portrayed courtly lover, Troilus. Chaucer's infusion of satire into his parody, however, is not an unusual maneuver in a narrative of this nature. As Hutcheon notes, 'Satire frequently uses parodic art forms for either expository or aggressive purposes' (43). In the case of the *Troilus*, Chaucer employs a parodic narrative structure that satirizes the same courtly love conventions with which the characters of Boccaccio's narrative are clearly invested – conventions also 'aggressively' exaggerated by the characters in Chaucer's poem. In this manner, then, Chaucer produces a parody that functions on a variety of narrative levels, as well as a parody that reveals Chaucer's principal motives for revising the characterization strategies of Boccaccio and his other literary precursors. As with our discoveries in the *Clerk's Tale*, an analysis of the *Troilus*'s narrative design demonstrates Chaucer's efforts, time and time again, to draw his readers into an enduring conversation with his texts.

8 Addressing Horizons of Readerly Expectation in Joseph Conrad's *Heart of Darkness* and Ford Madox Ford's *The Good Soldier*, or, How to Put the 'Reader' in 'Reader Response'

> The impulse to moralize, to pontify, is a very strong one, and comes in many treacherous guises.
>
> (Ford Madox Ford, *Joseph Conrad*)

As one of early modernism's most visible and fruitful collaborations, Joseph Conrad and Ford Madox Ford's literary relationship resulted in the publication of three, largely undistinguished novels, *The Inheritors* (1901), *Romance* (1903), and *The Nature of a Crime* (1909). More importantly, though, their decade-long collaboration completely altered the nature of each writer's aesthetic by providing Conrad and Ford with an explicit model for tapping into their reader-ship's textual expectations.[1] Their theories of the novel – most notably, their aspirations for honing a kind of 'literary impressionism' in their fictions – demonstrate each writer's attempts at creating a mechanism for eliciting reader response. Simply put, Conrad and Ford fashion a series of self-conscious appeals in their novels to what Hans Robert Jauss describes as the reader's 'horizon of expectations,' or the manner in which readers interact with and ultimately respond to literary works. Conrad's and Ford's literary impressionism, with its accent upon the reader's experiences when encountering literary texts, attempts to exploit these horizons of expectation in order to produce new and eminently more complicated layers of meaning in contrast with their literary precursors.

In *Aesthetic Experience and Literary Hermeneutics* (1982), Jauss creates a communicative model for understanding readerly expectations of literary works, as well as an interpretive framework for explaining the aesthetic pleasure that readers derive from literary texts. Jauss's reception theory includes five levels in which the reader achieves a sense of 'aesthetically mediated identification' with the text.[2] During Jauss's first level, the associative level of interaction, the reader experiences the text by aligning him- or herself with the protagonist, often through games or other rites of competition. The second level involves the reader's unadulterated admiration for the protagonist, while the third level reflects the reader's sympathy for the text's central character, which the reader now recognizes as flawed and innately human. The fourth, cathartic level of interaction invites further reflection on the reading experience, particularly in terms of the reader's capacity for rendering moral judgment about the literary work. Finally, the fifth or ironic level of interaction involves the reader's sense of critical perception as he or she begins to formulate and refine a more sustained perspective of the literary work's larger meanings beyond the confines of the text (159).

Reading Conrad's and Ford's literary impressionism in terms of the five levels of Jauss's reception theory reveals the ways in which Conrad and Ford's collaboration allowed them to develop a common theory of the novel that involves a detached narrative voice in collusion with concrete notions of literary character and irony of situation. Conrad and Ford's theory of the novel finds its origins in a form of shifting narrative authority that exists at the heart of their two greatest narrative achievements, *Heart of Darkness* (1899) and *The Good Soldier* (1915), respectively. The quality and nature of the first-person narratives in each of these two novels demonstrates Conrad's and Ford's hyper-awareness of their evolving textual authority, as well as of the capacity of their narrators – Marlow and Dowell, respectively – for eliciting highly particularized responses from their readership. In short, Conrad and Ford establish a reader-response model in their fictions that underscores the central tenets of the reader-response movement regarding the ways in which the construction of a given narrative shares in the ultimate production of its myriad possibilities of meaning. Conrad and Ford evinced a particular interest in the manner in which the peculiar fusion that emerges between writers and their readers serves to evoke meaning and varying shades of interpretation. As writers cum theorists, Conrad and Ford conceptualized what they describe as a form of literary impressionism – a mechanism explicitly designed in order to draw the reader into the text.

Engendering reader response through Conrad's and Ford's literary impressionism

In his important essay, 'On Impressionism,' Ford relates their idea of Impressionism in terms of its capacity for impacting – and, indeed, ultimately shifting – readerly perspectives: 'Always consider the impressions that you are making upon the mind of the reader,' he writes, 'and always consider that the first impression with which you present him will be so strong that it will be all that you can ever do to efface it, to alter it, or even quite slightly to modify it' (39). In Ford's postulation, the impressionist technique affords novelists with the ability to capture the nuances of genuine humanity that mark our lives and to ponder the occasional moments in which we reveal the nature of our inner selves: 'I suppose that Impressionism exists to render those queer effects of real life that are like so many views seen through bright glass,' Ford observes, 'through glass so bright that whilst you perceive through it a landscape or a backyard, you are aware that, on its surface, it reflects a face of a person behind you. For the whole of life is really like that,' Ford adds, and 'we are almost always in one place with our minds somewhere quite other' (41). Ford's impressionistic technique involves the careful construction of a series of layers of meaning that work in concert in order to evoke various images and emotions. As Max Saunders notes, Ford's fiction 'does not work to subordinate everything to his voice. It re-creates the play of conflicting voices, volitions, attitudes, and viewpoints' (2:211). Simply put, through their assembly of details and revelations in their novels concerning the lives and proclivities of their characters, Conrad and Ford attempt, in Ford's words, 'to produce an illusion of reality' in the mind of their readers ('On Impressionism' 44).

This notion of an 'illusion of reality' functions at the core of the writers' practice of literary impressionism in their novels. In his Preface to *The Nigger of the 'Narcissus'* (1897), Conrad contends that literary impressionism ensures a given reader's response via its capacity for entreating the reader to tap into his or her auditory and visual senses:

> To snatch a moment of courage, from the remorseless rush of time, a passing phase of life, is only the beginning of the task. The task approached in tenderness and faith is to hold up unquestioningly, without choice and without fear, the rescued fragment before all eyes in the light of a sincere mood. It is to show its vibration, its colour, its form; and through its movement, its form, and its colour, reveal the substance of its truth – disclose its inspiring secret: the stress and passion within the core of each convincing moment. (*Prefaces* 52)

For Conrad, then, literary impressionism involves particular attention to the interaction between the writer's descriptive capabilities and the reader's capacity for registering sensory impressions.[3] The synergy between these two aspects of the reading experience accounts for literary impressionism's power as a narrative construct. Albert J. Guerard describes Conrad's and Ford's literary impressionism as 'a narrative method of deceptive emphasis and constantly shifting perspective, depending for much of its beauty on swift oscillations between the long view and the close, between the moralizing abstract and the highly visualized particular' (77).

For this reason, Conrad's and Ford's imaginative composition of Marlow and Dowell, respectively, bears considerable examination in terms of each writer's capacity for engendering various forms of reader response to their narratives. Their narrators in *Heart of Darkness* and *The Good Soldier* fashion convoluted, often circular orations about the people and events that they encounter. In such instances, literary impressionism affords Conrad and Ford with the means, in Guerard's words, for coming 'closer to actual life by presenting experience as a sensitive witness would receive it – casually, digressively, without logical order' (126). Both Marlow and Dowell meander through their narratives in a decidedly human fashion, pausing here and there to reflect on a salient (or perhaps not so salient) point. Even more significantly, each storyteller finds himself confronted with the issue of truth and its relation – whether direct or converse – with the tenuous realities of human affairs. Conrad and Ford adopt similar forms of shifting narrative authority in *Heart of Darkness* and *The Good Soldier* in an effort to account for the ways in which human passions and ideologies inevitably shift over the course of a lifetime, a protracted narrative, or even a mere scene. Read under the guise of Jauss's five levels of readerly interaction, Conrad's and Ford's literary impressionism reveals the manner in which human desires and experiences become decidedly contingent upon the context of our actions, as well as upon the social or political ramifications of our relationships with others. In short, some moments in Conrad's and Ford's fictions enjoy substantially more authority – or reliability or validity – than others. These instances, in themselves, invite the interactive phenomenon of reader response.

Marlow's journey to the ethical void

Conrad's Marlow finds his origins in *Lord Jim* (1900), which features a similarly named narrator who is forced to render moral judgements amongst difficult personal and psychological circumstances.[4] In dramatic contrast, though, the Marlow of *Heart of Darkness* functions as a more committed and forceful exemplar of humanity. Unlike Dowell, Marlow intuitively understands his place in the world, as well as humanity's precarious role in an evolving society in which civilization can erode and ultimately topple at any moment. As the novel begins, Conrad establishes the reader's innate sense of identification with Marlow by highlighting the narrator's credentials as the novel's moral compass. In so doing, Conrad underscores the power of Jauss's associative level of interaction in which readers align themselves with the protagonist. Marlow narrates *Heart of Darkness* before an audience – an audience that includes, rather significantly, Conrad's readers – on a cruising yawl moored in the Thames Estuary, with London, seemingly a beacon of civilization and propriety, looming just beyond the *Nellie*, the vessel from which Marlow recites his tale. The Buddha-like Marlow tells his story about a woe-begotten visit to the Congo to four rapt listeners; soon, though, we find ourselves, as with Conrad's readers, equally transfixed by Marlow's vexing narrative. With 'sunken cheeks, a yellow complexion, a straight back, an ascetic aspect, and, with his arms dropped, the palms of hands outwards, [he] resembled an idol' (18). After Conrad's nameless narrator genuflects verbally to London's yen for conquest and civilization-building – 'What greatness had not floated on the ebb of that river in to the mystery of an unknown earth! . . . The dreams of men, the seed of commonwealths, the germs of empires' – Marlow interrupts with a flourish and explodes the narrator's sea of whitewashed praise: '"And this also," said Marlow suddenly, "has been one of the dark places of the earth"' (19).

Marlow's ostensible role as the novel's moral center allows Conrad's readers to identify with his protagonist. For this reason, Marlow pointedly inaugurates his story with a treatise on humankind's propensity for savagery, particularly when civilization's grasp begins to diminish. 'The conquest of the earth,' Marlow observes, 'which mostly means the taking it away from those who have a different complexion or slightly fatter noses than ourselves, is not a pretty thing when you look into it too much' (21). In this manner, Marlow invites us, as judges of a sort, to enter into his story ourselves. Conrad purposefully represents Marlow in the act of putting forth concepts and offering illustrative scenes, yet the writer never allows his storyteller the opportunity to render any final judgements, which he cedes to his readers. Marlow's journey begins, rather significantly, in Brussels, the picture of contemporary, civilized existence as revealed by Marlow's impressions of the city as 'a whited sepulchre' in contrast with the Congo's evolutionary darkness. Marlow's aunt blissfully hopes that her nephew – as an 'emissary of light, something like a lower sort of apostle' no less – will bring culture and the gleam of civilization to the Congo's ostensibly savage population. A pre-voyage visit to the company doctor seems even more ominous. Perfunctory at best, Marlow's physical examination occurs over drinks as the old doctor fumbles to check the narrator's pulse. The physician admits that he never sees his patients again after their initial appointments with him. Besides, he adds, the 'changes' that they experience 'take place inside' the psyche. As Marlow prepares to embark upon his voyage, the doctor soberly reminds him that 'in the tropics one must before everything keep calm' (26).

As Marlow's expedition takes him ever deeper into the Congo, Conrad exploits the attributes of Jauss's second level of interaction in which readers further align themselves with the protagonist by sharing in his experiences. Hence, as civilization's reach recedes, Marlow finds himself confronted with successively greater moral challenges via which to impress his audience. As with his listeners – indeed, his readers – Marlow admits to being struck by the deafening clash between the untamed, colossal jungle and the vague fabric of civilization. His ship itself seems 'incomprehensible' in relation to the jungle's vastness: 'Nothing could happen,' he notes. 'There was a touch of insanity in the proceeding, a sense of lugubrious drollery in the sight' of the steamship as it navigates Africa's 'formless' coast and its 'uniform sombreness' (28). Within the jungle itself, Marlow observes, nameless custom-clerks with flag-poles and tin sheds attempt to exert the power of civilization upon an unflinching wilderness. At the mouth of the river, Marlow transfers to another vessel, and his journey into the heart of darkness begins in earnest. At the first company station, he encounters a 'scene of inhabited devastation.' At one point, he sees a deserted boiler in the grass – an obvious symbol of civilization's defeat at the hands of the jungle – before happening upon a chain-gang of natives. Marlow grimly realizes that 'I also was a part of the great cause of these high and just proceedings' (29–30). Reduced to mere black shapes by civilization's relentless onslaught, the natives 'were dying slowly – it was very clear. They were not enemies, they were not criminals, they were nothing earthly now – nothing but black shadows of disease and starvation, lying confusedly in the greenish gloom' (31). For Conrad's readers, Marlow shines in comparison to what seem to be the jungle's deplorable and amoral ways.

During Jauss's third level of interaction, the reader begins to feel sympathy for the protagonist's human qualities. Conrad accomplishes this end by characterizing Marlow in dramatic contrast with the various, largely unsavory figures whom he encounters during his journey. In one of the novel's most telling scenes regarding the strange contradiction that occurs in the wilderness between civilized propriety and the jungle's untrodden ways, Marlow describes his meeting with the company's chief accountant, 'a white man, in such an unexpected elegance of get-up that in the first moment I took him for a sort of vision. I saw a high-starched collar, white cuffs, a light alpaca jacket, snowy trousers, a clean necktie, and varnished boots. No hat. Hair parted, brushed, oiled, under a green-lined parasol held in a big white hand. He was amazing, and had a pen-holder behind his ear' (32). The accountant – a 'miracle' of modern civilization loosed upon the jungle – evinces an utter devotion to his books, via which he attempts to effect pristine order upon the wilderness. In addition to training a native woman to do his ironing, the chief accountant toils in a brutally humid office in which humongous, stabbing flies buzz overhead. In one instance, an agonizingly sick employee appears on a gurney. Amazingly, the accountant dares to complain that the man's groans 'distract my attention. And without that it is extremely difficult to guard against clerical errors in this climate' (33). In this way, Marlow communicates to Conrad's audience the tragic fact that nothing, it seems, is worthy of interrupting society's amoralistic rage for order.

Jauss's third level of interaction is further revealed by Marlow's experiences with Mr Kurtz, as well as other characters whom he encounters in the Congo. It is through the accountant that Marlow first learns about the storied Mr Kurtz, a fabulously successful agent in the company's employ who trades in ivory in the jungle's interior. With a safari of 60 men in tow, Marlow begins his 200-mile journey to the Central Station. Along the way, Marlow encounters abandoned and pillaged villages, the devastating aftermath of slave traders. At this juncture, Marlow suffers another delay – his steamer will require nearly a month in order to undergo repairs – that will allow him to linger a bit and survey the jungle's psychologically overwhelming social and geographical landscape. The station manager, for example, suffers from the malaise engendered by life in the wilderness. 'He was neither civil nor uncivil,' Marlow observes. The jungle and his dreams of usurping Kurtz have reduced him to a 'chattering idiot' (36, 37). Later, Marlow happens upon the company's nefarious brickmaker, who plumbs Marlow for information about the firm and its plans. The brickmaker's conniving, immoral behavior prompts Marlow to declare that 'I hate, detest, and can't bear a lie, not because I am straighter than the rest of us, but simply because it appalls me. There is a taint of death, a flavour of mortality in lies – which is exactly what I hate and detest in the world – what I want to forget' (41).

Heart of Darkness engages Jauss's fourth level of interaction – the level in which readers begin to reflect upon their various interpretations of the novel and render moral judgments – almost entirely through Marlow's confused and often debilitating experiences as he nears and finally arrives at the Inner Station. Having heard Kurtz's name spoken of with a combination of reverence and fear, Marlow imagines the agent to be a man of moral determination and civilized demeanor – the antithesis of the Europeans whom he has encountered in the jungle thus far. In a supreme moment revealing Conrad's and Ford's well-honed literary impressionism, Marlow describes the natives' surprise attack – a 'tumultuous and mournful uproar' – on his steamer as the craft approaches the Inner Station. The death of his helmsman affects Marlow particularly deeply, and he is thunderstruck by the seemingly instantaneous calamity that the attack causes: 'The rest of the world was nowhere, as far as our eyes and ears were concerned,' Marlow remembers. 'Just nowhere. Gone, disappeared; swept off without leaving a whisper or a shadow behind' (55). From Marlow's uninitiated purview, the sight of the steamship must have filled the natives with so much 'extreme grief' that they had no other choice but to attack the vessel that was encroaching on the wilderness. Marlow feels even more dismay over the possibility of the natives having extinguished Kurtz as well: 'I was cut to the quick at the idea of having lost the inestimable privilege of listening to the gifted Kurtz' (63).

By establishing Marlow as inherently flawed and capable of gross mistakes in judgment, Conrad prepares his readers for Jauss's fifth level of interaction in which they enjoy an ironic view of the novel itself and its larger moral implications. Marlow subsequently learns that Kurtz orchestrated the natives' attack on the steamer in order to continue his dominion over the natives and the Inner Station. To Marlow's great surprise and dismay, Kurtz, it seems, had been undone by the jungle's 'solitude without a policeman' (64). In addition to encouraging and presiding over the natives' ritualistic self-sacrifices, Kurtz had been entrusted by the International Society for the Suppression of Savage Customs with the imperative of writing a report about the need to 'Exterminate all the brutes!' (66). Marlow eventually reaches the Inner Station, where he finds Kurtz's headquarters in a putrid building surrounded by posts ornamented with human skulls. Kurtz's soul, Marlow reports, had been seduced by the jungle: 'Being alone in the wilderness, it had looked within itself, and, by Heavens! I tell you, it had gone mad,' says Marlow. 'I saw the inconceivable mystery of a soul that knew no restraint, no faith, and no fear, yet struggling blindly with itself' (82). In short, the jungle's clash with civilization has left Kurtz hollow and soulless, virtually unable to draw upon any innate sense of ethics or human decency. An empty shell of a man, he dies with Marlow as the only witness to his terrible fate. As if entranced by the awful vision of his life in the wilderness, Kurtz mutters his notorious last words, 'The horror! The horror!' (85). Moments later, the manager's boy dismisses the natives' oppressor with contempt and scorn: 'Mistah Kurtz – he dead' (86).

Heart of Darkness completes its tour of Jauss's five levels of readerly expectation by returning Marlow to civilization, where he, as with Conrad's readership, can finally recognize the extent of humanity's depravity, as well as the corrosive power of myth despite our paralyzing belief that it can sustain civilization's self-aggrandizing desires for moral elevation. Hence, Marlow's experiences back in Europe – safe within the confines of Brussels, that sepulchral city – allow him to reflect upon his own encounter with the void, 'a vision of greyness without form filled with physical pain, and a careless contempt for the evanescence of all things' (86–87). He later presents a journalist with Kurtz's report on the 'Suppression of Savage Customs,' but only after having removed its most vile desideratum. Soon thereafter, Marlow visits the doomed agent's fiancée to return her correspondence and her portrait. When she demands to know Kurtz's last words, Marlow chooses to lie, despite his disgust for equivocation. 'The last word he pronounced,' Marlow tells her, 'was – your name' (93). For Marlow, 'it seemed to me that the house would collapse before I could escape, that the heavens would fall upon my head. But nothing happened' (94). As with Kurtz's listeners on the *Nellie*, Marlow's readers are left only to ponder the vast heart of darkness that exists just beyond the reach of civilization's grasp. It is within that horrible empty place that ethics loses its hold and where human beings fill the ensuing void with disillusion and a potentiality for evil. Conrad's narrative, with its affecting literary impressionism, asks us to look within that void as well.

Dowell's narrative circumlocution and the ethics of storytelling

For John Dowell and the readers of *The Good Soldier*, the void seems remarkably simple to comprehend, given that the narrative functions as the means via which Dowell comes to terms with the suicides of his wife Florence and of his friend Edward Ashburnham, as well as the untimely passing of Maisie Maidan and the spiritual death of Nancy Rufford. Yet, in many ways, *The Good Soldier* features layers of difficulty and textual complication that dwarf *Heart of Darkness*'s various attempts at ethical revelation and narrative circumlocution. Reading *The Good Soldier* in terms of Jauss's levels of interaction demonstrates Ford's self-conscious efforts at drawing his readership into the novel's remarkably dense layers of meaning. The composition of his narrative after their deaths allows Dowell to comprehend – slowly and often confoundingly – Florence, Edward, and Leonora Ashburnham's deceptive roles in the construction of his existence. As readers, we cannot help but align ourselves with Ford's protagonist as he variously describes the relationship between the Dowells and the Ashburnhams in *The Good Soldier* as a 'four-square coterie' and as an 'extraordinarily safe castle' (11). Ford's befuddled narrator only learns the extent of the Dowell's and the Ashburnham's collective dysfunctionality *after* Florence's and Edward's suicides. Before their deaths, Dowell consoled himself with the notion that they were all 'good people.' Yet Dowell's unsavory discoveries about his wife and friend force him to confront the awful reality of their relationship as he slowly comprehends the truth about the couples' nine-year association.

The atemporality of Dowell's narrative discoveries presents significant problems for Ford's readership as they attempt to unravel the mysterious threads of his past, while aligning themselves with his cause and empathizing with his precarious situation. Conrad and Ford's literary impressionism reveals Dowell in the act of telling and retelling his own story. By narrating the events of his life with Florence and Edward, Dowell hopes to make sense of their experiences together, to understand the desires that motivated the covert activities of his duplicitous wife and her lover, and to trace the events that resulted in their suicides. Dowell's utterances – which frequently vacillate between moments of genuine profoundness and instances of utter farce – must be necessarily understood in terms of the awkward and nonlinear emotional trajectory of his narrative experiences in *The Good Soldier*. As Saunders perceptively observes, Dowell's narrative 'insists on the complexity of human character, its contradictoriness and instability. It presents all these aspects as equally true, equally inescapable.' Ford's narrator 'foregrounds the difficulty of knowing and understanding,' Saunders adds. 'It articulates difficulty by chronological fragmentation, narrative and semantic intricacy' (1:407). Simply put, for all of his narratological quirks and moments of equivocation, Dowell reveals himself to be decidedly *human* in his textual attempts to make sense of his past.

In *The Good Soldier*, Dowell impinges upon Jauss's first level of interactivity when he addresses the background of his narrative directly to his (and Ford's) audience: 'You may ask why I write,' he remarks. 'And yet my desires are quite many. For it is not unusual in human beings who have witnessed the sack of a city or the falling to pieces of a people to desire to set down what they have witnessed for the benefit of unknown heirs or of generations infinitely remote; or, if you please, just to get the sight out of their heads' (11). In the novel,

Dowell ultimately chooses to share his story with a 'sympathetic' listener with whom he can work through his grief and rage:

> I shall just imagine myself for a fortnight or so at one side of the fireplace of a country cottage, with a sympathetic soul opposite me. And I shall go on talking, in a low voice while the sea sounds in the distance and overhead the great flood of wind polishes the bright stars. From time to time we shall get up and go to the door and look out at the great moon and say: 'Why, it is nearly as bright as in Provence!' And then we shall come back to the fireside, with just the touch of a sigh because we are not in Provence where even the saddest stories are gay. (15)

Evincing yet again a desire for self-delusion when confronted with the awfulness of his past, Dowell invokes a French provincial cottage as his setting in an effort to provide himself with the comfort of the fireside and to diminish the emotional trauma of his recent discoveries. Yet, in this circumlocutory manner, Dowell also intends both to reflect upon his memories of life with Florence and the Ashburnhams, as well as to contextualize their betrayal of him.

Jauss's first level of interaction concerns the protagonist's capacity for establishing a sense of association between himself, in Dowell's case, and his reading audience. Hence, Dowell goes to great lengths to demonstrate his complicated emotional state in order to win his audience's sympathy. In the process, he reveals himself to be in a perpetual state of flux as he vacillates between feelings of grief and torment. When reflecting upon his past with Florence and the Ashburnhams, for example, Dowell writes that 'our intimacy was like a minuet. No indeed, it can't be gone. You can't kill a minuet de la cour,' he continues. 'The mob may sack Versailles; the Trianon may fall, but surely the minuet – the minuet itself is dancing itself away into the furthest stars' (11). Yet within scant moments, Dowell seems to confront the reality of his past, only to deny it once more. 'No, by God it is false!' he writes. 'It wasn't a minuet that we stepped; it was a prison – a prison full of screaming hysterics. . . . And yet, I swear by the sacred name of my creator that it was true. It was true sunshine; the true music; the true plash of the fountains from the mouth of stone dolphins' (12). In this way, Dowell's conflicted memories of the intimate 'minuet' that he shared with Florence and the Ashburnhams slowly dissolve into a profound sense of isolation. Having finally confronted the truth about his life in Nauheim, Dowell finds himself alone with the images of death and duplicity that now mark his existence.

Dowell impinges upon Jauss's second level of interaction, which necessitates the audience's identification with the protagonist's admirable qualities, when he expresses his moral outrage regarding various aspects of his experiences in *The Good Soldier*. Dowell's anger manifests itself as he reflects upon a variety of issues, including his feelings about Florence and Edward's role in Maisie's death; his jealousy over Leonora's new marriage and her capacity to overcome the past and Edward's loss; and his disgust for Florence's conniving behavior and what he perceives to be her cowardly escape via suicide. Rather ironically, Maisie possesses the only *legitimate* heart condition in the novel, while Edward's condition of the heart finds its roots in his inability to control his romantic urges and Florence's heart palpitations are the stuff of pure invention. Maisie's heart attack occurs after she witnesses an intimate conversation between Edward and Florence. The chaste wife of one of Edward's junior officers, Maisie met her death as she prepared to leave Nauheim, and, perhaps even more significantly, Edward, for whom she harbored an innocent affection. Angry over Maisie's tragic entanglement in Florence and Edward's deceitful web, Dowell exclaims that 'such young things ought to have been left alone. Of course Ashburnham could not leave her alone' (56). As he compiles his narrative, Dowell remembers the surreal discovery of Maisie's body: 'Maisie had died in the effort to strap up a great portmanteau,' he writes. 'She had died so grotesquely that her little body had fallen forward into the trunk and it had closed upon her, like the jaws of a gigantic alligator,' he continues. 'Her dark hair, like the hair of a Japanese, had come down and covered her body and her face' (56).

Perhaps even more significantly, Dowell's anger reaches its jealous nadir during his textual reflections upon Leonora's life after Edward's suicide, as well as her more agreeable existence after the conclusion of their minuet's final, tragic movements. 'I am estranged from Leonora, who married Rodney Bayham,' Dowell writes. 'Leonora rather dislikes me, because she has got it into her head that I disapprove of her marriage with Rodney Bayham. Well, I disapprove of her marriage. Possibly I am jealous. Yes, no doubt I am jealous' (151). While he blames Leonora for her own manipulative behavior and for her ability to usurp her own loneliness and isolation, Dowell reserves particular loathing for Florence, for the woman who fabulated a heart condition on their honeymoon in order to set their sexless marriage into motion and to allow her to conduct her romantic affairs in secret. In one instance, Dowell fumes as he remembers Florence gazing seductively at him as she prepares to enter a Nauheim bathhouse: 'What the devil! For whose benefit did she do it? For that of the bath attendant? of the passers-by? I don't know,' he writes. 'Anyhow, it can't have been for me, for never, in all the years of her life, never on any possible occasion, or in any other place did she so smile to me, mockingly, invitingly. Ah, she was a riddle' (22–23).

As with Dowell, we find ourselves – as his ever-patient listeners – sympathizing with his plight. This aspect of reading *The Good Soldier* allows us to enter into the third level of Jauss's communicative model, which accounts for the ways in which we empathize with the protagonist precisely because of his human frailties and interpersonal flaws. For this reason, we forgive Dowell for his vituperative response to his duplicitous wife's death. After Florence commits suicide when she believes, mistakenly it turns out, that her husband has discovered the extent of her infidelities, an angry Dowell imagines an afterlife of isolation for his faithless wife:

> I hate Florence with such a hatred that I would not spare her an eternity of loneliness. She need not have done what she did. She was an American, a New Englander. She had not the hot passions of these Europeans. She cut out that poor imbecile of an Edward – and I pray God that he is really at peace, clasped close in the arms of that poor, poor girl! And, no doubt, Maisie Maidan will find her young husband again, and Leonora will burn, clear and serene, a northern light and one of the archangels of God. And me . . . Well, perhaps, they will find me an elevator to run . . . But Florence . . . . (53)

Vacillating between empathy for his late wife's social station and utter disdain for her betrayal of Edward, Dowell's utterances signal the profundity of his wide-ranging sympathies for the plights of *The Good Soldier*'s other beleaguered characters. Dowell's anger and understandable hatred for Florence in this passage demonstrate, moreover, the amplitude of his current hostility in the face of her loss, particularly because her death ensures that many of Dowell's most pressing questions about his existence during the past nine years will remain mysteries forever; the latter facet of his anger results in the bitter resentment that Dowell harbors for his late wife.

Of particular importance to our understanding of the ways in which the novel reflects Jauss's third level of interaction are Dowell's rumi-nations about what constitutes the notion of 'good people,' one of the most significant themes in Ford's novel. As Arthur Mizener notes: 'What *The Good Soldier* is showing us is that both within the private selves of people and in the relations between them that makes a society there is a terrible division' (275). Ford's concept of 'good people' operates within the narrow confines of this 'terrible division,' or the discrepancy between the outward personae that people share with the world around them and the less savory reality of their inter-nal selves. Dowell longs for a better fate than the one that awaits him at the conclusion of *The Good Soldier.* 'Is there any terrestrial paradise where, amidst the whispering of the olive-leaves, people can be with whom they like and have what they like and take their ease in shadows and in coolness?' Dowell asks. 'Or are all men's lives like the lives of us good people – like the lives of the Ashburnhams, of the Dowells, of the Ruffords – broken, tumultuous, agonized, and unro-mantic lives, periods punctuated by screams, by imbecilities, by deaths, by agonies? Who the devil knows?' (151). Dowell's irrationality in this instance – and, indeed, throughout much of the novel – under-scores his prevailing desire for self-delusion and for seeking a genuine paradise that would allow him to return to his earlier, albeit naïve world of comforting 'permanence' and 'stability.' Yet this self-delu-sion is, in itself, one of the principal aspects that allows us, as his audience, to sympathize with his increasingly emotionally debilitating plight.

Jauss's fourth level of interaction, with its concern for the protago-nist's capacity for enjoying catharsis and subsequently rendering moral judgment, underscores Dowell's sense of loss and intense feel-ings of depression after he experiences the effects of Edward's suicide and Nancy's subsequent catatonia. For his readers, these events prove equally traumatic, as we identify with Dowell's emotional trials and begin formulating moral judgments of our own. Edward's decision to take his own life finds its roots in his overwhelming love for Nancy, rather than Florence's suicide; like Dowell, Edward erroneously believed that she expired after an overdose of heart medication. Fearing the consequences of consummating his relationship with Nancy, his much younger ward, Edward sends her to join her father in India. 'It was a most amazing business,' Dowell writes, 'and I think that it would have been better in the eyes of God if they had all attempted to gouge out each other's eyes with carving knives. But they were "good people."' Later, after Edward tells Dowell that 'I am so desperately in love with Nancy Rufford that I am dying of it' (158), Edward kills himself with a penknife in the stables of his estate at Branshaw Teleragh after receiving a telegram from Nancy, who announces that she has arrived safely in Brindisi.

Similarly, Dowell's depression and anxiety regarding Nancy's madness draw Ford's readers into an even closer association with the narrator's vast moral quandaries. His despondency fosters a kind of exhaustion in Dowell's psyche, the kind of spiritual depletion that will result in the feelings of acceptance that mark his narrative's final pages. 'Anyhow, I don't know whether, at this point, Nancy Rufford loved Edward Ashburnham,' Dowell observes. 'I don't know whether she even loved him when, on getting, at Aden, the news of his suicide she went mad. Because that may just as well have been for the sake of Leonora as for the sake of Edward. Or it may have been for the sake of both of them. I don't know. I know nothing. I am very tired' (155–56). Particularly depressing for Dowell is the fact that he now functions as Nancy's platonic attendant, the same office that he fulfilled during his sexless marriage to Florence. 'I should marry Nancy if her reason were ever sufficiently restored to let her appreciate the meaning of the Anglican marriage service,' Dowell writes. 'But it is probable that her reason will never be sufficiently restored to let her appreciate the meaning of the Anglican marriage service. Therefore I cannot marry her, according to the law of the land. So here I am very much where I started thirteen years ago,' Dowell continues. 'I am the attendant, not the husband, of a beautiful girl, who pays no attention to me' (150–51).

Having recognized the ironic and circular nature of Dowell's situation, readers finally gain a larger perspective about the novel's ethical examination of human nature's destructive powers and its potential for exacting the moral debasement of others in pursuit of entirely self-motivated desires. For Dowell's audience, this aspect of the novel demonstrates the narrative's intersection with Jauss's fifth level of interaction, the moment in which readers themselves consider the narrative's social commentary beyond the text of *The Good Soldier*. For Dowell and his audience, a feeling of resignation characterizes his acceptance of the admittedly unfair state of affairs in which he finds himself at the novel's conclusion. 'Society must go on, I suppose, and society can only exist if the normal, if the virtuous, and the slightly deceitful flourish, and if the passionate, the headstrong, and the too-truthful are condemned to suicide and to madness,' he writes. 'But I guess that I myself, in my fainter way, come into the category of the passionate, of the headstrong, and the too-truthful. For I can't conceal from myself the fact that I loved Edward Ashburnham – and that I love him because he was just myself,' Dowell adds. 'He seems to me like a large elder brother who took me out on several excursions and did many dashing things whilst I just watched him robbing the orchards, from a distance. And, you see, I am just as much of a senti-mentalist as he was' (160–61). Despite Edward's betrayal of him, Dowell finally comes to terms with his previously unsettling memo-ries of their friendship, as well as with an arbitrary society in which virtue rarely goes rewarded and deceit frequently thrives.

In this way, Dowell invites his audience to render ethical judgments about the manner in which Florence, Edward, and Leonora's actions will continue to impact the nature of his existence. Resigned to his fate, he imagines his own spiritual death as years of sameness spread out before him in all of their predictable constancy: 'So life peters out. I shall return to dine and Nancy will sit opposite me with the old nurse standing behind her,' Dowell writes. 'Then she will say that she believes in an Omnipotent Deity or she will utter the one word "shut-tlecocks," perhaps. It is very extraordinary to see the perfect flush of health on her cheeks, to see the lustre of her coiled black hair, the poise of the head upon the neck, the grace of the white hands – and to think that it all means nothing – that it is a picture without a meaning' (161). For Dowell, life has become void of significance, 'a picture without a meaning.' Having resigned himself to the absurdity of fate – particularly revealed to him by Edward's senseless death and by Nancy's perpetual elegance, even in her madness – Dowell finally assents to the numbing circularity that will pervade his life in the present, as well as in the foreseeable future. Interestingly, Dowell's situation at the conclusion of the novel mirrors Marlow's remarks at the end of *Heart of Darkness*. Both narrators find themselves confronted with the awfulness of a void that they simply cannot evade.

As with *Heart of Darkness*, *The Good Soldier* draws us into the narra-tive via Conrad's and Ford's conception of literary impressionism. By enhancing the particularity inherent in their characterizations of Marlow and Dowell, respectively, Conrad and Ford provide their readership with a mechanism for evaluating each narrator's tale in relation to themselves and their own senses of ethics and humanity. In many ways, both narrators function as victims of civilization's situational ethics and misplaced value systems. Marlow's experiences demonstrate what happens when civilization wanes and human beings wallow in an ethical wilderness. Dowell's treatment at the hands of Florence, Edward, and Leonora reveals the manner in which human beings elevate the needs of the self over basic moral considerations and simple magnanimity. Exploring the five levels of Jauss's communicative model underscores the ways in which Conrad's and Ford's narratives establish vital interrelationships with their readers that entreat us to ponder the texts within the contexts of our own experiences, to proffer our own interpretations of the 'meaning as an event,' in Stanley Fish's words. And that act, in itself, embodies the theoretical imperatives of reader-response criticism.

Conclusion: Beyond Formalist Criticism and Reader-Response Theory

So what now then?

(Paul Thomas Anderson, *Magnolia*)

Despite the increasing hegemony of new, often politically conscious forms of literary critique, the contemporary theoretical project clearly holds a revered place for formalist criticism and reader-response theory. Until recently, formalist and New Critical ideologies were dismissed almost universally in a derisory fashion as decidedly 'old school' ways of reading and thinking about literature. During the 1990s, though, formalist criticism began to enjoy a renaissance of sorts, particularly as a number of theorists sought to historicize the New Criticism's place within critical theory's relatively brief heritage. Steven Knapp, for example, has questioned the validity and value of contemporary literary theory's denigration of formalism as a primitive interpretive methodology. As the title of his thoughtful volume suggests, in *Literary Interest: The Limits of Anti-Formalism* (1993) Knapp demonstrates the inherent limits of our collective rage against our theoretical precursors. As Knapp and others have revealed in their scholarship, the fundamental attributes of close reading continue to resound within the interpretive methodologies of the present.[1] Aligned as they are with an overarching identity politics, our contemporary schools of criticism differentiate themselves almost exclusively in terms of their particular political imperatives. Yet the scholarly fruits of their inquiries inevitably find their origins in some form of close, formalistic readings of the texts that they choose to further their ideological aims.

As with formalism and the New Criticism, reader-response theory is reaping the benefits of critical theory's interest in historicizing its place in the intellectual continuum. As Jane Tompkins's *Reader-*

Response Criticism: From Formalism to Poststructuralism (1980) demonstrates, the reader-response movement began engaging in acts of historicism long before its influence waned within the academy's vaunted corridors. As one of the principal driving forces behind the advent of the cultural studies movement, reader-response theory's basic premises about the complex nature of the reading process continue to exert a substantial influence upon the ways in which we consider the peculiar interrelationships that emerge between ourselves and literary texts. In many ways, the genesis of reader-response theory explains much of the identity politics that pervades contemporary literary criticism. As the present volume reveals, the reader-response movement emerged amidst a flurry of competing voices engaging in debate about various aspects of the reading experience. Their spirited disagreements, however well-intentioned, invariably led to ideological entrenchment and theoretical bifurcation. While the reader-response movement resulted in vast intellectual riches regarding our understanding of the reading process itself, its ongoing debate about the problematics of canonicity and the politics of interpretation played a role in engendering the vitriolic 'culture wars' of the 1980s and 1990s, as well as the theoretical entrenchment of the present.

If nothing else, the culture wars have demonstrated identity politics – with the left and the right drawing upon literary studies as their battleground – at its collective nadir. The conservative right's political preeminence during the 1980s served as the catalyst for the ensuing culture wars that tested the resiliency of cultural studies and multiculturalism while also challenging the intellectual dominion of the academy. Students of the culture wars typically attribute the inauguration of the intellectual crisis in higher education to Secretary of Education William J. Bennett's 1984 governmental report on the humanities, *To Reclaim a Legacy*, in which he fans the flames of nationalism and charges American academics with having lost their senses of moral and intellectual purpose when they enacted policies of canon expansion and multicultural study. While the power and publicity concomitant with Bennett's cabinet post provided him with the public voice necessary to strike a strident initial chord within the American public, Allan Bloom's *The Closing of the American Mind: How Higher Education Has Failed Democracy and Impoverished the Souls of Today's Students* (1987) imbued the culture wars with the intellectual cachet of a scholarly voice. As the culture wars advanced into the 1990s, proponents of the right continued the culture warriors' onslaught against canon revision, while also increasingly objecting to the manner in which contemporary scholars resorted to the politicization of literary and cultural studies. In its attempt to respond to the right's political and cultural attacks upon its missions, the academy set about solidifying the ideologies of difference that function at the core of its identity politics. Hence, the culture wars not only resulted in a renewed interest in cultural studies, but also in the institutionalization of the aims of the multicultural project. By responding to the explicit threats posed by the culture wars waged by the right, the theoretical project renewed its interpretive claims and clarified its position as an ideologically based form of critique. It also erected a rigid, often dogmatic system of identity politics that frequently measures success in terms of the failures of what it perceives to be its opponents – and nothing can be more oppositional than the interpretive mechanism that receives credit for authoring the truth claims of the past.

Yet formalist criticism and reader-response theory are lessons in themselves about the value – indeed, the necessity – for fluid and flexible modes of literary interpretation. In its less-ideologically narrow manifestations, formalism exists at the bedrock of most close readings of literary texts. Similarly, understanding the nature of our reading experiences allows us to comprehend the remarkable synergy that occurs between writers and readers. In short, both critical modes afford us with essential means for understanding the many ways in which we, as writers and readers, produce meaning. All novels, plays, poems, and short stories possess specific formal structures that will determine, in part, a given reader's response; likewise, every reader has a set of preconceived notions about aesthetics, culture, and gender that will determine how the formal structure of a text is read and comes to evoke particular kinds of meanings. Hence, as theorists we enjoy the benefits, often unknowingly and almost certainly uncritically, of the interpretive aspects of the reading process that formalism and reader-response criticism seek to reveal. Although they no longer exist at the zenith of literary fashion, both schools of criticism nevertheless continue to operate at the forefront of literary studies. While we set about renaming them and crediting their good work to seemingly more prescient and contemporaneous ideological goals, formalism and reader-response theory will always remain as viable as the close readings that we, as theorists, continue to propound.

Notes

Introduction: Moving beyond the politics of interpretation

1. We must acknowledge that even this assumption – that an artist must move beyond imitation to something 'original' – is grounded in Western thought. There are numerous cultures, even within the Western world, that do not embrace originality or the idea of ownership in the arts. Certainly, Bloom's theory would not even seem applicable to Neoclassicism in the Western literary tradition.

2. The professionalization of the academy affects artists and critics. These days one is hard-pressed to find a critic who does not have an institutional affiliation or a PhD. The public critic whose work appeared in magazines and who made a living with the publication of such criticism belongs to another era, as does the artist without an MFA who works independently of some college or university. In fiction and poetry, one of the more common complaints in the profession is that creative writing programs have become so ubiquitous and influential that one may tell by the particular style of the writer what MFA program he or she attended. Most writers do not make a living by writing, but rather by teaching. With the shift to professionalization – replete with its own set of standards and degrees – colleges and universities have become the true benefactors of the arts.

3. In *The Politics of Interpretation: Ideology, Professionalism, and the Study of Literature* (1990), Patrick Colm Hogan explains how he was 'dumbfounded to find critics such as Walter Benn Michaels and Terry Eagleton debating whether or not literary interpretation could or could not be political': 'I had always conceived criticism to be often *actually* political,' Hogan remarks. 'A debate on the possibility of such seemed to me redundant' (4). At this point in literary history, there would be few who would contend that the act or reading and writing is apolitical. The power wielded by the critic, not only in a single interpretation, but in the effect of that interpretation on what texts will and will not be taught most widely, continues to be a matter of much concern and does raise ethical issues that need to be addressed by the discipline.

4. The manner in which we originally experienced our domiciles, we should note, no longer exists. With the passing of each moment, the way things once were may only be represented by memory and language. Such a condition, however, does not negate the idea of transition and collaboration. To the contrary, this notion only further strengthens the validity of the importance of transition and collaboration. Both memory and language coalesce around their ability to change and transform depending upon our needs.

PART I   FORMALIST CRITICISM AND READER-RESPONSE THEORY: A CRITICAL INTRODUCTION

1   Twentieth-century formalism: Convergence and divergence

1. While the later pedagogical programs established by some New Critics suggest that New Criticism's doctrinal lines for membership and practice were clearly delineated, the actual theoretical positions of many formalist critics with ties to this movement contradict such an idea. The critics who debated about the shape and concepts of formalism in scholarly journals and groundbreaking monographs did not draw such boundaries as facilely or exclusively as many literary historians imply. The influential work of I. A. Richards, for example, in developing a foundational theory of formalism – found in such works as *Principles of Literary Criticism* (1924) and *Practical Criticism* (1929) – is nuanced and perceptive, offering nothing as crass or authoritative as its later permutations in the classroom texts developed by such American New Critics as Cleanth Brooks and Robert Warren. Brooks and Warren make fine use of Richards's techniques in *Understanding Poetry* (1938) and *Understanding Fiction* (1943), as does Brooks and Robert Heilman in *Understanding Drama* (1945). But in taking Richards's theory into the classroom via such texts, the theoretical underpinnings of the various techniques was often omitted or ignored.

2. Perhaps postmodern theory owes Krieger a debt for his reluctance to abandon humanism altogether. In recent years such postmodern theorists as Ihab Hassan in *The Postmodern Turn* (1987) and Stephen Yarbrough in *Deliberate Criticism: Toward a Postmodern Humanism* (1992) have attempted to negotiate a space for what may be seen as a permutation or evolution of Krieger's own desire for faith in human connection.

3. See Gerald Graff's *Professing Literature: An Institutional History* (1987).

Graff makes a compelling case for the anxieties and insecurities of the newly formed departments of English in the late nineteenth- and early twentieth-century universities of the West. In light of the more established departments of science, many professors of literature wished for a systematic and objective means of criticism – easily appropriated for classroom use and clearly identifiable in terms of the production of knowledge through scholarship.

4. This instance brings to mind recent developments in feminist thought that call for a move away from our sole reliance upon the logos and suggest ways to 'think' with one's body. Having said this, in many ways Brooks's understanding of criticism fits neatly with other critics of the day. For example, Brooks was adamant about the exclusion of history from the study of literature. Attacking historicism, Brooks asserts that 'almost every English professor is diligently devoting himself to discovering "what porridge had John Keats." This is our typical research: the backgrounds of English literature. And we hopefully fill our survey textbooks with biographical notes on the poets whose poems are there displayed. But one may know what the poet ate and what he wore and what accidents occurred to him and what books he read – and yet not know his poetry' (35–36).

5. Frye damns criticism that he refers to as 'aesthetic superstition,' a form of criticism that sees its work as an end in itself. Frye calls for a criticism that does not believe the 'aesthetic or contemplative aspect of art' is 'the final resting place of art or criticism' (349). Instead, he contends that 'the moment we go from the individual work of art to the sense of the total form of art, the art becomes no longer the object of aesthetic contemplation but an ethical instrument, participating in the work of civilization' (349).

2   Russian Formalism, Mikhail Bakhtin, heteroglossia, and carnival

1. Quoted from *Problems of Dostoevsky's Poetics*, trans. Caryl Emerson, Minneapolis: University of Minnesota Press, 1984.

2. Gary Saul Morson and Caryl Emerson astutely observe that American and Russian formalists conspicuously diverge in their competing definitions of 'literariness.' In Western formulations of the concept, literariness refers exclusively to the nature of poetic language. Russian formalists, however, advocate a more expansive definition of the term, which, in their estimation, accounts for the aesthetic and material components inherent in a wide range of literary forms (18, 64).

3. Morson and Emerson caution against confusing the notion of heteroglossia with the concept of polyphony. Quite obviously, both terms refer to aspects of multiple-voiced narratives, yet 'polyphony is not even roughly synonymous with heteroglossia,' Morson and Emerson write. 'The latter term describes the diversity of speech styles in a language, the former has to do with the position of the author in a text . . . The two concepts pertain to fundamentally different kinds of phenomena, although the critical practice of conflating Bakhtin's categories has tended to blur the distinction for many readers' (232).

4. As Michael Gardiner reminds us, though, it is important to remain cognizant of the official culture's significant place in the same social phenomenon that produces the carnivalesque moment. Synchronous with carnival's utopian effervescence, officialdom's hegemonic nature ensures that it will attempt to stabilize the cultural continuum via a series of staid, conservative, and potentially oppressive gestures. As Gardiner observes: 'A crucial aspect of carnival is its critical function, the refusal to acquiesce to the legitimacy of the present social system which, for many theorists, is the hallmark of the oppositional utopia' (260).

5. Bakhtin first encountered the term in the work of Soviet physiologist A. A. Ukhtomsky. Bakhtin attended Ukhtomsky's lecture on the intersections between the chronotope and biology in 1925 (Bakhtin, *Dialogic* 84).

3 Reader-response theory, the theoretical project, and identity politics

1. Rosenblatt's signal contributions to reader-response theory receive special attention in Terence R. Wright's review essay, 'Reader Response under Review: Art, Game, or Science?' The value of Rosenblatt's transactional theory of reading, Wright argues, 'lies in its recognition of both sides of the 'reading transaction,' reader and text' (542). For an expansive discussion of Rosenblatt's efforts on behalf of reader-response criticism, see *The Experience of Reading: Louise Rosenblatt and Reader-Response Theory* (1991), edited by John Clifford.

2. Rosenblatt derives *efferent* from the Latin *effere*, which means 'to carry away' (24).

3. More specifically, ethical criticism functions as a self-reflexive means for critics to explain the contradictory emotions and problematic moral stances that often mask literary characters, as well as a mechanism for positing socially relevant interpretations by celebrating the Aristotelian

qualities of living well and flourishing. As a reader-response theory of sorts, ethical criticism finds its contemporary manifestations in several important volumes, including J. Hillis Miller's *The Ethics of Reading: Kant, de Man, Eliot, Trollope, James, and Benjamin* (1987), Martha C. Nussbaum's *Love's Knowledge: Essays on Philosophy and Literature* (1990), and Adam Zachary Newton's *Narrative Ethics* (1995). For a more expansive discussion of ethical criticism's wide-ranging interpretive possibilities, see *Mapping the Ethical Turn: A Reader in Ethics, Culture, and Literary Criticism* (2001), edited by Todd F. Davis and Kenneth Womack.

4. See Genette's *Figures III* (1972) and Prince's seminal essay, 'Introduction à l'étude du narrataire' (1973). As Suleiman notes: 'By analyzing the relationships between the various narrators and narratees – relationships that are indicated by linguistic markers in the text – one can not only make manifest the complex circuits of communication established in a given work, but also arrive at a typology of narratives based on the kinds of narrative situations they involve and the place(s) they assign to the narratee(s)' (14).

5. In *Structuralist Poetics: Structuralism, Linguistics, and the Study of Literature* (1975), Culler questions the efficacy of Barthes's codes because they 'do not seem exhaustive or sufficient.' Moreover, they 'vary according to the perspective chosen and the nature of the texts one is analyzing.' While Culler ultimately describes them as a 'major flaw in Barthes's analysis,' their rudimentary postulation nevertheless served to foment productive debate in the annals of literary criticism regarding our collective understanding of the reading process (203). See Roland Champagne's illuminating *Literary History in the Wake of Roland Barthes: Re-Defining the Myths of Reading* (1984) for additional discussion of Barthes's epistemological claims, as well as of the thinker's considerable impact upon twentieth-century letters.

6. In *The Return of the Reader: Reader-Response Criticism* (1987), Elizabeth Freund sharply questions Culler's postulation of readerly competence. 'It seems to me that Culler's discourse,' she writes, 'voices its own limits, manifesting (to repeat a metaphor that has become a cliché of contemporary discourse) the blind spot in a vision on the edge of discovering its limitations but recoiling from the discovery. The discovery is that reading is not by any means a "mastery"' (85).

7. Interestingly, Mailloux also acted as one of Stanley Fish's staunchest critics during reader-response theory's theoretical heyday because of Mailloux's position that Fish intentionally abdicated the movement's important evaluative functions as a critical paradigm. As Mailloux argues in 'Evaluation and Reader-Response Criticism: Values Implicit in

Affective Stylistics': 'Though outwardly embracing only the descriptive capabilities of his method, Fish appears to be restraining a desire to bring in evaluative criteria.' For Mailloux, the assumptions and theoretical methodologies behind Affective Stylistics, as with reader-response criticism, are 'value laden' (340–41).

8. In *Families and Larger Systems: A Family Therapist's Guide through the Labyrinth* (1988), Evan Imber-Black astutely observes that 'all families engage with larger systems.' Healthy, differentiated families, moreover, 'are able to function in an interdependent manner with a variety of larger systems, utilizing information from these systems as material for their own growth and development' (14). Differentiated family members have the transgenerational potential for producing yet other selves with full senses of identity (Barnard and Corrales 36–37).

9. For additional discussion regarding family systems psychotherapy as a means for explicating literary works, see Barbara A. Kaufman's 'Training Tales in Family Therapy: Exploring *The Alexandria Quartet.*' Kaufman argues that 'inclusion of novels in didactic contexts encourages trainees to search their own experiences, thereby maximizing the opportunity for positive therapeutic interaction and highlighting the variety of treatment approaches in the field' (70). See also Janine Roberts's *Tales and Transformations: Stories in Families and Family Therapy* (1994), which features an appendix that enumerates a host of existing 'family systems novels.'

10. Family therapists often employ narrative therapy as a means for assisting their clients in overcoming homeostasis and establishing morphogenesis in their lives. Despite its considerable danger to a given family member's ability to achieve selfhood beyond the family system, homeostasis is the process by which the family as a whole preserves its various – and often unhealthy – value systems. Conversely, functional family systems possess the capacity for allowing family members to evolve as individuals through morphogenesis, which family therapists define as the process that allows a given family system 'to deviate from its usual relationship among component parts and even to amplify that deviation' (Knapp 67). In *Systemic Family Therapy: An Integrative Approach* (1986), Williams C. Nichols and Craig E. Everett explain morphogenesis as the mechanism through which families effect radical, meaningful change. Morphogenesis, they write, 'involves altering the nature of the system itself so that new levels of functioning are achieved' (130).

11. Miller's concept of overreading is remarkably similar to Annabel Patterson's notion of 'reading between the lines,' which functions as a kind of informed reading strategy in which readers negotiate the

complexities of overtly masculinized texts by such figures as Milton, Donne, and Spenser. As postulated in *Reading between the Lines* (1993), Patterson's reading schema recognizes 'a strong connection between the debates on the canon and pedagogical priorities and the sociopolitical values for which, by synecdoche, literary values have come to stand' (7).

4 Stanley Fish, self-consuming artifacts, and the professionalisation of literary studies

1. William E. Cain takes particular issue with Fish's humanistic claims about the significance of the individual in his conceptualization of reader-response theory. 'Fish fails to explain the relation between his regard for "human beings,"' Cain writes, 'and his insistence that their responses are to be accorded different degrees of value' (77).
2. In *The Practice of Reading* (1998), Denis Donoghue takes issue with Fish's claims about the relevance of interpretive communities to the reading process. 'This is a doubtful claim,' Donoghue writes. 'Who are those who constitute a community, and how can we assume that their being a community depends on the way they read texts? It may depend on consanguinities of social class, family income, race, religious observance, and many other considerations' (84). As Annette Patterson, Bronwyn Mellor, and Marnie O'Neill observe (1994), Fish's conceptualization of interpretive communities eschews individualism in favor of group praxis. 'Rather than claiming that individuals produce different readings because everyone is personally different, it is argued that a specific group produces a particular reading because its members share something which is *intrinsic* to the group. That "something,"' they add, 'is often conceptualized in essentialist terms as "essence"' (65). In *Stories of Reading: Subjectivity and Literary Understanding* (1989), Michael Steig chides Fish for advancing the notion of interpretive communities that he 'never really describes' in terms of any concrete social context (7).
3. See Richard H. Weisberg's *Poethics, and Other Strategies of Law and Literature* (1992), which, as with Martha C. Nussbaum's *Poetic Justice: The Literary Imagination and Public Life* (1995), explores the ethical interconnections between the study of law and the interpretation of literary texts.

PART II   READINGS IN FORMALIST CRITICISM AND READER-RESPONSE THEORY

5   Travelling through the valley of ashes: Symbolic unity in F. Scott Fitzgerald's *The Great Gatsby*

1. For an introduction to some of the most influential work on Fitzgerald's life, see Scott Donaldson's *Fool for Love: F. Scott Fitzgerald* (1983) and *Hemingway vs. Fitzgerald: The Rise and Fall of a Literary Friendship* (1999), Rose Adrienne Gallo's *F. Scott Fitzgerald* (1978), and Jeffrey Meyers's *Scott Fitzgerald* (1994).

2. As with Ford Madox Ford and Joseph Conrad, Fitzgerald's popular success tormented him. While he enjoyed the financial rewards that such success brought him, he was not satisfied with his work aesthetically and set out to create a book that focused solely upon the artistic integrity of it as a novel.

3. The idea that different forms of criticism might work together, producing a more profitable and holistic reading of a work was addressed in the introduction. Sadly, identity politics have made criticism a domain ruled by competition, where one critic tries to silence another based upon arbitrary lines of division.

6   Charlotte Brontë and Frye's *Secular Scripture*: The structure of romance in *Jane Eyre*

1. In *The Stone and the Scorpion* (1994), Judith Mitchell contends that 'in *Jane Eyre* we have the quintessential Harlequin Romance, the love story of conflict, misunderstandings and seemingly insurmountable obstacles, complete with a dark Byronic hero who turns out to be capable of great tenderness toward the heroine, who reaps her reward in the end in the form of marriage and a child' (44). Mitchell frames the success of the novel, however, in terms of its power as an erotic story of domination, of female submission and, ultimately, role-reversal.

2. A fine contrast to Jane's faith might be found in *Uncle Tom's Cabin*. In Stowe's text, there is little doubt as to how we are to interpret Eva and her faith. No less than a saint, Eva preaches a Christianity that knows no doubt. No lack of certainty clouds Eva's sky, even in the face of death, and with her unblemished goodness she saves others. While Jane does 'save' Rochester, there is far less clarity in such a resolution in Brontë's text than in Stowe's.

3. In this context, Frye's idea of sexual purity mirrors cultural practice before the first wave of feminism in the twentieth century. If a woman lost her virginity or was with child, she had two options, both of which meant a loss of her independence: one, the woman could have the child out of wedlock, a course of action that usually meant she and her child would be ostracized by the community; or two, she could marry the man, becoming his property, based upon nineteenth-century law.

7 'Telle us som myrie tale, by youre fey!': Exploring the reading transaction and narrative structure in Chaucer's *Clerk's Tale* and *Troilus and Criseyde*

1. Because the Clerk is the implicit, although fictionalized, author of this tale, this essay calls into question the notions of author and authority, as well as the fundamental differences in the reception of oral and written narratives. Moreover, the 'author' of the tale self-consciously employs what essentially function as highly complex narratological constructs, according to Anne Middleton, who notes that in the *Clerk's Tale*, 'like its immediate antecedents in Latin and French, the story is offered and received primarily as *read* rather than *heard*; its narrator has within it the status of author rather than actor, and so, it seems, his fellow pilgrims take him' (147). Thus, we will consider the tale as a written text self-consciously constructed by an author for a particular audience.

2. For yet another paradigmatic example of Chaucer's use of an explicit ellipsis in the *Clerk's Tale*, see the instance in the sixth part of the tale when Griselda acknowledges – without hesitation – her usurper with kindness and regard for the maiden's brother: 'In al this meene while she ne stente/ This mayde and eek hir brother to commende/ With al hir herte, in ful benyngne entente,/ So wel that no man koude hir pris amende' (1023–26).

3. Chaucer later utilizes an implicit ellipsis – the age of Walter's daughter – to acknowledge the time that has passed before Walter implores 'the court of Rome' for an annulment: 'Whan that his doghter twelve yeer was of age,/ He to the court of Rome, in subtil wyse/ Enformed of his wyl, sente his message,/ Comaundynge hem swich bulles to devyse/ As to his cruel purpos may suffyse' (736–40)

4. In this instance, diegesis refers to the 'story' or the 'act of narration' in the parlance of Genette's narratological schema. Genette ascribes the term's origins to the 'theoreticians of cinematographic narrative' (27).

5. In his essay, 'The Style of the *Clerk's Tale* and the Functions of Its

Glosses,' Thomas J. Farrell examines the Latin glosses that accompa-
nied the text of the *Canterbury Tales*, and notes that in the gloss to this
particular passage, Walter explains to Griselda, 'et patri tuo placet
inquid et michi vt vxor mea sis et credo idipsum tibi placeat set habeo
ex te querere.' In this way, then, the Clerk 'is more forceful in anticipat-
ing Walter's later behavior' (294). Remarkably, Farrell's acknowledg-
ment of this particular gloss underscores Chaucer's – and moreover, the
Clerk's – attention to the process of composition, and the tropes and
figures upon which it functions.

6. On the composition and value of the Envoy to the *Clerk's Tale*, Ganim
remarks: 'The manuscript evidence seems to indicate that the Envoy
was added after the tale itself was written, perhaps much later. I shall
assume, however, that the Envoy and the ending were intended by
Chaucer and are part of the meaning and context of the tale' (113).

7. Although Pratt acknowledges the substantial influence of Boccaccio's
text upon Chaucer's composition of the *Troilus*, he also notes that
establishing the textual differences between the two poems poses a
particular problem for textual scholars, for more than 50 extant manu-
scripts of Boccaccio's poem have survived. For further discussion
regarding this dilemma, as well as a close textual analysis of the linguistic parallels between the two poems, see Pratt's essay, 'Chaucer and *Le
Roman de Troyle et de Criseida*' (509–39).

8. In *Chaucer and the French Tradition: A Study in Style and Meaning*
(1957), Muscatine discusses further the operation of courtly love
conventions in literature, while especially noting the influence of C. S.
Lewis upon twentieth-century Chaucerian scholarship regarding this
widely debated literary construct. See, especially, 128–31. For additional
analysis of courtly love and literature, see Richard Firth Green's text,
*Poets and Princepleasers: Literature and the English Court in the Late
Middle Ages* (1980), in which he examines the fourteenth-century view
of the courtly love tradition. Finally, see E. Talbot Donaldson's *Speaking
of Chaucer* (1970) for a dissenting view regarding the existence of the
courtly love tradition in literature, and moreover, the works of Chaucer
(154–63).

9. See R. K. Gordon's translation of *Il Filostrato*, collected in *The Story of
Troilus* (1978). Additional references to this text will be denoted with a
G in the text, followed by the appropriate page citation.

10. For further analysis regarding the history and evolution of Criseyde's
problematic reputation in medieval literature, see Gretchen
Mieszkowski's essay, 'The Reputation of Criseyde, 1155–1500' (71–153).

8 Addressing horizons of readerly expectation in Joseph Conrad's *Heart of Darkness* and Ford Madox Ford's *The Good Soldier*, or, how to put the 'reader' in 'reader response'

1. Conrad and Ford's biographers continue to debate the exact nature of the writers' collaboration, as well as about the degree of its impact and influence upon their future novels. Richard A. Cassell argues that, for Ford at least, 'the collaboration with Conrad had permanently altered Ford's creative talents on writing and led to his years of intense literary activity' (9). Leo Gurko contends that the collaboration merely provided Conrad with the opportunity to work with a native English speaker who possessed considerable aesthetic sensibilities. 'Conrad's motive was apparently linguistic and technical,' Gurko writes (103). Norman Sherry reveals, moreover, that Ford often exaggerated his influence upon Conrad, especially regarding his role in the genesis of Conrad's *The Secret Agent* (1906). Yet many, if not all, of their biographers and critics agree that Conrad's and Ford's conception of literary impressionism exerted a resounding impact upon their individual novels. Carl D. Bennett, for example, describes their collaboration and its aesthetic rewards as 'unquestionably symbiotic' (28).

2. Jauss distinguishes his five levels of interaction from Northrop Frye's typology of the hero by noting that his own levels of reception exist 'as a nexus of functions of the aesthetic experience,' particularly as they 'are derived from an examination of historically attested interaction patterns.' In Jauss's estimation, Frye's five-pronged typology substitutes the generalities inherent in archetypal mythology for an understanding of the peculiar modalities of readerly reception that impinge upon the ways in which we encounter and ultimately ascribe meaning to literary texts (154).

3. In his essay memorializing Conrad's life and work, Ford writes that 'we agreed that the general effect of a novel must be the general effect that life makes on mankind. A novel must therefore not be a narration, a report . . . We in turn, if we wished to produce on you an effect of life,' Ford adds, 'must not narrate but render . . . impressions' ('Joseph Conrad' 72–73).

4. While *Lord Jim* was published a year later than *Heart of Darkness*, it was written for serialization before Conrad began working on the novella. Hence, the Marlow of *Heart of Darkness* represents a later, more mature incarnation of the character. See Bennett 75.

Conclusion: Beyond formalist criticism and reader-response theory

1. For additional examples of literary criticism's recent efforts at histori-
cizing formalism and the New Criticism, see J. Timothy Bagwell's
American Formalism and the Problem of Interpretation (1986), Mark
Jancovich's *The Cultural Politics of the New Criticism* (1993), and
William J. Spurlin and Michael Fischer's *The New Criticism and
Contemporary Literary Theory: Connections and Continuities* (1995).

Annotated Bibliography

Bakhtin, Mikhail. *The Dialogic Imagination: Four Essays.* 1975. Trans. Caryl Emerson and Michael Holquist. Austin: University of Texas Press, 1981.

Bakhtin's important volume elaborates upon many of the theorist's most significant contributions to literary criticism, including his conception of heteroglossia, which refers to the manner in which literary works function on microlinguistic levels by intersecting a wide variety of competing utterances and speech acts. Bakhtin also differentiates between monologic and dialogic texts. In Bakhtin's terminology, monologic works are dominated by single, controlling voices or discourses. Dialogic texts allow for the existence and convergence of a wide range of disparate voices and discourses. Bakhtin's notion of the chronotope refers to the aesthetic or envisioning of the human subject as it is situated materially within a specific geotemporal location or spatial/temporal structure that determines the shape of a narrative.

Barthes, Roland. *S/Z.* 1970. Trans. Richard Miller. New York: Hill and Wang, 1974.

In addition to discussing the reading experience as a reflexive process that involves a fusion of sorts between text and reader, Barthes explores the reader's function as the *de facto* producer of a given text's meaning. Barthes devotes particular emphasis to making distinctions between 'readerly' and 'writerly' texts. Readerly texts require little special effort on behalf of the reader in order to create meaning, while writerly texts are more difficult to interpret because their meanings are not immediately evident. Barthes identifies five codes of reading that provide a semantic model for the ways in which readers construct meaning, including the proairetic code, the hermeneutic code, the semic code, the symbolic code, and the referential code.

Booth, Wayne C. *The Rhetoric of Fiction.* 1961. Chicago, IL University of Chicago Press, 1983.

Booth examines the ways in which fictional forms work, as well as the manner in which authors make their texts accessible to their readership. Booth identifies the roles of implied authors and readers in the reading process, as well as the ideological and ethical ramifications of our reading experiences. According to Booth, the implied author functions as the actual author's 'second self,' the persona that the reading process invariably constructs or reconstitutes during the act of reading. Booth's implied author is responsible for the text's ultimate verbal meanings, as well as for the value systems that undergird those meanings.

Brooks, Cleanth. *The Well-Wrought Urn: Studies in the Structure of Poetry.* New York: Reynal and Hitchcock, 1947.

Brooks's central formalist text discusses the tension between the movement's focus upon structure and humanism's embrace of art as representative of humanity's range of emotional or spiritual life. Brooks argues that formalism, as practiced by the New Critics, must always be seen as praxis, as an act that cannot be dissected or parsed into distinct theoretical categories without ceasing to be the act itself – in much the same way that a poem ceases to be a poem if the formalist critic merely attends to its mechanical workings. Brooks emphasizes the practical implications of *doing* literary criticism as opposed to merely addressing it in a theoretical vacuum.

Brooks, Cleanth, John T. Purser, and Robert Penn Warren. *An Approach to Literature.* New York: Appleton-Century-Crofts, 1964.

Brooks, Purser, and Warren address literature as a mechanism that provides readers with a form of scientific, aesthetically informed truth. According to Brooks, Purser, and Warren, science forces readers to indulge in processes of classification, as well as more conceptual and abstract possibilities for understanding language. Literature, on the other hand, allows readers to illuminate language in a more concretized, particularized, and individual fashion. In short, they argue, literature offers readers the opportunity for imaginatively encountering the meaning inherent both in life and in language.

Culler, Jonathan. *Structuralist Poetics: Structuralism, Linguistics, and the Study of Literature.* Ithaca, NY: Cornell University Press, 1975.

Culler devotes attention to a wide range of linguistic foundations, including distinctions between *langue* and *parole,* as well as to the nature of signs and signifiers. In addition to contending that a knowledge of language and its components will enhance the quality of the reading experience, Culler argues for the existence of a 'competent' reader, the educated or literate reader who employs various interpretive conventions in his or her analysis of literary works such as poems or novels. Culler describes two reading conventions, including the primary convention of reading in which the literary work is interpreted in terms of humankind's metaphorical relationship to the universe. Culler's second readerly convention involves the notion of 'metaphorical coherence' that dictates the fashion in which readers understand a given text's place in the larger historical-literary continuum, as well as its capacity for generating meaning on a personal level.

Eliot, T. S. *The Sacred Wood: Essays on Poetry and Criticism.* London: Methuen, 1920.

Eliot's influential collection of essays advances the idea that the decadent devolution of the contemporary world represents a marked turning from the ordered, unified world whose very creation implies a sacrosanct, higher order – a complexity and wholeness that can only be found in a turn away from skepticism and science. Eliot argues that the alienation of modernity results from our turn to secularism and industrialization, a condition that may only be overcome in a return to myth and religion. For this reason, Eliot champions texts and forms of criticism that value what he calls a 'unified sensibility' – a complexity of thought and wholeness birthed from some religious or mythical order.

Empson, William. *Seven Types of Ambiguity.* London: Chatto and Windus, 1930.

Empson argues for an analytical form of criticism that advocates a rhetorical approach to close reading based upon the scientific method. In addition to addressing the relationship between the art object and its human creator, Empson discusses the double-bind that critics face during the act of interpretation. Empson argues that critics must find a balance between the close, objective analysis of the art object and their more passionate appreciation or connection with it. Yet Empson contends that while such an idea may appear contradictory, perhaps even impossible, it remains clear that humans do in fact hold such antinomies within themselves at the same time.

Fish, Stanley E. *Is There a Text in This Class?: The Authority of Interpretive Communities.* Cambridge, MA: Harvard University Press, 1980.

Fish's influential volume propounds two models of self-actualization that intersect with his imperatives regarding reader-response theory. In the first model of self-actualization, the self becomes constituted via conventional ways of thinking about literature. In the second model, an autonomous self explores conventional ways of thinking about literature and chooses a methodology that suits the self's needs and perspectives. Fish's conception of interpretive communities accounts for those readers 'who share interpretive strategies not for reading (in the conventional sense) but for writing texts, for constituting their properties and assigning their intentions.' Fish identifies two models of critical activity, including the demonstration or fact-based model and the persuasion or self-motivated model of reading.

Fish, Stanley E. *Self-Consuming Artifacts: The Experience of Seventeenth-Century Literature.* Berkeley: University of California Press, 1972.

Fish's landmark volume broadens reader-response theory conceptually in an effort to provide the movement with a vocabulary for engendering further debate about the symbiotic nature of the reading process. Fish identifies two kinds of literary presentation, including what he deems, respectively, as rhetorical presentation and dialectical presentation. Rhetorical presentation refers to the kind of literary works that mirror and reinforce readers' existing interpretations. Conversely, texts that evince dialectical presentation techniques challenge readers to establish their own meanings for literary works. These latter texts – 'self-consuming artifacts,' in Fish's terminology – often feature contradictory elements that countermand the aspects of unity and symmetry extolled by the New Critics.

Frye, Northrop. *Anatomy of Criticism: Four Essays.* Princeton, NJ: Princeton University Press, 1957.

Frye's archetypal criticism argues that literature inhabits language structures that differ from common speech and writing, that language in literary texts is elevated and manipulated in ways that transform it from the utilitarian tool of communication into the realm of art. For Frye, plot motif, character type, image, and symbol are the tools of the literary artist and the subject of investigation for the critic. Frye views the relationship between literature and reality as latent and ever-changing, as a place that does not offer the critic solid footholds. While he argues that literature exists within a separate realm from such other fields as theology, philosophy, politics, or science, he nevertheless advocates the usurpation of disciplinary boundaries as a means of defeating dogmatism and insecurity.

Genette, Gérard. *Narrative Discourse: An Essay in Method.* Trans. Jane E. Lewin. Ithaca, NY: Cornell University Press, 1980.

In addition to formulating the concept of the 'narratee' in an effort to account for the audience's role in the production of narrative, Genette examines the various levels of narration that comprise the reading experience. Genette explains these different levels of narration and meaning in terms of their relation to the 'diegesis' (or story). Genette also examines the elements of narratology that drive narrative movements within a literary work. These narrative movements – specifically, summary, ellipsis, descriptive pause, and scene – illustrate the temporal foundations that produce the overall impression that a given narrative evokes. Such movements establish a tempo within a literary work, and their effectiveness can be measured by the effects they create within that narrative.

Graff, Gerald. *Professing Literature: An Institutional History.* Chicago, IL: University of Chicago Press, 1987.

Graff surveys the history of English departments and makes a compelling case for the anxieties and insecurities of the newly formed departments of English in the late nineteenth- and early twentieth-century universities of the West. In light of the more established departments of science, Graff argues that many professors of literature wished for a systematic and objective means of criticism – easily appropriated for classroom use and clearly identifiable in terms of the production of knowledge through scholarship.

Holland, Norman N. *The Dynamics of Literary Response.* 1968. New York: Norton, 1975.

As one of the proponents of reader-response criticism's 'subjectivist' modes of inquiry, Holland contends that a given reader's responses to literary texts are often influenced by that individual's fundamental psychological needs. Holland's identity theme – his mechanism for understanding the manner in which readers search for remnants of the self in literary texts – attempts to account for the systemic ways that humans interact with (and, indeed, respond to) the larger psychosocial worlds in which they live. Drawing upon his own theory regarding the nature of our readerly suspension of belief, Holland argues that the psychoanalytic concept of affect exists at the core of our textual desires. Holland's reader-response schema locates affect at the nexus of our anxieties, our desires for wish-fulfillment, and our drives for gratification and self-replication.

Iser, Wolfgang. *The Implied Reader: Patterns of Communication in Prose Fiction from Bunyan to Beckett.* 1972. Baltimore, MD: Johns Hopkins University Press, 1974.

Iser's phenomenological approach to theorizing reader response accounts for the text itself, as well as for the various activities involved in the act of critical interpretation. Iser contends that authors must fashion literary works that engage readers and establish an active and creative fusion between writer and reader. This synergy creates, in turn, what Iser refers to as *Konkretisation* – the realization (or comprehension) of the literary text by the reader. This process involves two poles: the artistic pole allows for the text created by the author; the aesthetic pole refers to the consumption and – perhaps more importantly – the realization of the text by the reader. For Iser, this aspect of the reader experience constitutes the 'unwritten' nature of the reading process, the vague spaces of comprehension that result from the interaction between the text and the reader.

Jauss, Hans Robert. *Aesthetic Experience and Literary Hermeneutics.* Trans. Michael Shaw. Minneapolis: University of Minnesota Press, 1982.

Jauss establishes a communicative model for understanding readerly expectations of literary works, as well as an interpretive framework for explaining the aesthetic pleasure that readers derive from literary texts. Jauss's communicative model regarding a given reader's 'horizon of expectations' involves an intuitive comprehension of the ways in which readers interact with, and ultimately respond to, literary works. Drawing upon the insights of Aristotle and Montaigne, Jauss ascribes the reader's need for catharsis to his or her desire to experience the 'exemplary' aspects of the reading experience. Jauss defines the concept of the exemplary as the quality of reflection that the reader enjoys when contemplating the interaction between the aesthetic experience and the invariably shifting nature of the self.

Krieger, Murray. *The New Apologists for Poetry.* Minneapolis: University of Minnesota Press, 1956.

Krieger examines the nature of the creative process, with particular emphasis upon the intersections among, science, poetry, and the imagination. In addition to addressing the influence of such figures as T. E. Hulme, T. S. Eliot, and I. A. Richards upon the direction of twentieth-century literary studies, Krieger postulates the requirements for an organic theory of poetic creation. Krieger devotes special attention to conceptualizing the aesthetic object in terms of science, poetry, and language. Krieger concludes his study with a survey of various theories about poetry and truth, as well as with an analysis of Richards's contextual theory of the aesthetic object.

Richards, I. A. *Practical Criticism.* London: K. Paul, Trench, and Trubner, 1929.

Richards examines the variety of difficulties students have in apprehending both the content and meaning of a poem, as well as in deciphering its structural or formal qualities. In addition to proffering ten descriptive categories that illustrate the elements of confusion or misreading that plague his students, Richards discusses his students' problematic disengagement with their personal experience – as well as the oppressive theoretical baggage, of which students are likely ignorant. Richards contends that these moves lead to an emphasis upon the text and the act of 'close reading.'

Rosenblatt, Louise M. *Literature as Exploration.* 1938. New York: MLA, 1995.

Rosenblatt argues that literary critics must differentiate between the text and the meaning that it evokes. In addition to reframing our larger conception of the reading experience, Rosenblatt contends that reading functions as a constructive and selective process that shifts over time, as well as within particular contexts. Rosenblatt advocates a transactional theory of reading that demonstrates the reciprocal nature of the reading process and that reveals the ways in which the literary experience exists as a particularized event contingent upon sets of specific circumstances.

Wimsatt, W. K., and Monroe C. Beardsley. *The Verbal Icon: Studies in the Meaning of Poetry.* Lexington: University Press of Kentucky, 1954.

Wimsatt and Beardsley discuss the foolishness in considering biographical or extra-textual information of any kind during the interpretive act. In addition to dogmatically asserting the preeminence of the literary art object – its position outside the constraints of authorial intention, cultural influence, or historical forces – Wimsatt and Beardsley suggest that the critic also should not look to the poems impact upon the reader – in other words, the reader's response should be given no deliberation. Theories of catharsis, didacticism, or delight, Wimsatt and Beardsley insist, should not be considered when evaluating or judging art. Finally, Wimsatt and Beardsley fashion a poetics that rejects temporality, the very strictures of human finitude. Instead, they create a theory that is ahistorical, one that suggests art may transcend the very context out of which it emerges.

Works Cited

Anderson, Paul Thomas. *Magnolia: The Shooting Script.* New York: Newmarket, 2000.

Bagwell, J. Timothy. *American Formalism and the Problem of Interpretation.* Houston, TX: Rice University Press, 1986.

Bakhtin, Mikhail. 'Toward a Methodology for the Human Sciences.' *Speech Genres and Other Late Essays.* Ed. Caryl Emerson and Michael Holquist. Trans. Vern W. McGee. Austin: University of Texas Press, 1986. 159–72.

——. *Rabelais and His World.* 1968. Trans. Hélène Iswolsky. Bloomington: Indiana University Press, 1984.

——. *The Dialogic Imagination: Four Essays.* 1975. Trans. Caryl Emerson and Michael Holquist. Austin: University of Texas Press, 1981.

——. 'Discourse in the Novel.' Bakhtin, *The Dialogic Imagination* 259–422.

——. 'Forms of Time and of the Chronotope in the Novel: Notes Toward a Historical Poetics.' Bakhtin, *The Dialogic Imagination* 84–258.

——. *Problems of Dostoevsky's Poetics.* 1929. Trans. R. W. Rotsel. Ann Arbor, MI: Ardis, 1973.

Barnard, Charles P., and Ramon Garrido Corrales. *The Theory and Technique of Family Therapy.* Springfield, IL: Thomas, 1979.

Barney, Stephen A. '*Troilus and Criseyde.*' *The Riverside Chaucer.* Ed. Larry D. Benson. Boston, MA: Houghton Mifflin, 1987. 471–72.

Barthes, Roland. *Image-Music-Text.* Trans. Stephen Heath. New York: Hill and Wang, 1977. 155–64.

——. *The Pleasure of the Text.* 1973. Trans. Richard Miller. New York: Hill and Wang, 1975.

——. *S/Z.* 1970. Trans. Richard Miller. New York: Hill and Wang, 1974.

Bennett, Carl D. *Joseph Conrad.* New York: Continuum, 1991.

Bennett, William J. *To Reclaim a Legacy: A Report on the Humanities in Higher Education.* Washington, DC: NEH, 1984.

Bleich, David. *Subjective Criticism*. Baltimore, MD: Johns Hopkins University Press, 1978.

Bloom, Allan. *The Closing of the American Mind: How Higher Education Has Failed Democracy and Impoverished the Souls of Today's Students*. New York: Simon and Schuster, 1987.

Bloom, Harold. *The Anxiety of Influence: A Theory of Poetry*. New York: Oxford University Press, 1973.

Booth, Stephen. *An Essay on Shakespeare's Sonnets*. New Haven, CT: Yale University Press, 1969.

Booth, Wayne C. *The Company We Keep: An Ethics of Fiction*. Berkeley: University of California Press, 1988.

——. *The Rhetoric of Fiction*. 1961. Chicago, IL: University of Chicago Press, 1983.

Brontë, Charlotte. *Jane Eyre*. 1847. Ed. Richard J. Dunn. New York: Norton, 1987.

Brooks, Cleanth. 'Irony as a Principle of Structure.' *The Critical Tradition: Classic Texts and Contemporary Trends*. Ed. David H. Richter. New York: St. Martin's Press – now Palgrave, 1989. 799–807.

——. 'The Heresy of Paraphrase.' *Critical Theory since Plato*. Ed. Hazard Adams. New York: Harcourt Brace Jovanovich, 1971. 1033–41.

——. 'The Formalist Critic.' *Kenyon Review* 13 (1951): 72–81.

——. *The Well-Wrought Urn: Studies in the Structure of Poetry*. New York: Reynal and Hitchcock, 1947.

——.'The Poem as Organism: Modern Critical Procedure.' *English Institute Annual, 1940*. New York: Columbia University Press, 1941.

Brooks, Cleanth, and Robert B. Heilman. *Understanding Drama*. New York: Holt, 1945.

Brooks, Cleanth, and Robert Penn Warren. *Understanding Fiction*. New York: F. S. Crofts, 1943.

——. *Understanding Poetry*. New York: Holt, 1938.

Brooks, Cleanth, and W. K. Wimsatt. *Literary Criticism: A Short History*. Chicago, IL: University of Chicago Press, 1978.

Brooks, Cleanth, John T. Purser, and Robert Penn Warren. *An Approach to Literature*. New York: Appleton-Century-Crofts, 1964.

Burke, Kenneth. *The Philosophy of Literary Form: Studies in Symbolic Action*. 3rd edn Berkeley: University of California Press, 1973.

——. *Language as Symbolic Action: Essays on Life, Literature, and Method*. Berkeley: University of California Press, 1966.

——. *Counter-Statement*. 1931 2nd edn Los Altos, CA: Hermes, 1953.

——. 'Kinds of Criticism.' *Poetry* 68 (1946): 278–79.

Cain, William E. 'Constraints in Politics in the Literary Theory of Stanley Fish.' *Theories of Reading, Looking, and Listening.* Ed. Harry R. Garvin. Lewisburg, WV: Bucknell University Press, 1981. 75–88.

Cassell, Richard A. *Ford Madox Ford: A Study of His Novels.* Baltimore, MD: Johns Hopkins University Press, 1962.

Champagne, Roland. *Literary History in the Wake of Roland Barthes: Re-Defining the Myths of Reading.* Birmingham: Summa, 1984.

Chaucer, Geoffrey. *The Riverside Chaucer.* Ed. Larry D. Benson. Boston, MA: Houghton Mifflin, 1987.

Clausen, Christopher. 'Reading Closely Again.' *Commentary* 103.2 (1997): 54–57.

Clifford, John, ed. *The Experience of Reading: Louise Rosenblatt and Reader-Response Theory.* Portsmouth: Heinemann, 1991.

Conrad, Joseph. *Heart of Darkness.* 1899. Ed. Ross C. Murfin. New York: St. Martin's Press – now Palgrave, 1989.

——. *Prefaces to His Work.* London: Dent, 1937.

Crosman, Robert. 'Do Readers Make Meaning?' *The Reader in the Text: Essays on Audience and Interpretation.* Ed. Susan R. Suleiman and Inge Crosman. Princeton, NJ: Princeton University Press, 1980. 149–64.

——. *Reading Paradise Lost.* Bloomington: Indiana University Press, 1980.

Culler, Jonathan. *Structuralist Poetics: Structuralism, Linguistics, and the Study of Literature.* Ithaca, NY: Cornell University Press, 1975.

Davis, Todd F., and Kenneth Womack, eds. *Mapping the Ethical Turn: A Reader in Ethics, Culture, and Literary Criticism.* Charlottesville: University Press of Virginia, 2001.

Donaldson, E. Talbot. *Speaking of Chaucer.* New York: Norton, 1970.

Donaldson, Scott. *Hemingway vs. Fitzgerald: The Rise and Fall of a Literary Friendship.* Woodstock, NY: Overlook, 1999.

——. *Fool For Love: F. Scott Fitzgerald.* New York: St. Martin's Press – now Palgrave, 1983.

Donoghue, Denis. *The Practice of Reading.* New Haven, CT: Yale University Press, 1998.

Eagleton, Terry. *Literary Theory: An Introduction.* Minneapolis: University of Minnesota Press, 1983.

Eble, Kenneth. *F. Scott Fitzgerald.* Boston, MA: G. K. Hall, 1977.

Eliot, T. S. 'Hamlet and His Problems.' *Critical Theory since Plato.* Ed. Hazard Adams. New York: Harcourt Brace Jovanovich, 1971. 788–90.

——. 'Tradition and the Individual Talent.' *Critical Theory since Plato.* Ed. Hazard Adams. New York: Harcourt Brace Jovanovich, 1971. 784–87.

——. *To Criticize the Critic.* New York: Farrar, Straus, and Giroux, 1965.

——. *The Sacred Wood: Essays on Poetry and Criticism.* London: Methuen, 1920.

Ellmann, Maud. *The Poetics of Impersonality: T. S. Eliot and Ezra Pound.* Cambridge, MA: Harvard University Press, 1987.

Emerson, Ralph Waldo. *Selections from Ralph Waldo Emerson: An Organic Anthology.* Ed. Stephen E. Whicher. Boston, MA: Houghton Mifflin, 1960.

Empson, William. *The Structure of Complex Words.* London: Chatto and Windus, 1951.

——. *Some Versions of Pastoral.* London: Chatto and Windus, 1935.

——. *Seven Types of Ambiguity.* London: Chatto and Windus, 1930.

Farrell, Thomas J. 'The Style of the *Clerk's Tale* and the Function of Its Glosses.' *Studies in Philology* 86 (1989): 286–309.

Fetterley, Judith. *The Resisting Reader: A Feminist Approach to American Fiction.* Bloomington: Indiana University Press, 1978.

Fish, Stanley E. *Professional Correctness: Literary Studies and Political Change.* Oxford: Clarendon, 1995.

——. *There's No Such Thing as Free Speech, and It's a Good Thing, Too.* Oxford: Oxford University Press, 1994.

——. *Doing What Comes Naturally: Change, Rhetoric, and the Practice of Theory in Literary and Legal Studies.* Durham, NC: Duke University Press, 1989.

——. *Is There a Text in This Class?: The Authority of Interpretive Communities.* Cambridge, MA: Harvard University Press, 1980.

——. 'What Is Stylistics and Why Are They Saying Such Terrible Things About It?' *Approaches to Poetics: Selected Papers from the English Institute.* Ed. Seymour Chatman. New York: Columbia University Press, 1973. 109–52.

——. *Self-Consuming Artifacts: The Experience of Seventeenth-Century Literature.* Berkeley: University of California Press, 1972.

——. *Surprised by Sin: The Reader in Paradise Lost.* Berkeley: University of California Press, 1971.

Fitzgerald, F. Scott. *The Letters of F. Scott Fitzgerald.* Ed. Andrew Turnbull. New York: Scribner's, 1963

——. *The Crack-Up.* Ed. Edmund Wilson. New York: New Directions, 1945.

——. *The Great Gatsby*. New York: Scribner's, 1925.

Flynn, Elizabeth A. 'Gender and Reading.' Flynn and Schweickart, *Gender and Reading* 267–88.

Flynn, Elizabeth A., and Patrocinio P. Schweickart, eds. *Gender and Reading: Essays on Readers, Texts, and Contexts*. Baltimore, MD: Johns Hopkins University Press, 1986.

Ford, Ford Madox. *The Good Soldier*. 1915. Ed. Martin Stannard. New York: Norton, 1995.

——. 'On Impressionism.' *Critical Writings of Ford Madox Ford*. Ed. Frank MacShane. Lincoln: University of Nebraska Press, 1964. 33–55.

——. 'Joseph Conrad.' *Critical Writings of Ford Madox Ford*, pp. 72–88.

——. *Joseph Conrad: A Personal Remembrance*. London: Duckworth, 1924.

Franklin, Benjamin. *The Autobiography and Other Writings*. 1789. Ed. Kenneth Silverman. New York: Penguin, 1986.

Freund, Elizabeth. *The Return of the Reader: Reader-Response Criticism*. London: Methuen, 1987.

Frye, Northrop. *The Secular Scripture: A Study of the Structure of Romance*. Cambridge, MA: Harvard University Press, 1976.

——. *The Critical Path: An Essay on the Social Context of Literary Criticism*. Bloomington: Indiana University Press, 1971.

——. *Anatomy of Criticism: Four Essays*. Princeton, NJ: Princeton University Press, 1957.

Gallo, Rose Adrienne. *F. Scott Fitzgerald*. New York: Ungar, 1978.

Ganim, John M. 'Carnival Voices and the Envoy to the *Clerk's Tale*.' *Chaucer Review* 22 (1987): 112–27.

Gardiner, Michael. 'Bakhtin's Carnival: Utopia as Critique.' *Critical Essays on Mikhail Bakhtin*. Ed. Caryl Emerson. New York: G. K. Hall, 1999. 252–77.

Genette, Gérard. *Narrative Discourse: An Essay in Method*. Trans. Jane E. Lewin. Ithaca, NY: Cornell University Press, 1980.

——. *Figures III*. Paris: Éditions du Seuil, 1972.

Gibson, Walker. 'Authors, Speakers, Readers, and Mock Readers.' Tompkins, *Reader-Response Criticism* 1–6.

Gilbert, Sandra M., and Susan Gubar. *No Man's Land: The Place of the Woman Writer in the Twentieth Century*. 3 vols. New Haven, CT: Yale University Press, 1988–94.

——. *The Madwoman in the Attic: The Woman Writer and the*

Nineteenth-Century Literary Imagination. New Haven, CT: Yale University Press, 1979.

Goldhurst, William. *F. Scott Fitzgerald and His Contemporaries.* New York: World, 1963.

Gordon, R. K., trans. and ed. *The Story of Troilus.* Toronto: University of Toronto Press, 1978.

Graff, Gerald. *Professing Literature: An Institutional History.* Chicago, IL: University of Chicago Press, 1987.

Green, Richard Firth. *Poets and Princepleasers: Literature and the English Court in the Late Middle Ages.* Toronto: University of Toronto Press, 1980.

Greetham, D. C. *Theories of the Text.* Oxford: Oxford University Press, 1999.

Gubar, Susan. *Racechanges: White Skin, Black Face in American Culture.* Oxford: Oxford University Press, 1997.

Guerard, Albert J. *Conrad the Novelist.* Cambridge, MA: Harvard University Press, 1962.

Gurko, Leo. *Joseph Conrad: Giant in Exile.* New York: Macmillan, 1962.

Hassan, Ihab. *The Postmodern Turn: Essays in Postmodern Theory and Culture.* Columbus: Ohio State University Press, 1987.

Hogan, Patrick Colm. *The Politics of Interpretation: Ideology, Professionalism, and the Study of Literature.* New York: Oxford University Press, 1990.

Holland, Norman N. *The Dynamics of Literary Response.* 1968. New York: Norton, 1975.

——. 'Unity, Identity, Text, Self.' Tompkins, *Reader-Response Criticism* 118–33.

——. 'Why This Is Transference, Nor Am I Out of It.' *Psychoanalysis and Contemporary Thought* 5 (1982): 27–34.

Hutcheon, Linda. *A Theory of Parody.* London: Routledge, 1984.

Imber-Black, Evan. *Families and Larger Systems: A Family Therapist's Guide through the Labyrinth.* New York: Guilford, 1988.

Irigaray, Luce. *An Ethics of Sexual Difference.* Trans. Carolyn Burke and Gillian C. Gill. Ithaca: Cornell University Press, 1993.

Irving, John. *The World According to Garp.* New York: Random House, 1978.

Iser, Wolfgang. *The Implied Reader: Patterns of Communication in Prose Fiction from Bunyan to Beckett.* 1972. Baltimore, MD: Johns Hopkins University Press, 1974.

Jakobson, Roman, and Morris Halle. *Fundamentals of Language.* The Hague: Mouton, 1956.

Jancovich, Mark. *The Cultural Politics of the New Criticism.* Cambridge: Cambridge University Press, 1993.

Jarrell, Randall. *Poetry and the Age.* New York: Vintage, 1959.

Jauss, Hans Robert. *Aesthetic Experience and Literary Hermeneutics.* Trans. Michael Shaw. Minneapolis: University of Minnesota Press, 1982.

Kaufman, Barbara A. 'Training Tales in Family Therapy: Exploring *The Alexandria Quartet.' Journal of Marital and Family Therapy* 21.1 (1995): 67–75.

Kavanagh, James H. 'Ideology.' *Critical Terms for Literary Study.* Ed. Frank Lentricchia and Thomas McLaughlin. Chicago, IL: University of Chicago Press, 1990. 306–20.

Knapp, John V. *Striking at the Joints: Contemporary Psychology and Literary Criticism.* Lanham, MD: University Press of America, 1996.

Knapp, Steven. *Literary Interest: The Limits of Anti-Formalism.* Cambridge, MA: Harvard University Press, 1993.

Krieger, Murray. *Poetic Presence and Illusion: Essays in Critical History and Theory.* Baltimore, MD: Johns Hopkins University Press, 1979.

——. *Theory of Criticism: A Tradition and Its System.* Baltimore, MD: Johns Hopkins University Press, 1976.

——. *The New Apologists for Poetry.* Minneapolis: University of Minnesota Press, 1956.

Lauter, Paul. *Canons and Contexts.* New York: Oxford University Press, 1991.

Leavis, F. R. *The Great Tradition: George Eliot, Henry James, Joseph Conrad.* London: Chatto and Windus, 1948.

Lodge, David. *Changing Places: A Tale of Two Campuses.* 1975. New York: Penguin, 1978.

Luelsdorff, Philip A., ed. *The Prague School of Structural and Functional Linguistics.* Amsterdam: John Benjamins, 1994.

MacFarquhar, Larissa. 'The Dean's List: The Enfant Terrible of English Lit Grows Up.' *The New Yorker* 11 June 2001: 62–71.

Mailloux, Steven. *Interpretive Conventions: The Reader in the Study of American Fiction.* Ithaca, NY: Cornell University Press, 1982.

——. 'Evaluation and Reader-Response Criticism: Values Implicit in Affective Stylistics.' *Style* 10 (1976): 329–43.

Merod, Jim. *The Political Responsibility of the Critic.* Ithaca, NY: Cornell University Press, 1987.

Meyers, Jeffrey. *Scott Fitzgerald: A Biography*. New York: Harper Collins, 1994.

Middleton, Anne. 'The Clerk and His Tale: Some Literary Contexts.' *Studies in the Age of Chaucer* 2 (1980): 121–50.

Mieszkowski, Gretchen. 'The Reputation of Criseyde, 1155–1500.' *Transactions* 43 (1971): 71–153.

Miller, J. Hillis. *The Ethics of Reading: Kant, de Man, Eliot, Trollope, James, and Benjamin*. New York: Columbia University Press, 1987.

Miller, Nancy K. *Subject to Change: Reading Feminist Writing*. New York: Columbia University Press, 1988.

Mitchell, Judith. *The Stone and the Scorpion: The Female Subject of Desire in the Novels of Charlotte Brontë, George Eliot, and Thomas Hardy*. Westport, CT: Greenwood, 1994.

Mizener, Arthur. *The Saddest Story: A Biography of Ford Madox Ford*. New York: World, 1971.

Morson, Gary Saul. *Narrative and Freedom: The Shadows of Time*. New Haven, CT: Yale University Press, 1994.

Morson, Gary Saul, and Caryl Emerson. *Mikhail Bakhtin: Creation of a Prosaics*. Stanford, CA: Stanford University Press, 1990.

Muscatine, Charles. *Chaucer and the French Tradition: A Study in Style and Meaning*. Berkeley: University of California Press, 1957.

Newton, Adam Zachary. *Narrative Ethics*. Cambridge, MA: Harvard University Press, 1995.

Nichols, William C., and Craig A. Everett. *Systemic Family Therapy: An Integrative Approach*. New York: Guilford, 1986.

Nussbaum, Martha C. *Poetic Justice: The Literary Imagination and Public Life*. Boston, MA: Beacon, 1995.

——. *Love's Knowledge: Essays on Philosophy and Literature*. New York: Oxford University Press, 1990.

O'Connor, Flannery. *Mystery and Manners: Occasional Prose*. New York: Farrar, Strauss and Giroux, 1969.

Patterson, Annabel. *Reading between the Lines*. Madison: University of Wisconsin Press, 1993.

Patterson, Annette, Bronwyn Mellor, and Marnie O'Neill. 'Beyond Comprehension: Poststructuralist Readings in the Classroom.' *Knowledge in the Making: Challenging the Text in the Classroom*. Ed. Bill Corcoran, Mike Hayhoe, and Gordon M. Pradl. Portsmouth: Boynton/Cook, 1994. 61–72.

Pearsall, Derek. *The Life of Geoffrey Chaucer: A Critical Biography*. Oxford: Blackwell, 1992.

Pratt, R. A. 'Chaucer and *Le Roman de Troyle et de Criseida*.' *Studies in Philology* 53 (1956): 509–39.

Prince, Gerald. 'Introduction à l'étude du narrataire.' *Poétique* 14 (1973): 178–96.

Propp, Vladimir. *Morphology of the Folktale*. 1928. Trans. Laurence Scott. Austin: University of Texas Press, 1968.

Rabinowitz, Peter. *Before Reading: Narrative Conventions and the Politics of Interpretation*. Ithaca, NY: Cornell University Press, 1987.

Radway, Janice A. *Reading the Romance: Women, Patriarchy, and Popular Literature*. 1984. Chapel Hill: University of North Carolina Press, 1991.

Ransom, John Crowe. *The World's Body*. 1938. Baton Rouge: Louisiana University Press, 1968.

Rhodes, Chip. 'Dialogism or Domination?: Language Use in Proust's *À la recherche du temps perdu*.' *MLN* 111.4 (1996): 760–74.

Rhys, Jean. *Wide Sargasso Sea*. 1966. New York: Norton, 1996.

Richards, I. A. *Practical Criticism: A Study of Literary Judgment*. London: K. Paul, Trench, and Trubner, 1929.

——. *Principles of Literary Criticism*. New York: K. Paul, Trench, and Trubner, 1924.

Roberts, Janine. *Tales and Transformations: Stories in Families and Family Therapy*. New York: Norton, 1994.

Rosenblatt, Louise M. *Literature as Exploration*. 1938. New York: MLA, 1995.

——. *The Reader, the Text, the Poem: The Transactional Theory of the Literary Work*. Carbondale: Southern Illinois University Press, 1978.

——. 'Towards a Transactional Theory of Reading.' *Journal of Reading Behavior* 1.1 (1969): 31–49.

Saunders, Max. *Ford Madox Ford: A Dual Life*. 2 vols. Oxford: Oxford University Press, 1996.

Schweickart, Patrocinio P. 'Reading Ourselves: Toward a Feminist Theory of Reading.' Flynn and Schweickart, *Gender and Reading* 31–62.

Selden, Raman. *Practicing Theory and Reading Literature*. Lexington: University Press of Kentucky, 1989.

Sherry, Norman. *Conrad's Western World*. Cambridge: Cambridge University Press, 1971.

Shklovsky, Victor. 'Literature beyond Plot.' 1921. *Theory of Prose*, by Shklovsky. 1929. Trans. Benjamin Sher. Elmwood Park: Dalkey Archive, 1990. 226–45.

———. 'Art as Device.' 1916. *Russian Formalist Criticism: Four Essays.* Ed. L. T. Lemon and M. J. Reis. Lincoln: University of Nebraska Press, 1965. 5–24.

Sklar, Robert. *F. Scott Fitzgerald: The Last Laocoön.* New York: Oxford University Press, 1967.

Smith, Barbara Herrnstein. *Contingencies of Value: Alternative Perspectives for Critical Theory.* Cambridge, MA: Harvard University Press, 1988.

Spurlin, William J., and Michael Fischer, eds. *The New Criticism and Contemporary Literary Theory: Connections and Continuities.* New York: Garland, 1995.

Steig, Michael. *Stories of Reading: Subjectivity and Literary Understanding.* Baltimore, MD: Johns Hopkins University Press, 1989.

Steiner, Peter, ed. *Russian Formalism: A Metapoetics.* Ithaca, NY: Cornell University Press, 1984.

———. *The Prague School: Selected Writings, 1929–1946.* Trans. John Burbank, Olga Hasty, Manfred Jacobson, Bruce Kochis, and Wendy Steiner. Austin: University of Texas Press, 1982.

Stowe, Harriet Beecher. *Uncle Tom's Cabin or, Life Among the Lowly.* London: Penguin, 1981.

Striedter, Jurij. *Literary Structure, Evolution, and Value: Russian Formalism and Czech Structuralism Reconsidered.* Cambridge, MA: Harvard University Press, 1989.

Suleiman, Susan R. 'Introduction: Varieties of Audience-Oriented Criticism.' *The Reader in the Text: Essays on Audience and Interpretation.* Ed. Susan R. Suleiman and Inge Crosman. Princeton, NY: Princeton University Press, 1980. 3–45.

Tate, Allen. *Essays of Four Decades.* Chicago, IL: Swallow, 1968.

———. *Collected Essays.* Denver, CO: Alan Swallow, 1959.

Thompson, Ewa M. *Russian Formalism and Anglo-American New Criticism: A Comparative Study.* The Hague: Mouton, 1971.

Tillotson, Kathleen. *Novels of the 1840s.* Oxford: Oxford University Press, 1956.

Tompkins, Jane P. 'An Introduction to Reader-Response Criticism.' Tompkins, *Reader-Response Criticism* ix–xxvi.

———. 'The Reader in History: The Changing Shape of Literary Response.' Tompkins, *Reader-Response Criticism* 201–32.

———. ed. *Reader-Response Criticism: From Formalism to Poststructuralism.* Baltimore, MD: Johns Hopkins University Press, 1980.

Tynyanov, Yuri. 'Dostoevsky and Gogol: Toward a Theory of Parody.' *Texte* 1 (1921): 300–70.

Vachek, Josef. 'Phonology and Graphemics.' Luelsdorff, *The Prague School of Structural and Functional Linguistics* 13–43.

Vodichka, Felix. 'The Concretization of the Literary Work: Problems of the Reception of Neruda's Works.' Steiner, *The Prague School* 103–34.

Weisberg, Richard H. *Poethics, and Other Strategies of Law and Literature*. New York: Columbia University Press, 1992.

Wellek, René. 'The New Criticism: Pro and Contra.' *Critical Inquiry* 4 (1978): 611–24.

Wellek, René, and Austin Warren. *Theory of Literature*. New York: Harcourt, Brace, 1942.

Wentersdorf, Karl P. 'Chaucer's Clerk of Oxenford as Rhetorician.' *Mediaeval Studies* 51 (1989): 313–28.

White, Michael, and David Epston. *Narrative Means to Therapeutic Ends*. New York: Norton, 1990.

Wimsatt, W. K., and Monroe C. Beardsley. *The Verbal Icon: Studies in the Meaning of Poetry*. Lexington: University Press of Kentucky, 1954.

Wittig, Monique. *The Straight Mind and Other Essays*. Boston, MA: Beacon, 1992.

Wolfreys, Julian. *Readings: Acts of Close Reading in Literary Theory*. Edinburgh: Edinburgh University Press, 2000.

Wright, Terence R. 'Reader Response under Review: Art, Game, or Science?' *Style* 29 (1995): 529–48.

Yarbrough, Stephen R. *Deliberate Criticism: Toward a Postmodern Humanism*. Athens: University of Georgia Press, 1992.

Index

aesthetic reading   54–5
affective fallacy   18, 20, 21, 23
Agrarians   14, 16
Alger, Horatio   34, 96
Anderson, Paul Thomas   154
Aristotle   27, 35, 63
Arnold, Matthew   16–17
Auden, W. H.   16
Austin, J. L.   87

Bagwell, J. Timothy   168
Bakhtin, Mikhail   39, 47–50, 160
   Rabelais and His World   48
Barnard, Charles P.   72
Barthes, Roland   47, 58–60,
   129–30, 161
   'The Death of the Author'   59
   The Pleasure of the Text   59
   S/Z   58–9
Beardsley, Monroe C.   14, 18,
   19–20, 21–2, 23, 93
Bely, Andrey   40
Bennett, Carl D.   167
Bennett, William J.   155
Blake, William   15
Bleich, David   65–6, 67, 68
   Subjective Criticism   65
Bloom, Allan   155
Bloom, Harold   2, 3, 36, 38, 157
   Anxiety of Influence: A Theory of
      Poetry   2–3, 36
Boccaccio, Giovanni   129–35
   Il Filostrato   129–35
Booth, Stephen   81–2
Booth, Wayne C.   53, 55–7
   The Company We Keep   56
   The Rhetoric of Fiction   56
Brontë, Charlotte   107–22, 164
   Jane Eyre   107–22, 164

Brooks, Cleanth   14, 22, 25–6, 27,
   28, 158, 159
   The Well-Wrought Urn   25, 27
Burke, Kenneth   14, 28, 30–3, 37,
   38

Cain, William E.   163
carnival   39, 47, 48–9, 50, 160
Cassell, Richard A.   167
Champagne, Roland   161
Chaucer, Geoffrey   123–35, 165–6
   Clerk's Tale   23–9, 135, 165–6
   Troilus and Criseyde   129–35,
      165–6
chronotope   49–50
Clausen, Christopher   38
Clifford, John   160
coduction   57
Columni, Guido de   129
Conrad, Joseph   136–45, 152–3,
   164, 167
   Heart of Darkness   136, 137, 139,
      140–5, 152–3, 167
   The Inheritors   136
   Lord Jim   140, 167
   The Nature of a Crime   136
   The Nigger of the Narcissus   138
   Romance   136
   The Secret Agent   167
Corrales, Ramon Garrido   72
Criterion, The   15
Crosman, Robert   66–7
   Reading Paradise Lost   67
Culler, Jonathan   58, 60–1, 161
   Structuralist Poetics   60, 161

Dante Alighieri   15, 19
   The Divine Comedy   19
Davis, Todd F.   161

defamiliarization   41, 42, 44
Derrida, Jacques   16, 87
descriptio   125
Dial, The   98
dialogic text   49
dialogism   48, 50
Dickens, Charles   110
diegesis   57, 165
diegetic level   57
Donaldson, E. Talbot   166
Donaldson, Scott   164
Donne, John   163
Donoghue, Denis   163
doppelgänger   114, 115
Dostoevsky, Fyodor   42

Eagleton, Terry   29–30, 157
Eble, Kenneth   102
efferent (nonaesthetic) reading   55
Eichenbaum, Boris   39, 43
Eliot, T. S.   9, 14, 15, 17, 18–19, 21, 30, 31, 93, 95, 97–8
    To Criticize the Critic   15
    The Sacred Wood   15
    The Waste Land   98
Ellman, Maud   19
Emerson, Caryl   48, 159–60
Emerson, Ralph Waldo   5
Empson, William   13, 14, 15, 24–5
    Seven Types of Ambiguity   24
Epston, David   72–3
Everett, Craig E.   162
extradiegetic level   58

Farrell, Thomas J.   166
Fetterley, Judith   77
Fischer, Michael   168
Fish, Stanley   38, 80–9, 153, 161–2, 163
    Doing What Comes Naturally   86–7, 88
    Is There a Text in This Class?   80, 85
    Professional Correctness   88, 89
    Self-Consuming Artifacts   81, 82–3, 84
    Surprised by Sin   83–4

There's No Such Thing as Free Speech, and It's a Good Thing, Too   88–9
Fitzgerald, F. Scott   93–106, 164
    The Great Gatsby   93–106, 164
Flynn, Elizabeth A.   75–7
Ford, Ford Madox   136, 137, 138, 140, 164, 167
    The Good Soldier   136, 137, 139, 145–53, 167
    The Inheritors   136
    The Nature of a Crime   136
    Romance   136
foregrounding   44
Franklin, Benjamin   100
Freund, Elizabeth   51, 65, 161
froda   113, 114, 115, 121
Frye, Northrop   33–6, 107–22, 159, 164–5, 167
    Anatomy of Criticism   33, 34, 37, 38
    The Secular Scripture   108–22
Fugitives   14
Fugitive, The   14

Gallo, Rose Adrienne   164
Ganim, John M.   123–4, 166
Gardiner, Michael   160
Genette, Gérard   56, 57, 123, 124, 125, 127, 128, 129, 161, 165
    Narrative Discourse   57–8, 124
Gibson, Walker   52
Gilbert, Sandra M.   4
    The Madwoman in the Attic   4
    No Man's Land   4
Gogol, Nikolai   42, 43
Goldhurst, William   98
Gordon, R. K.   166
Gould, Stephen Jay   6
Graff, Gerald   1, 4, 7, 13, 158–9
Green, Richard Firth   166
Greetham, D. C.   68–9
Gubar, Susan   4–5
    The Madwoman in the Attic   4
    No Man's Land   4
Guerard, Albert J.   139
Gurko, Leo   167

Hassan, Ihab   158

Heilman, Robert   158
Hemingway, Ernest   93, 164
heteroglossia   39, 47–8, 50, 160
Hogan, Patrick Colm   7, 157
Holland, Norman N.   63–5, 67, 68
  *The Dynamics of Literary
    Response*   64
Holocaust   5
homeostasis   162
Hutcheon, Linda   130

identity theme   63
Imber-Black, Evan   162
intentional fallacy   18, 20
interpretive communities   85–6,
  163
intertextuality   129
Irigaray, Luce   78–9
Irving, John   6
  The World According to Garp   6
Iser, Wolfgang   61–2
  The Implied Reader   61

Jakobson, Roman   39, 40, 41, 44,
  45, 46, 58
Jameson, Fredric   47
Jancovich, Mark   168
Jarrell, Randall   32–3
Jauss, Hans Robert   62–3, 136,
  140–53, 167
  *Aesthetic Experience and Literary
    Hermeneutics*   62, 137
Joyce, James   98
  Ulysses   98
Jung, Carl   33

Kant, Immanuel   26, 40
Kaufman, Barbara A.   162
Kavanagh, James H.   8
Keats, John   159
Kenyon Review   14
Knapp, John V.   162
Knapp, Steven   154
konkretisation   61
Krieger, Murray   8, 16–17, 18, 31,
  158

langue   49
Lauter, Paul   1

Lawrence, D. H.   30
Leavis, F. R.   14, 18, 28, 29–30, 31
  The Great Tradition   30
Lentricchia, Frank   38
Lévi-Strauss, Claude   58
Lewis, C. S.   166
lisible   59
literaturnost   40
Lodge, David   80–1
  Changing Places   80–1

MacFarquhar, Larissa   81
Mailloux, Steven   67–70, 161–2
  Interpretive Conventions   67–70
Mathesius, Vilém   44, 45, 46
Mellor, Bronwyn   163
Melville, Herman   96, 106
Merod, Jim   7
metadiegetic level   58
Meyers, Jeffrey   164
Michaels, Walter Benn   157
Middleton, Anne   127, 165
Mieszkowski, Gretchen   134, 166
Miller, J. Hillis   161
Miller, Nancy K.   77–8, 162
Milton, John   83–4, 162
  Paradise Lost   83–4
Mitchell, Judith   164
mnemonic irrelevancies   23
mock reader   52
monologic text   49
Montaigne, Michel Eyguem de   63
morphogenesis   162
Morson, Gary Saul   48, 49, 159–60
Moscow Linguistics Circle   39
Mukarovsky, Jan   39, 44
Muscatine, Charles   128, 129,
  130–1, 132, 133, 166

narratee   57, 58, 161
Neruda, Pablo   46
New Republic, The   98
Newton, Adam Zachary   161
Nichols, Williams C.   162
Nussbaum, Martha C.   161, 163

objective correlative   19, 95–6, 97
O'Connor, Flannery   28
O'Neill, Marnie   163

ostranenie   41, 42, 43

parole   49
Patterson, Annabel   162–3
Patterson, Annette   163
Pearsall, Derek   127
Perkins, Maxwell   94
polyphony   160
Posner, Richard   88
Pound, Ezra   30
Prague Linguistic Circle   44, 45
Prague Structuralists   39, 40, 44–7
Pratt, Robert A.   130, 166
priem   41
Prince, Gerald   57, 161
Propp, Vladimir   42–3
   Morphology of the Folktale   43
Proust, Marcel   124
Purser, John   27

Rabelais, François   48
Rabinowitz, Peter J.   70–1
   Before Reading   70
Radway, Janice A.   73–4
   Reading the Romance   73–4
Ransom, John Crowe   9, 13–14, 26
Rhodes, Chip   49
Rhys, Jean   113–14
   Wide Sargasso Sea   114
Richards, I. A.   9, 14, 15, 22–3, 24,
   53, 158
   Practical Criticism   23, 53, 158
   Principles of Literary Criticism
   22, 158
Roberts, Janine   162
Rorty, Richard   38
Rosenblatt, Louise M.   53–5, 160
   Literature as Exploration   53–4,
   55
   The Reader, the Text, the Poem
   53–5

Sainte-Maure, Benoît de   129
Saunders, Max   138, 146
Saussure, Ferdinand de   45, 47,
   49
Schweickart, Patrocinio P.   74–5,
   77
scriptible   59

Scrutiny   29
Selden, Raman   17–18
Sewanee Review   14, 20
Shakespeare, William   34
Sherry, Norman   167
Shklovsky, Victor   39, 40–1, 42
simulacrum   27
skaz   43
Sklar, Robert   98
Smith, Barbara Herrnstein   1
Spenser, Edmund   163
Society for the Study of Poetic
   Language   39
Sophocles   3
   Oedipus the King   3
Southern Review   14
Spurlin, William J.   168
Steig, Michael   163
Steiner, Peter   40, 43
Stevens, Wallace   16
Stowe, Harriet Beecher   164
   Uncle Tom's Cabin   164
Striedter, Jurij   41
Suleiman, Susan R.   56, 161
syuzhet   42, 43

Tate, Allen   14, 22, 28
Tesnière, Lucien   44
Tillotson, Kathleen   107
Tompkins, Jane P.   51, 52, 154
   Reader-Response Criticism   52,
   154–5
transactive criticism   64–5
Trnka, Bohumil   45
Tynyanov, Yuri   39, 42, 44

Ukhtomsky, A. A.   160

Vachek, Josef   45
Vodichka, Felix   46–7

Warren, Austin   47
Warren, Robert   9, 17, 27, 158
Weisberg, Richard H.   163
Wellek, René   14, 16, 29, 44, 45, 47
Wentersdorf, K. P.   125
White, Michael   72–3
Williams, William Carlos   27
Wilson, Edmund   98

Wimsatt, W. K.   14, 18, 19–20,
    21–2, 23, 28, 93
Winters, Yvor   14
Wittig, Monique   78
Wolfreys, Julian   59

Womack, Kenneth   161
Wordsworth, William   25
Wright, Terence R.   160

Yarbrough, Stephen R.   158